C. G. Warnford Lock

Tobacco: growing, curing, & manufacturing

A handbook for planters in all parts of the world

C. G. Warnford Lock

Tobacco: growing, curing, & manufacturing
A handbook for planters in all parts of the world

ISBN/EAN: 9783744715065

Printed in Europe, USA, Canada, Australia, Japan

Cover: Foto ©Andreas Hilbeck / pixelio.de

More available books at **www.hansebooks.com**

TOBACCO:
GROWING, CURING, AND MANUFACTURING.

TOBACCO:

GROWING, CURING, & MANUFACTURING.

A HANDBOOK FOR PLANTERS

IN ALL PARTS OF THE WORLD.

EDITED BY

C. G. WARNFORD LOCK, F.L.S.

E. & F. N. SPON, 125, STRAND, LONDON.

NEW YORK: 35, MURRAY STREET.

1886.

PREFACE.

TOBACCO growing is one of the most profitable branches of tropical and sub-tropical agriculture; the "weed" has even been proposed as a remunerative crop for the British farmer, and is very extensively grown in continental Europe. The attention recently drawn to the subject has resulted in many inquiries for information useful to the planter desirous of starting a tobacco estate. But beyond scattered articles in newspapers and the proceedings of agricultural societies, there has been no practical literature available for the English reader. It is a little remarkable that while our neighbours have been writing extensively about tobacco growing, of late years, no English book devoted exclusively to this subject has been published for nearly thirty years. A glance at the bibliography given at the end of this volume will show that the French, German, Swiss, Italian, Dutch, Sicilian, and even Scandinavian planter has a reliable handbook to guide him in this important branch of agriculture, while British settlers in our numerous tobacco-growing colonies must glean their information as best they may from periodical literature.

To supply the want thus indicated, the present volume

has been prepared. The invaluable assistance of tobacco-planters in both the Indies and in many other tropical countries, has rendered the portion relating to field operations eminently practical and complete, while the editor's acquaintance with agricultural chemistry and familiarity with the best tobacco-growing regions of Asiatic Turkey, have enabled him to exercise a general supervision over the statements of the various contributors.

CONTENTS.

CHAPTER I.
		PAGE
THE PLANT		1

CHAPTER II.
| CULTIVATION | | 7 |

CHAPTER III.
| CURING | | 67 |

CHAPTER IV.
| PRODUCTION AND COMMERCE | | 137 |

CHAPTER V.
| PREPARATION AND USE | | 231 |

CHAPTER VI.
| NATURE AND PROPERTIES | | 253 |

CHAPTER VII.
| ADULTERATIONS AND SUBSTITUTES | | 267 |

CHAPTER VIII.

IMPORTS, DUTIES, VALUES, AND CONSUMPTION 271

CHAPTER IX.

BIBLIOGRAPHY 276

INDEX 281

LIST OF ILLUSTRATIONS.

FIG.		PAGE
1.	Cuban Tobacco Plant	4
2.	Maryland Tobacco Plant	5
3.	Amersfort Tobacco Plant	6
4.	Straw Mat for Covering Seed-beds	47
5.	Shade Frames used in Cuba	49
6.	Quincunx Planting	52
7.	Tobacco Worm and Moth	56
8.	Shed for Sun-curing Tobacco	83
9.	Hanging Bunches of Leaves	95
10.	Tobacco Barn	95
11.	Interior of Tobacco Barn	96
12.	Hand of Tobacco	108
13.	Packing Hogshead	133
14 to 17.	Tobacco-cutting Machine	234
18.	Machine for making Plug Tobacco	237
19 to 21.	Machine for making Twist or Roll Tobacco	238
22, 23.	Diagrams of Segment Rollers of Twist Machine	240
24 to 26.	Andrew's Improvements in Twist Machine	243-4
27.	Machine for Cutting and Sifting Scrap Tobacco	246
28.	Machine for making Cigarettes	247
29.	Resweating Apparatus	249
30.	Machine for Weighing out Small Parcels of Tobacco	250
31.	Tobacco-cutting Machine	252

TOBACCO:

GROWING, CURING, AND MANUFACTURING.

CHAPTER I.

THE PLANT.

NEXT to the most common grains and pulses, probably no plant is so widely and generally cultivated as tobacco. In what country or at what date its use originated has little to do with us from a practical point of view, though interesting enough as a subject for the student of ethnography and natural history. Suffice it to say that it has been grown and smoked since pre-historic times in many tropical and sub-tropical countries, and has assumed an importance in modern daily life only surpassed by a few prominent food plants and cotton.

This long-continued and widespread cultivation has helped to produce local varieties or races of the plant which have sometimes been mistaken for distinct species, and caused a multiplication of scientific names almost bewildering. The following epitome comprehends the species and varieties of *Nicotiana* possessing interest for the cultivator:—

I. *N. Tabacum macrophylla* [*latifolia, lattissima, gigantea*] —Maryland tobacco. Of this, there are two sub-species

TOBACCO.

—(1) Stalkless Maryland, of the following varieties: (*a*) *N. macrophylla ovata*—short-leaved Maryland, producing a good smoking-tobacco, (*b*) *N. macrophylla longifolia*—long-leaved Maryland, yielding a good smoking-tobacco, and excellent wrappers for cigars, (*c*) *N. macrophylla pandurata* —broad-leaved, or Amersfort, much cultivated in Germany and Holland, a heavy cropper, and especially adapted for the manufacture of good snuff; (2) Stalked Maryland, of the following varieties: (*a*) *N. macrophylla alata*, (*b*) *N. macrophylla cordata*—heart-shaped Maryland, producing a very fine leaf, from which probably the finest Turkish is obtained. Cuban and Manilla are now attributed to this group.

II. *N. Tabacum angustifolia* — Virginian tobacco. Of this, there are two sub-species—(1) Stalkless Virginian of the following varieties: (*a*) *N. angustifolia acuminata*, grown in Germany for snuff, seldom for smoking, (*b*) *N. angustifolia lanceolata*, affords snuff, (*c*) *N. angustifolia pendulifolia*, another snuff tobacco, (*d*) *N. angustifolia latifolia*—broad-leaved Virginian, used chiefly for snuff, (*e*) *N. angustifolia undulata*—wave-like Virginian, matures quickly, (*f*) *N. angustifolia pandurata*, furnishes good leaves for smoking, produces heavily, and is much grown in Germany, and said to be grown at the Pruth as "tempyki," and highly esteemed there; (2) Stalked Virginian, of the following varieties: (*a*) *N. angustifolia alata*, (*b*) *N. angustifolia lanceolata* [*N. fructiosa*], growing to a height of 8 ft., (*c*) *N. angustifolia oblonga*, (*d*) *N. angustifolia cordata*—E. Indian, producing heavily in good soil, and well adapted for snuff, but not for smoking. Latakia and Turkish are now accredited to *N. Tabacum.*

III. *N. rustica*—Common, Hungarian, or Turkish tobacco. Of this, there are two varieties: (*a*) *N. rustica cordata*—large-leaved Hungarian, Brazilian, Turkish, Asiatic, furnishing leaves for smoking ; (*b*) *N. rustica ovata*—small-leaved Hungarian, affords fine aromatic leaves for smoking, but the yield is small. Until quite recently, Latakia, Turkish, and Manilla tobaccos were referred to this species; Latakia is now proved to belong to *N. Tabacum*, and Manilla is said to be absolutely identical with Cuban, which latter is now ascribed to *N. Tabacum macrophylla*.

IV. *N. crispa.*—This species is much grown in Syria, Calabria, and Central Asia, and furnishes leaves for the celebrated cigars of the Levant.

V. *N. persica.*—Hitherto supposed to be a distinct species, affording the Shiraz tobacco, but now proved to be only a form of *N. Tabacum*.

VI. *N. repanda.*—A Mexican plant, with small foliage. Long thought to be a distinct species peculiar to Cuba, but none such is now to be found in Cuba, whether wild or cultivated, and all the Cuban tobacco is now obtained from *N. Tabacum macrophyllum*.

Among the many other forms interesting only to the botanist or horticulturist, the principal are *N. paniculata*, *N. glutinosa*, *N. glauca*, attaining a height of 18 ft., and *N. clevelandii*, exceedingly strong, quite recently discovered in California, and supposed to have been used by the early natives of that country.

Thus the bulk of the best tobaccos of the world is afforded by the old well-known species *Nicotiana Tabacum*.

A good idea of the foliage and inflorescence of commonly cultivated tobaccos may be gained from a study of the accompanying illustrations.

Fig. 1 is a Cuban tobacco, and much grown on the continent of Europe, notably in Holland, Germany, and Switzerland, and there known as *goundie*, from the name

Fig. 1.

of an American consul who introduced the plant into Germany in 1848. It has a broad yet somewhat pointed leaf, with the ribs not arranged in pairs; it is fine, soft, thin, and esteemed for smoking in pipes and for wrappers of cigars.

One variety of the Maryland plant is shown in Fig. 2. The leaves spring from a tall stem at considerable intervals, and are broad and rounded at the end. This

Fig. 2.

kind is valued for cigar-wrappers, and assumes a fine light brown colour when well cured.

A broad-leaved Cuban or Maryland growth long naturalized in Germany, and now familiar as Amersfort, is represented in Fig. 3. It is distinguished by unusual length of leaf accompanied by a corresponding narrowness. A stem and flower are shown at *a*, a leaf at *b*, a flower in section at *c*, a capsule at *d*, a seed at *e*, and a cross-section of a leaflet at *f*.

Fig. 3.

These three examples represent the most successful kinds grown in Europe and at the same time some of the most marked diversities of form of leaf.

CHAPTER II.

CULTIVATION.

THE following observations on the methods of cultivating tobacco have reference more particularly to the processes as conducted in Cuba, India, and the United States; this branch of agriculture has been brought to great perfection in the last-named country, and the supervision of the operations in India is mostly entrusted to skilled Americans.

Climate.—Of the many conditions affecting the quality of tobacco, the most important is climate. The other conditions that must be fulfilled in order to succeed in the cultivation of this crop may be modified, or even sometimes created, to suit the purpose; but cultivators can do little with reference to climate: the utmost they can do is to change the cultivating season, and this only in places where tobacco can be grown nearly throughout the year. The aromatic principles, on the presence of which the value of a tobacco chiefly depends, can only be properly developed in the plant by the agency of high temperature and moisture. The fame that Cuban and Manilla tobaccos enjoy is mostly due to the climate. The article produced in Cuba is most highly esteemed; up to this time, no other country has been able to compete successfully with it. However it cannot be doubted that there are many places whose climate justifies the assumption that a tobacco could be grown there, not inferior to that produced in the West Indies. The more closely the climate of a place corresponds with that of Cuba, the greater chance is there that a Havanna variety will preserve its peculiar aroma. In such places, a fine and valuable tobacco may be grown with less expenditure on labour, &c., than it is necessary to bestow in raising an inferior article in less suitable climes. In countries where a low temperature rules, the plants must be raised in hot-beds, and there is also a great risk that the young plants may be destroyed by frost, or afterwards by hail-stones. When damp weather prevails during the tobacco harvest, it is often injured; and to give the required flavour, &c., to make the article marketable, macerating has often to be resorted to, thus involving great risk and expenditure. But in spite of these drawbacks, tobacco cultivation is often very remuneratively carried out in countries possessing an unfavourable climate. The deficient climatic conditions are here partly compensated for by making the other conditions affecting the quality of tobacco, and which can be controlled by the cultivator, the most favourable possible.

Soil.—The soil affects to a great extent the quality of a tobacco. The plant thrives best in a soil rich in vegetable mould; this, however, is not so much required to supply the necessary plant food, as to keep the soil in a good physical condition. No other plant requires the soil in such a friable state. A light soil, sand or sandy loam, containing an average amount of organic matter, and well drained, is considered best adapted for raising smoking-tobacco; such a soil produces the finest leaves. The more organic matter a soil contains, the heavier is the outturn; but the leaves grow thicker, and the aroma becomes less. As, in tropical climates, the physical properties of the soil play a prominent part in its productive capabilities generally, and the presence of organic matter in the soil tends to improve these properties, it will rarely occur that in such places a soil will contain too much humus. The more clay in a soil, the less is it adapted to the production of fine smoking-tobacco, on account of its physical properties being less favourable to the development of the aromatic principles; the leaf becomes also generally thick and coarse, but the outturn on such soils is commonly heavier than on a more sandy one. A clay soil possessing a great amount of humus may, if properly tilled, produce an ordinary smoking-tobacco, and may even, if great attention be paid to the selection of the variety, &c., produce leaves for cigar-wrappers.

Of less importance than the physical properties of the soil is its chemical composition. By proper tillage and heavy manuring, tobacco is sometimes grown on comparatively poor soils. From analysis of the plant, it is clear that it contains a large amount of ash constituents, which it extracts from the soil; the most important of these are potash and lime. A soil destitute of these constituents would require a great quantity of manure to supply the wants of tobacco.

An experienced Ohio planter, Judson Popenoe, speaking of soil, says "A rich, sandy, second bottom, I believe to be the best for raising tobacco, although our chocolate-coloured uplands, when very rich and highly manured, will grow an excellent quality of tobacco, but will not yield as much to the acre. Black river-bottoms will yield more to the acre than any other kind of land, but the tobacco is not of so fine a quality; it grows larger, has coarser stems, and heavier body, and consequently, in my opinion, is not so good for wrappers or fine cut as the second bottom or upland tobacco."

On the same subject, an Illinois grower observes, "for us in the West, and for all the localities that have not an over-amount of heat, experience has proved, that a dry, warm soil (loam or sandy loam), rich, deep, and containing lime, is most suitable for tobacco. The more sandy, to a certain degree, the soil is, the better will be the quality of the tobacco; the nearer the soil is to clay, the poorer will be the crop under similar circumstances, although the yield may yet be satisfactory. Clayey soil will hardly produce tobacco suitable for cigars. Wet and tough clay soils are under no circumstances suitable to tobacco."

Situation.—Land intended for tobacco-culture should have good drainage, and be sheltered from high winds. In Holland, where tobacco-cultivation is carried out to great perfection, each field is surrounded by a hedge about 7 ft. high; the fields are divided into small plots, which are again bordered by rows of plants that are able to break the force of the wind, which would injure the leaves, and render them of comparatively little value. To this circumstance must chiefly be attributed the fact that Dutch growers succeed in getting as much as 50 per cent. of leaves of the first quality, whereas in most other countries 25 per cent. is considered to be a very good outturn.

In the United States, several rows of pole beans, i. e. scarlet runners, a few steps apart, are sometimes planted as a wind-screen.

Manure.—In its natural state, the soil will rarely possess the elements of plant food in such a form as is most conducive to the production of a fine tobacco-leaf. Any deficiency must be supplied in the shape of suitable manure. Schlösing found that a bad burning tobacco was produced on a soil containing little potash, on unmanured soil, on soil manured with flesh, humus, calcium chloride, magnesium chloride, and potassium chloride. A good burning tobacco was produced on a soil manured with potassium carbonate, saltpetre, and potassium sulphate. More recent experiments carried out by other investigators tend to corroborate these conclusions. It is generally assumed that a soil rich in nitrogenous organic matter produces a strong tobacco that burns badly.

The results of Nessler's experiments clearly show that it is not sufficient to apply the element most needed by the plant—potash—in any form, but that, to produce a good tobacco, it is necessary to apply it in a particular combination. It was found that potash carbonate applied as manure produced the best tobacco: it burned for the longest time, and its ash contained most potash carbonate; whereas potash chloride produced a much inferior tobacco. The assertion of other experimenters that chlorides produce a bad tobacco is thus confirmed. Potash sulphate and lime sulphate produced a good tobacco. It may be noticed here that tobacco which was manured with gypsum contained a great amount of potash carbonate in the ash, probably due to the fact that gypsum is a solvent for the inert potash salts. From the foregoing, it may be concluded that in tobacco cultivation, the elements potassium and calcium should be restored to the soil in the form of carbonate, sulphate, or nitrate, but not as chlorides. Poudrette, or prepared night-soil, generally contains a considerable amount of chlorides, and is not well suited as manure for fine tobacco. It has been found that fields manured with chlorides produced heavily; a small proportion of chlorides may therefore be applied in this form, whenever quality is of less importance than quantity. Farmyard manure may suffice when tobacco is cultivated in proper rotation, but here also, unless the soil be very rich in potassium and calcium, the application of some special manure will greatly enhance the value of the outturn. Wood-ashes are a valuable supplement to stable dung. Gypsum is an excellent dressing for soils in a good manurial condition : it supplies the lime needed by the tobacco, and acts as a solvent on the inert potash salts. Gypsum applied on poor land, however, hastens the exhaustion of the soil. It is said that crops manured with gypsum suffer less from the effects of drought, and require less irrigation, than when manured otherwise: the leaves of plants that had been manured with gypsum exhaling less water than when manured with other substances. If this assertion be correct, gypsum would be invaluable to the Indian cultivator.

With regard to the amount of manure to be employed, it may be observed that, with farmyard manure properly rotted, there is no theoretical limit, especially when the tobacco is intended for snuff, and is grown in a hot climate, where the physical properties of the soil are of the utmost importance. It is said that some Rhenish-Bavarian soils contain as much as 15 per cent. of organic matter, yet the cultivator considers it necessary to heavily manure each tobacco crop. Dutch growers apply to the rich alluvial soil as much as 25 tons an acre of well-rotted cattle-manure. In America, it is reported that the heaviest crops are obtained on soil newly taken up, and very rich in vegetable mould. It is considered nearly everywhere that tobacco will pay best when heavily manured. The first care of even the poorest peasant in the tobacco districts of Germany, Holland, &c., as soon as he sells his tobacco, is to purchase the manure which he considers essential to his success.

The amount of any special manure which can be applied without injury to the plants depends very much on the solubility of the stuff, and the manner of applying it. Highly soluble salts, such as soda or potash nitrate, should be applied in smaller quantities than salts which dissolve slowly. With regard to the manner of applying concentrated manures, it is evident that, when a salt is applied in close proximity to the plant, less will be required than when strewn over the whole field. When applied in solution, not more than 300 lb. of nitrate per acre should be used at one time. The amount to be applied varies also with the soil; a sandy soil, which has little absorptive power, should receive less than a clay. Salts easily disintegrating should not be applied before tobacco has been planted, especially not before heavy rains which would carry off the salt. To supply the potash required by the tobacco plant, 200 lb. of good salt-petre per acre would be sufficient in most cases. Lime, although removed from the soil in large quantities, is rarely applied to tobacco as a special manure. Where wood-ashes can be had at a moderate price, lime may be applied in this form. Some ashes are very rich in lime. It has been found that ashes obtained from beech-wood contain 52 per cent. of lime, and those from oak-wood as much as 75.

Whilst most growers are agreed that tobacco is a crop demanding a rich soil, there is a want of uniformity of opinion as to the best method of manuring. On this point, C. Schneider, a successful Illinois planter, says "manuring cannot be done too early, or too heavily. The manures are very different, and equally useful for the different kinds of tobacco. We may classify them as follows:—

"To be applied shortly before planting, and in equal quantities, for all kinds of tobacco: 1. Guano, 200 to 300 pounds on the acre; 2. Poultry-droppings, 400 to 500 pounds; 3. Green manure in any quantity; 4. Sheep-dung, 6 two-horse loads; 5. Cattle manure, 10 two-horse loads.

"For chewing-tobacco and snuff: 1. Sheep-dung, 10 to 12 loads per acre; 2. Cattle manure, 20 to 30 loads; 3. Horse-dung, 15 to 25 loads; 4. Hog manure, 20 to 30 loads. The last two are useless for smoking-tobacco, or for that to be used for cigars.

"The first three manures (guano, poultry-droppings, and green manure) must be followed after the tobacco-crop, by a plentiful supply of stable-manure. The tobacco-stalks themselves, rotted or burned to ashes, sown over the field before the transplanting, or in the planting-furrows, will act as a good manure, but are not sufficient. In highly-worked farms, that is, where the soil is valuable, and cannot remain idle, it will pay every way, to sow rye for fodder on the tobacco-land in the fall; this may be made into hay, or turned under as manure at the beginning of July, just as may seem most profitable. Deep ploughing for the rye, and afterward for the tobacco, must not be forgotten."

R. E. Burton, in the *Sugar Cane*, translating from Mitjen's essay on tobacco growing in the most renowned district of Cuba, has the following sensible remarks on the all-important subject of manuring:—

"Each veguero or farmer should make a hole or rotting-bin in which he should deposit as much muck and leaves as he may be able to accumulate, and, before giving the last ploughing to prepare his field for planting the tobacco, he should spread over it all the prepared rotten manure he can procure. Manure that is not thoroughly rotten injures the plants more than benefits them. A piece of land, well manured and thoroughly worked up, will produce four times more tobacco than one badly prepared would. Consequently no expense or labour is so remunerative as that which is applied to the soil. This is a very important point which should fix the attention of every agriculturist who desires to prosper.

"Agriculturists acknowledge the advantage of manuring. In tobacco cultivation it produces the most brilliant results, but in Vuelta-Abajo it is very difficult to procure sufficient country manure. Yagues (i. e. strips of palm bark used as screens, and for baling) and all the refuse from palm trees are excellent; grass from the savannahs and all kinds of vegetables in a thoroughly putrid state are very good, but it requires a great quantity, and the immense labour to collect and prepare these, frightens the greater number of vegueros, and few have sufficient constancy to enable them to collect enough properly prepared manure for their fields.

"The most which some manage to do is to spread refuse over some portions of land, where it rots and fertilizes the soil; but this system is inefficacious, because the vegetable substances being very light, the heavy rains wash away the greater portion of the decomposed matter, and fully nine-tenths are lost. If the system was adopted of depositing this manure in holes or trenches, from which it can be removed when thoroughly rotted and fit for the fields, it would produce much more with much less labour; for although at first sight the labour appears to be doubled; by having to carry it twice, it must be remembered that one load of well-prepared manure is better than ten or twenty of grass or bush that is not rotten.

"But in every way there is great difficulty in collecting vegetable manure in sufficient quantities; recently, guano has been tried with the most brilliant success.

"Peruvian guano is the most compact fertilizer known, and a very small quantity suffices to manure a tobacco field; its cost is not excessive, and is very frequently less than the carriage of other manures to the spot where they are to be used. Its most active results are shown on light and sandy soil; it quickens vegetation, and experience has shown that it increases prodigiously the quantity and value of crops; we therefore recommend the use of guano as a fertilizer of the first order for tobacco cultivation, and as light and sandy soils possess in themselves the substances most suitable for the development of the tobacco plant, on such soils guano acts as a stimulant to the plant.

" Before using Peruvian guano, it should be sifted; all the stones and lumps remaining should be broken up, and again sifted, so that nothing may be lost. After this, three or four times its weight of dry sandy soil should be thoroughly mixed with it, and it should remain thus 6–8 days before being used. This preparation should be made under cover, to avoid the possibility of rain falling on the mixture, and the heap should be covered with the empty guano bags, or anything else, to prevent the evaporation of the volatile alkali which it contains.

" It is better to prepare this mixture in detail, each heap containing one bag of guano, whose weight is 150–160 lb., so as to facilitate the calculation of the quantity that should be applied, and prevent mistakes. We will start, therefore, on this calculation.

" On lands of good quality, but which, nevertheless, require manure, from having been overworked, one pound of guano should be applied to each 15–20 superficial yards, or, say one heap of compost for each 2500–3000 yards, or, otherwise said, one heap of manure will suffice for a surface that contains 5000–6000 plants.

" In sandy unproductive soil, and on sterile savannah lands, 1 lb. of guano to 9–12 yards; or a heap of compost guano to 1500–2000 yards; or one heap for 3000–4000 plants.

" These are the proportions to be used for the first year;

for the second, and forward, two-thirds of that employed the first year will be sufficient.

"When crops of tobacco and corn are grown on the same lands, half the guano should be applied to the corn and the other half to the tobacco; but then a somewhat larger quantity will be required. The manure should be applied shortly before transplanting, and after the ground has been well cross-ploughed and prepared, and the ground should be plotted out into squares or beds of 50 yards square. The manure should then be spread and ploughed in, and the land should at once be furrowed and planted.

"Under this system of applying Peruvian guano as manure for tobacco the best results have been obtained, and, of all the various trials made, this is the most simple and the easiest to execute."

The remarks of the last-quoted essayist are good so long as guano is to be had. But there is a limit to the supply, and in many places it would be unprocurable.

The necessity for more definite knowledge concerning the actual wants of the tobacco plant in the matter of food, led to an investigation of the subject some years ago by Prof. S. W. Johnson on behalf of the Connecticut State Board of Agriculture, and more recently by Schiffmayer for the Agricultural Department of the Madras Presidency.

Prof. Johnson aptly observes it to be "a well-established fact that plants may receive from the soil and retain a larger portion of ash-ingredients than is needful for nutrition. This is especially marked in case of the lime, potash, and soda salts. The excess of these substances thus taken up may either be deposited in the solid state in the cells of the plant, or may remain dissolved in the juices. In tobacco, a part of the nitrogen usually exists as a nitrate, in combination with potash. That is to say, portions of the nitrogenous food of the plant—the nitrates of the soil—are not completely worked over into albuminoids, and into nicotine, the nitrogenous constituents of tobacco, but accumulate and remain in considerable quantity in the sap. When a dry tobacco-leaf is set on fire, it often burns like 'touch paper' (paper soaked in a solution of saltpetre and dried) with bright sparkles of fire, indicating the points where the nitre has gathered in minute crystals as the juice of the leaf evaporated. The quantity of superfluous salts in the plant depends upon its succulence, and upon the supply of them in the soil. Doubtless certain definite amounts of potash, lime, magnesia, iron, sulphuric acid and phosphoric acid are absolutely necessary to produce a given weight of tobacco. In case several or all these substances are superabundant in the soil, the plant has no power to exclude any unnecessary surplus of one or all of them from its interior altogether, although there are good reasons known to prevent their entrance beyond a certain limit. In one soil potash may be relatively most abundant, and may for that reason be found in the crop in greater quantity than was necessary for the growth of that crop. In another soil lime may be in surplus, and there the crop may have the minimum of potash, and a considerable excess of lime.

"The crop is a result of the working together of a number of causes or conditions; these are the heat and light of the sun, carbonic acid and oxygen of the atmosphere, water, nitrates and ammonia, and the ash-elements enumerated in our table of analyses. The crop is limited in quantity by that condition of growth, which is presented to it most sparingly. The richest and best prepared soil without solar warmth, or without due supplies of rain, cannot give a crop, and if weather be most favourable, then in one field it may be too little potash, in another too little phosphoric acid, in another too little nitrogen, which lowers the yield, or reduces the quality of the product.

"It is usual in tobacco culture to manure very heavily, and in many cases it is probable that all the various forms of plant food are present in available abundance. But soils differ in the nature of the supplies which they are able to yield to crops, and fertilizers even, when the same in name, may be very unlike in fact. The chief reliance of the tobacco farmer is stable manure. This, however, is by no means uniform in origin, appearance, evident quality, or chemical composition. The manure from bullocks, wintered on hay and roots, is very different from that of horses maintained chiefly on oats or corn. The yard manure that contains much strawy litter or much wasted hay, differs again from that of the city stables, from which the straw is carefully raked out to be used over and over again for bedding. The farm-made manure is likely to be much richer in potash and lime, and the city manure is richer in phosphates and nitrogen. Yet in the reports of the farmer, these two essentially different fertilizers are designated as stable manure simply.

"Every one understands that a fertilizer acts upon the plant to supply it with food, and to favour its growth; everybody is also convinced that some fertilizers act upon the soil, improving its texture and composition and increasing its fertility. It is an equally well ascertained fact that the soil acts upon fertilizers to modify their effect. A very wet or very dry soil is known to nullify the benefit which might be expected of a fertilizer in a simply moist soil; but more than this, more than by the accident of external circumstances, it is a fact that each kind of soil has a special action of its own on fertilizers, so that if it were asserted of two soils, which, unmanured, were of equal fertility, that a given fertilizer applied to both, greatly improved the crop on one, and had little effect on the other, such a statement might not only be accepted as a fact, but an explanation might be given in general terms for such a fact.

"Now experiments have shown that different soils when mixed with like quantities of various fertilizing elements and then treated with water, in imitation of rain, manifest very different behaviour toward the admixed substances. One soil will lay hold of the potash in a fertilizer, and fix it in a kind of chemical combination so firmly that water can dissolve it but with extreme slowness; another soil puts its grasp on the lime of a fertilizer, and at the same time allows potash which belongs to itself to be dissolved out freely. There is, in fact, always a complicated series of changes set in operation whenever any fertilizer is incorporated with the soil, be it animal, vegetable, or mineral; be it alkali, acid, or saline; be it made on the farm or imported from abroad; be it natural or artificial. The fertilizer acts on the soil, and the soil reacts on the fertilizer; but the point we wish to make prominent is this, that different soils are differently affected by one and the same application, or in other words, a given manure fertilizes a given crop unequally in degree, and unlike in kind, on different soils, by virtue of the different assimilating or fixing power, which the soil exerts upon its ingredients.

"We know of the existence of these peculiarities of soils, and something of their causes and of the laws by which they act; but the real necessities of the tobacco crop, or of any other crop, as respects soil-ingredients, cannot be arrived at by chemical analysis of a single sample, nor of a dozen samples." Thus analyses of a dozen New England tobaccos showed the following highest and lowest percentages of each ash-ingredient, and of nitrogen:—

Silica .. .. 0·05 to 0·30	Magnesia .. .. 0·94 to 2·21
Chlorine .. 0·08 „ 2·55	Potash .. .. 3·90 „ 7·45
Sulphuric acid 0·52 „ 1·69	Soda .. .. 0·08 „ 1·81
Phosphoric acid 0·47 „ 0·80	Nitrogen .. 3·20 „ 5·11
Lime .. .. 3·17 „ 8·22	

"It appears that the percentages of nitrogen, phosphoric acid and potash are nearly twice as great in some samples as in others; that the proportions of magnesia and lime are about $2\frac{1}{2}$ times greater in some samples than in others, and that sulphuric acid is 3 times more in one case than in another. The variation of silica is still greater, and the disparity rises to its extreme in case of soda and chlorine, whose maxima are respectively 20 and 30 times greater than their minima."

The three ingredients chlorine, silica, and soda cannot be considered in the light of essentials to tobacco culture; but the other substances are absolutely indispensable to plant growth, and the absence of any one of these would render a soil incapable of sustaining agricultural vegetation of any kind. "The variation in the percentage of these ingredients depends somewhat upon the fact that the leaves of different crops are unequally developed, and therefore their nutritive needs are unlike; but it is, no doubt, chiefly connected with the fact that the plant takes up from a highly fertilized soil more of each or every element than is essential for growth. The nearly certain conclusion is that every one of the crops analysed contains more of some elements than belongs to its nutrition. It is quite certain that the average of the analyses of the New England tobaccos is fully up to the mark as regards the necessities of the crop. It is, indeed, not improbable that the lowest percentages of each ingredient are quantities sufficient for a perfect crop. Still, it is not proved that lime may not partially take the place of potash, or the reverse. The probability of such a substitution is great upon the face of most of the analyses. As a rule, those which show most potash show least lime and *vice versâ*; but in one sample both ingredients are considerably below the average. The practical issue of these considerations is to give great probability to the view that the tobacco crop is fed unnecessarily (and wastefully?) high." (Prof. Johnson.)

Tobacco is usually characterized as a very exhausting crop. This is not true as regards the amount of nutriment taken from the soil, for in this respect tobacco is less exacting than hay, potatoes, or rye. It demands chiefly potash and lime, with phosphoric acid and nitrogen. Prof. Johnson recommends for the manuring of one acre, besides ploughing in the stalks of the plants, 500 lb. rock guano or 800 lb. fish guano, 500 lb. kainit (potash salts), and 50 lb. quicklime. But surely it cannot be advisable to mix quicklime with an ammoniacal manure like guano; it seems to the writer that gypsum, or spent calcium oxide from gasworks, would be a far preferable medium for conveying lime to the soil.

As observed by Johnson, the "demand made on the soil or on fertilizers by the tobacco crop, is for certain reasons greater than that made by other crops which receive more of nearly every kind of plant food. Hay is more exhausting than tobacco as measured by total export from the soil, but grass grows the whole year throughout, save when the ground is frozen or covered with snow, or for more than 8 months. The period of active growth which is required to mature a hay crop, begins indeed in April, and is finished by July, a period of 3 months, but during the year previous, for at least 5 months, in case of the first crop, the grass plants have been getting a hold upon the soil, filling it with their roots, and storing up food in their root-stocks or bulbs, for the more rapid aftergrowth. Tobacco on the other hand cannot be set out in the field before about the 10th of June, and should be in the shed in about 3 months. Its growth then must be a very rapid one, and the supplies of food in the soil must be very abundant so that the quick-extending roots may be met at every point with their necessary pabulum. A crop of 1260 lb. dry leaves requires about 1100 lb. of dry stalks to support the leaves, making a total of 2360 lb. of dry vegetable matter. As new hay contains not less than one-sixth of moisture, we increase the above dry weight of the tobacco crop by one-sixth, to make a fair comparison, and obtain as the yield of an average tobacco field 2750 lb. of air-dry vegetable matter, or more than 1¼ tons. The matter stands then thus: An acre of first-rate grass land yields as the result of 8 months' growth, 2¾ tons of crop, while the tobacco land must yield 1⅓ tons in 3 months.

"If the above data are correct, the *average* rate of growth of tobacco is greater than that of a corresponding hay crop, in the ratio of 9 : 7. The real disparity is, however, much greater. The principal growth of tobacco is accomplished in the hottest summer weather, and in a period of some 40–50 days. Very heavy manurings are therefore essential to provide for its nourishment, and the more so because the best tobacco lands are light in texture, and may suffer great loss by drainage, evaporation, and decomposition."

From these premises, Prof. Johnson advances to the question of what should or should not be presented to the plant in the form of manure. He commences with a caution that, in general, growers must "avoid employing fertilizers which contain salt or other chlorine compound in raising wrapping or smoking tobacco. It is evident, also, that there is no occasion to use any fertilizer for the special object of supplying phosphoric acid, since the heaviest export of this substance does not exceed 10 lb. per acre, annually. It may be well to mention here that phosphates which may be put upon a tobacco field, in guano, &c., cannot suffer waste by washing out, and will come to use when grain or grass shall follow in the rotation."

He observes of gypsum (lime sulphate) that it is "a valuable application to tobacco, not because it is very largely taken up by the crop, for the greatest export of sulphuric acid, viz. 20 lb. per acre, is restored by 50 lb. of plaster, and the greatest export of lime, 120 lb., is made good by 400 lb. of the sulphate, but because lime sulphate dissolves in 400 times its weight of water, and may rapidly wash out of the porous tobacco lands, and especially because the solution of lime sulphate in the soil is a very effective agent in rendering soluble and accessible to crops the potash and magnesia, which too often exist in close-locked combinations. The average annual rainfall (snow included) in our latitudes, is no less than 10,000,000 lb. per acre. This enormous quantity of water would be enough to dissolve and wash out of the soil 25,000 lb. of gypsum per acre if it had time to saturate itself, and then flowed off. In fact, but a small proportion of the rainfall runs through and out of the soil, not more than 10 to 20 per cent., according to its porosity and situation; but it is plain that there is nothing to hinder the waste of a hundred pounds or more of gypsum per acre yearly, since all investigations go to show that the soil has no retaining power for lime sulphate as it has for potash and for phosphoric acid. In Nessler's experiments, gypsum had an excellent effect on the burning quality of the tobacco raised under its application, an effect attributable, he believes, to the fact that this fertilizer often liberates potash in the soil, as Liebig and Deherain have demonstrated, and is therefore equivalent to an application of potash, provided the latter actually exists in the soil.

"Potash is exported in the tobacco crop to the amount of 70–80 lb. per acre yearly, and is required for the stalks to the extent of some 50 lb., making a total of 120–130 lb. As already intimated, potash does not commonly waste from the soil by washing. It is seldom found in appreciable quantity in well or drain water, and most soils absorb it and fix it so firmly that water can remove it but very slowly. It does, however, appear in the drain water from very heavily dunged fields, though in small proportion. Stable or yard manure on the average contains one-half per cent. of potash, or 10 lb. per ton. Twelve or thirteen tons of stable manure would therefore contain the potash needful to produce a crop. The dressing of 20 tons of 10 cords of stable manure, per acre, which is often employed on tobacco, is doubtless enough to fully supply the crop, and the application of additional potash is apparently quite unnecessary. The employment of potash salts upon tobacco lands would therefore seem to be uncalled for unless the amount of stable manure is greatly diminished, or its quality is very inferior. In case potash salts are to be applied, the best form to make use of is potash sulphate, of which 250 lb. contains 135 of potash. Next to this is probably potash carbonate, i. e. the ordinary potash of commerce, which contains some 70 per cent. of potash; 200 lb. of this would be sufficient for an acre. To apply it I would suggest breaking it up into small pieces and soaking it in two or three times its weight of water until the lumps crush easily, and mixing these with so much ground gypsum as will make a mass dry enough to handle.

"Kainit, which contains some 15 to 20 per cent. of potash, but also 10 per cent. or more of chlorine, is not so good for leaf tobacco, and least of all to be recommended is potassium chloride (muriate of potash) which is nearly half chlorine.

"Magnesia is an element which is abundantly provided for in stable manure, every ton of which, according to analyses on record, contains some 3 lb. of this substance.

"Lime is supplied in relative abundance in stable manure, the average ton of which contains some 15 lb. We have seen that 600 lb. of gypsum contain as much lime as the average tobacco crop: guano, dry fish, and superphosphate, each contains some 5–10 per cent. of lime. There is, furthermore, little likelihood that any soil intended for tobacco would not of itself contain enough lime to support the crop. Lime in the caustic state has, however, a value independent of its direct nutritive power, which is well worth the attention of the tobacco raiser. Of this I shall write briefly in a subsequent paragraph.

"Nitrogen in absolutely dry New England tobacco leaf ranges from 3·2 to 5·1 per cent., or 4·24 as the average. This is a larger proportion than exists in any of our ordinary field crops, except the seeds of legumes. The grain of wheat and red clover hay contain when dry scarcely 2½ per cent., and they exceed all other usually raised vegetable products, except the leguminous seeds. The pea and bean contain, when dry, 4·5 to 4·7 per cent. of nitrogen. The acreage export of nitrogen is nevertheless not large according to the data of our tables. It should be remembered, however, that the average is derived from 5 samples only. . . . There are reasons to suppose that this result is too low. Furthermore it is not improbable that tobacco loses nitrogen during the curing process."

The advantages of artificial manuring have been made manifest in all branches of agriculture, and there is no doubt that the nitrogenous qualities of farmyard dung may be replaced by soda nitrate, ammonia sulphate, &c., only it must be remembered that these have not nearly the lasting effect of dung, the latter liberating its ammonia but slowly. Indeed "when a soil has been heavily dunged for a term of years, it accumulates a large quantity of nitrogen, which is comparatively inert and therefore nearly useless to crops. Quicklime assists to convert this nitrogen into the active forms of ammonia or nitrates," hence Prof. Johnson's suggestion that an "application of lime may sometimes be advantageously substituted for one of stable manure. In fact, it is not improbable that moderate doses of lime might be turned under with stable manure or green crops, with the effect of exalting the action of these fertilizers, and obtaining from them a larger return of nitrogenous plant food. Lime, however, gives effect to the nitrogen of the soil by causing the destruction of the organic matters—*humus*—in which this nitrogen lies in an inactive state. These organic matters have themselves a value independent of their nitrogen, which must be taken account of, and therefore the use of lime must be undertaken cautiously, and with an intelligent comprehension of the various effects which it may produce."

Rotation.—A proper rotation of crops is particularly

advantageous for the cultivation of tobacco, since it requires a great amount of readily accessible inorganic matter in the soil, especially potash and lime. Although the importance of cultivating tobacco in rotation is admitted, there may be circumstances that justify the growth of this crop consecutively for several years in the same field. In America, tobacco is grown successively for several years on new land, where the elements of plant food exist in such abundance that the crop may be thus cultivated without for a time showing any notable decrease in yield; it is even said that the outturn of the second year is heavier than that of the first. In Hungary and Holland, the best tobacco is grown for many years in succession on the same land. There the plan is adopted partly out of necessity and partly for convenience. The small landholder is often obliged to grow tobacco on the same field, because he has only one properly fitted for it; for convenience, he grows it every year on the same place near his homestead, to allow of the closest attention to the crop, but he manures heavily. Nessler, in Carlsruhe, cultivated tobacco during six consecutive years in the same field, without noticing any perceptible decrease in yield or quality. To admit of such a system, the soil must either be very rich in the essential elements, or be heavily manured, as is the practice in Holland. It is generally assumed that, when tobacco is grown on the same field in succession, the leaves do not become so large after the first year, but grow thicker and more gummy, and contain less water.

From the foregoing, it would appear that, although tobacco may be grown successfully on the same land uninterruptedly under special circumstances, the cultivator will find it advantageous to adopt some plan of rotation. Cereals and pulses are very well adapted for this purpose, the reason being that tobacco removes but little phosphoric acid from the soil, and thus leaves it rich in the element most necessary for the growth of cereals. It has also been found that hemp thrives particularly well after tobacco.

Judson Popenoe suggests that there " should be a good coat of clover to plough under; if the ground is naturally rich, this alone will make a good crop, but hog and stable manure, well rotted, is what the tobacco, as well as any other crop, delights in, and the more manure the better the tobacco. The plan that I am now experimenting on is, as soon as I cut my tobacco in the fall I give the ground a good harrowing, and then drill in wheat; the ground being well cultivated all the fall, is clear of weeds and mellow and needs no ploughing. In the spring I sow clover, after the wheat is off; I keep the stock off until about September, to give the clover a chance to harden and spread. I then let the stock eat as low as they want to, which drives the clover to root, and causes the crown to spread; I do not suffer stock to run on the clover during winter or spring; about the last of May or first of June I plough the clover under, which is now in blossom, and so I alternately keep two fields in tobacco and wheat, at the same time feeding the ground a crop of clover every two years; in this way I expect my land to increase in fertility all the time. The clover turned under makes food for the cut-worms, and they trouble the tobacco-plants but little."

Selection of Sort.—The cultivator must carefully compare the requirements of the different sorts, and the means at his disposal to satisfy them, before making his selection. Though tobacco is a hardy plant, and grows under varied conditions, yet to become a remunerative crop, the plant should not be placed under circumstances very dissimilar from those to which it has been accustomed. By importing seed of a fine sort directly from its native land, the plants will not retain in the new habitat all their special qualities, unless climate, soil and treatment are nearly the same. Climate must first be considered. Fine and valuable tobacco is a product of tropical countries: in a warm and humid climate, by employing common means, tobacco may be made to yield a profit not attainable in less favoured regions. A warm, moist climate permits the selection of those sorts that command the highest prices; if to this be added a suitable soil, and proper treatment, the cultivation of tobacco yields a profit not easily obtainable from any other crop.

As the Havanna tobaccos command the highest prices, the cultivator nearly everywhere attempts to introduce and cultivate them. There is no great difficulty in raising plants of these varieties, but they speedily degenerate and form new varieties, if the climatic conditions, &c., are not favourable. Virginian tobacco was previously extensively cultivated, but has of late been frequently replaced by the Maryland kind. It is still much favoured by cultivators in temperate climates, as it does not require a high temperature. On account of its botanical characteristics, it is usually not much liked by manufacturers of cigars; some varieties, however, that have less of the marked specific characters, yield tolerably fine leaves for cigars. As the price of this tobacco is rather low, it is not so well suited for export. Hungarian tobacco is considered to be very hardy, but is less valuable than the foregoing. The leaves are generally small, and possess a peculiar aroma.

A high price is generally commanded, irrespective of the species, by those tobaccos that possess a large, smooth, thin, elastic leaf, possessing a fine golden colour and a good aroma; the ribs and veins should be thin, and the former should branch off from the midrib at nearly right angles, and should be far apart from each other. The lower the percentage of the weight in ribs, the thinner and broader the leaf, and the fewer the leaves torn, the more wrappers can be cut out of 1 lb. of tobacco, other conditions being equal, and consequently the higher is the price of the article. The cigar-manufacturer often does not appreciate the aroma so much as the other qualities. He can do nothing to improve the botanical characters: the finest aromatic leaf would be of little value to him if it were torn; but he is to a certain extent able artificially to improve defects in flavour. Of all kinds, Maryland is considered to possess the qualities that distinguish a good tobacco in the highest degree. Some of the Havanna tobaccos belong to this sort, as also the Ohio, Amersfort, Turkish, and Dutten tobaccos. Its cultivation assumes larger proportions every year, and the number of varieties and sub-varieties increases accordingly. Perhaps the finest wrappers for cigars are grown in Manilla.

On this subject, Judson Popenoe remarks that he has

" cultivated various kinds of tobacco, but have come to the conclusion that what we call the Ohio seed-leaf is the best and most profitable kind for general cultivation. There are other kinds of tobacco that sometimes are profitable, and do well, but most of these do not cure out so well, nor colour so evenly, nor are they so fine and saleable as t   seed-leaf. The Havanna tobacco is too small and has not the fine flavour of the imported. The Connecticut seed-leaf I believe to be identical with our Ohio seed-leaf; the difference in the climate may make a slight variation in the quality, but we plant the Connecticut seed-leaf here in Ohio, and I do not think they can be told apart."

Schneider recommends the following varieties: " 1. Connecticut seed-leaf, principally for cigar-wrappers; 2. Cuba, for fillers and wrappers; 3. Maryland; 4. Virginia, the last two principally for smoking and chewing tobacco. For snuff everything may be used, the refuse and even the stems. The Connecticut, Maryland, and Virginia yield the largest crops, the Cuba the smallest but best. The first varieties yield about one thousand pounds, the latter five hundred pounds. In very favourable seasons double the amount may be raised. All tobacco-seed, which is removed from its native clime and soil, will deteriorate, and the seed must be renewed from its native place, although the seed may, when it finds favourable soil, &c., yield just as good, if not a better variety."

In Virginia, remarks Thomas, there are "as many varieties of tobacco-seed as of corn or wheat. I will name a few: The Big Frederic, the Little Frederic, the

Blue Stalk, the Brittle Stem, the Big Orinoco, the Little Orinoco, and half-a-dozen others, each having, or supposed to have, some characteristic distinguishing it from all the others. But the Brittle Stem and the Orinocos were the varieties mostly cultivated, the former for its early maturity, the latter for its comparative heaviness. There are several varieties, also, in this vicinity, such as the Brittle Stem, the Graham Tobacco, and the Cuban, but the names convey little certain information, as the same varieties bear different names in different localities. But some varieties are evidently to be preferred to others—one noted for early maturity, all things else equal, is preferable to another that ripens late. One distinguished for fineness of texture, all things else equal, is better than another of coarser fibre, &c. Upon the whole, the surest and most profitable variety is that which ripens earliest, and yields the largest number of pounds, cured, to a given number of hills planted."

In the opinion of Perry Hull, a grower in Litchfield county, Connecticut, " the variety best adapted to our purpose is that known in this State as the Bull Tongue. The leaf is neither too long nor too short; the length and width being in such good proportion that manufacturers considered there is less waste than there is to a very long narrow leaf, or a very broad short leaf. It yields well, and ripens at least one week earlier than many of the broader varieties. Almost any of the seed-leaf varieties will do well; but never patronize any of the humbugs sent from the Patent Office, under the name of Graham tobacco, Maryland broad leaf, &c. They are a Southern tobacco, and when grown upon that soil, make chewing-tobacco; but here it is good for nothing for that purpose, and is too coarse for cigar-wrappers."

According to Dennis, an Indiana planter, "selection of seed depends upon the kind of land you have and the quality of tobacco you wish to raise. Rich, fertile bottom-lands will grow only heavy, strong tobacco, and it is the interest of the farmer to select that kind of seed that will produce the plant of the greatest weight; in other words, to make weight the prominent object in the result of the crop. Thinner, poorer land will produce tobacco of lighter weight, but of finer and more desirable quality, and one that will bring a correspondingly higher price. The Orinoco tobacco is raised extensively in Missouri and Kentucky for heavy tobacco, and is known in market as Kentucky Leaf. The seed for the finer qualities passes (as does the other also) under different names, but may be procured in Pike and Calloway counties, Missouri, and in Virginia; the Orinoco, and kindred kinds, in Howard and Chariton counties in Missouri. I should suggest that the seed may be procured through the agents of express-companies at Glasgow, Brunswick, and Renick for the Orinoco, and at Louisiana or Fulton for the other qualities. I would recommend the culture of the coarser, heavier kinds, for the reason that the finer quality needs much more care and experience in the handling, in order that it may go into market in a condition to command such a price as its quality, when well handled, entitles it to."

In the words of Libhart, a Pennsylvanian farmer, the "best variety for cultivation in a high northern latitude is the Connecticut seed-leaf, as it ripens two weeks earlier than most any other variety, cures and colours better, and commands the highest price in the market. The Pennsylvania seed-leaf outstrips the Connecticut in size and weight, but owing to its requiring a longer time to mature in, is not so well adapted to climates north of 41° or 42°."

An experienced Missouri grower, named Pursley, remarks that there " are more than twenty distinct varieties, of which I will only mention the most valuable :—The Yellow Prior, Blue Prior, Orinoco, Little Frederic, Big Frederic, Cuba, and Spanish tobacco. These are considered the most valuable in this State. The Yellow Prior and Orinoco are the most profitable.

" I prefer the Yellow Prior, as it is the easiest cultivated and is the most fine and smooth of the many varieties. Some growers prefer the Orinoco, on account of it being the heaviest. I do not for various reasons: it has large stiff fibres and ruffled stalks, which afford hiding-places for insects; it moulds easier, is harder to cure, and generally does not bring as good a price as the Yellow Prior."

Seed.—The best and strongest plants are selected for affording seed. These are not "topped" like the remainder of the crop, and are left standing when the crop is gathered. All suckers are carefully removed from the stems, and sometimes from the leaves also. When the crop is cut, the seed-stalks should be staked, to prevent their destruction by the wind. As soon as the seed-pods blacken, the seed is ripe; the heads are then cut off below the forks of the plant, and are hung in a dry and safe place to cure. Care must be taken to gather them before frost has impaired their vitality. During leisure time, the pods are stripped from the stalks, and the seed is rubbed out by hand, and winnowed. Its vitality is proved by its crackling when thrown upon a hot stove.

Seed-beds.—A very light friable soil is necessary for the seed-beds; to obtain this, it should be broken up to a depth of 1½ ft. some months before the sowing season. A drain is dug around the beds, and the soil is utilized in raising the surface. In America, a very warm and sheltered situation, such as the south end of a barn, is selected for the seed-beds. It is a common plan there to burn a brush-heap over the ground, thus supplying potash and killing weeds. The time for sowing in America is usually from the middle of March to the 10th of April, or as soon as the ground admits of working in the spring; in India, it depends upon the locality: when the monsoon rains are very heavy, it should follow them; in other cases, it may precede them.

Unless the soil be very rich in humus, it should be heavily manured with well-preserved farmyard manure soon after breaking up. The soil of a tobacco nursery cannot contain too much organic matter; the presence of much humus will prevent, to a great extent, the formation of a surface crust, which is so detrimental to the development of the plants during their early growth, and will also facilitate the extraction of the plants when transplanting takes place. After a few weeks have elapsed, the soil should be dug over a second time, and the whole be reduced to a fine tilth. The land may now remain untouched until the sowing-time, unless weeds should spring up: these must be eradicated.

CULTIVATION. 39

The area required for a nursery depends on the area of ground to be planted, and on the distance separating the plants in the field. About 1 sq. in. space should be allotted to each of the young plants in the nursery. Taking the number to be 7260 plants required for an acre (at 3 ft. × 2 ft.), and giving each plant 1 sq. in. of room, an area of 7000 sq. in. or 50 sq. ft. would raise plants sufficient for an acre. But as some are injured during growth, many rendered useless in lifting them for transplanting, and more needed to replace those that die after transplanting, double the number should be raised, or 100 sq. ft. of nursery bed for an acre.

The amount of seed required for an acre depends chiefly on its vitality. An ounce contains about 100,000 seeds, or sufficient for nearly 7 acres if all grew; but as even the best has not a very high percentage of vitality, $\frac{1}{2}$–1 oz. is generally sown to produce the plants required for one acre.

Sowing-time having arrived, the nursery is divided into beds, most conveniently, 10 ft. long and 5 ft. wide, making 50 sq. ft. each, on which plants for $\frac{1}{2}$ acre can easily be raised. As, even with a small tobacco plantation, several days are required for transplanting, all the beds should not be sown at one time, but at intervals of a few days. This will also lessen the risk of the young plants being all destroyed by a storm, insects, &c. Before sowing the seed, the soil is dug over to the depth of 6 inches, and levelled with a rake. The seed must then be sown evenly on the surface, and beaten down slightly with the hand or otherwise. The seed being very small, many cultivators mix it with ashes, or pulverized gypsum, in order to distribute it regularly over the bed. The seed must be covered only slightly, best done by strewing a little fine compost manure over it. Ants, which often destroy the seeds, may be kept off by sprinkling some ashes over the bed. Finally cut straw may be scattered over the surface. In India, to protect the nursery from the sun and rain, the whole is covered with a roof made of straw, leaves, or cloth, supported by poles, at only a few feet above the ground. The soil must be kept constantly moist, but not wet; weak liquid manure may be used for watering. Much time is saved by starting the seed in a warm room before sowing.

The plants, which will appear about a week after sowing, are very tender during the first stage of their growth, and require frequent watering through a fine rose. The straw will now prevent the water falling with any force immediately on the plants, and its tendency to wash the soil from the fine rootlets. If the plants spring up thickly, they are thinned out, when about a week or two old, leaving about 1 sq. in. for each. Those taken out may be used to fill blanks in the nursery bed, or, if more plants are taken out than are required for this purpose, they should be planted in a separate bed. It is universally acknowledged that plants transplanted when very young develop more roots, grow more vigorously, and become more hardy afterwards, than when not transplanted at this stage. When the plants are about two weeks old, they require less attention, and should be watered less frequently, to harden them before transplanting. Any weeds appearing must be removed, and injurious insects must be killed. In about 7–8 weeks after sowing, the plants will be fit for transplanting.

Bowie, a Maryland planter, gives his experience in the following words :—"After a thorough burning of brush, dig deep, and continue to dig, rake, and chop until every clod, root, and stone be removed; then level and pulverize nicely with a rake. As to the variety to plant, I think the Cuba is a very good kind for our climate. The Connecticut seed-leaf is the best, but culture has more than anything else to do with the quality. Mix 1 gill of seed for every 10 square yards with a quart of plaster or sifted ashes, and sow it regularly in the same manner that gardeners sow small seeds, only with a heavier hand; roll with a hand-roller or tramp it with the feet. If the bed is sown early, it ought to be covered with brush free from leaves; but it is not necessary to cover it after the middle of March. Tobacco-beds may be sown at any time during the winter if the ground be not too wet or frozen. The best time for sowing is from the 10th to the 20th of March, though it is safest to sow at intervals, whenever the land is in fine order for working. Never sow unless the land is in good order, for the work will be thrown away if the land be too moist or be not perfectly prepared. The beds must be kept free from grass or weeds, which must be picked out one at a time by the fingers. It is a tedious and troublesome operation, therefore you should be very careful not to use any manures on your beds which have grass or weed-seeds in them. After the plants are up, they should receive a slight top-dressing of manure once a week, sown broadcast by the hand. This manure should be composed of ½ bushel of unleached ashes (or 1 bushel of burnt turf), 1 bushel of fresh virgin woods-earth, 1 gallon of plaster, ½ gallon of soot, 1 quart of salt dissolved in 2 gallons of liquid from barnyard, and 4 lb. of pulverized sulphur, the whole well intermixed. Let a large quantity be got together early in the spring, or winter rather, and put away in barrels for use when wanted. This, and other such mixtures, have been found efficacious in arresting the ravages of the fly—both from the frequent dusting of the plants and the increased vigour which it imparts to them, thereby enabling the plant the sooner to get out of the tender state in which the fly is most destructive to it. The fly is a small black insect, somewhat like the flea, and delights in cold, dry, harsh weather, but disappears with the mild showers and hot suns of opening summer. If possible, the plants should stand in the bed from $\frac{1}{2}$ inch to 1 inch apart, and if they are too thick they must be raked when they have generally become as large as 5 or 10-cent pieces. The rake proper for the purpose should be a small common rake, with iron teeth 3 inches long, curved at the points, teeth flat, and $\frac{3}{8}$ inch wide, and set $\frac{1}{2}$ inch apart."

Schneider, whose success as an Illinois planter has already been mentioned, expresses himself thus:—"Raising tobacco-plants from seed is somewhat similar to raising cabbage-plants, but is different in two important things: It takes considerably more time for the seed to sprout (six weeks), and, on account of disturbing the roots, cannot well stand weeding. Therefore the principal care in providing the seed-bed is, to prepare for the early starting of the seed, and to have the bed free from all weed-seeds. In the West we prepare the seed-bed in the following manner: we take a plot of land—newly cleared land is preferred—sloping southward, and protected against winds. The bed should be 4 feet broad and 8 feet long; on this we pile brush, wood, and heavy logs, sufficient to keep up a strong fire for at least one hour, and burn it. When the coals begin to die out, or before the soil is cold, the bed is cleared off, and only the fine ashes are left; then it is hoed thoroughly and as deep as the strongest heat has penetrated, after which it is raked cross and lengthwise, until the soil is entirely pulverized. Everything that might hinder the growing of the plants, and their taking out afterwards, is carefully removed. On this bed a thimbleful of seed, well mixed with a few handfuls of ashes or earth, is sown broadcast, and tramped in with the feet, or slapped with the under side of the spade or any other suitable instrument. After this, the bed is thoroughly wetted with a weak manure-water, 12 lb. of hen-droppings, or 1 lb. of soot in 10 gallons of water, and lightly covered with straw. The seed-bed does not need much attention at first, if the weather remains mild; but if there is danger of night-frosts, a layer of brush must be made, and on this a layer of straw 2 to 4 inches thick, according to the degree of frost. The straw is removed in the morning, and put on again at evening, leaving it off entirely when the nights are mild. Although the seed-bed is ready now, it must not be left to itself, and requires some care. The plants must always have sufficient moisture, and if timely rains do not fall, they must be watered with weak liquid manure as often as needed. Should weeds appear, notwithstanding all precautions, they must be removed with the utmost care. The above-mentioned quantity of seed is sufficient to raise plants for one acre.

"Whoever is in possession of a hot-bed can raise the plants much easier; he can sow later and have plants earlier and with more certainty. But even the common bed may be made into a kind of hot-bed. The burned and hoed surface soil is removed and put on one side, then one foot of fresh horse-dung is laid on the subsoil, and the surface soil put back again. Boards may be placed around, cross-pieces laid over them, and the straw covering put on these.

"The earlier the young plants are ready for transplanting the surer the tobacco crop will be. March is the latest to make the seed-bed in the open air, and June the latest for transplanting. Some time may be gained by keeping the seed in damp earth in the room, and sow it in the seed-bed just before it commences to sprout."

Having selected a suitable location, says White, a Connecticut grower, "next consider how large a bed you will need. That depends on the surface you intend to plant out. A bed 2 rods long, by 12 feet wide, will produce a sufficient number of good plants to set an acre. On such a bed you should spread a heavy coat of good, fine, well-rotted manure, at least 2 inches thick; let it be free from straw or other litter. Then, with a good strong back, and long-handled spade (or other as you prefer), spade up the bed, mixing in the manure very fine. Have ready some fine dry brush, or the like, and spread over the whole surface; set it on fire and burn to ashes. A small quantity will answer better than a very large one, for if very much is burned, it is apt to do injury by burning the soil. The less quantity will tend to destroy any foreign seed turned up, and warm the ground. Having reduced the brush to ashes, take a fine iron or steel rake, and proceed to pulverize very finely the whole surface spaded up. After reducing it to as fine a state as possible, and having made it flat and level, leave it till the next day. Then, with your rake, carefully rake over the whole bed; it is now ready for the seed. Sow the seed on broadcast; be careful to sow it even and true. About two thimblefuls, or a little less, will be sufficient for such a bed. It is better to have too little than too much, as in the first instance, the plants will have room to form thick stalky roots and well-spread leaves, while in the latter they will be crowded with spindling tops as well as small roots. Having sowed your seed, take a good heavy garden-roller and roll the surface down hard and smooth. In the absence of a roll, a very good substitute can be made by taking a piece of 2-inch plank, say 18 inches long by 14 inches wide; in the centre, place an upright handle. With this spat the bed over, being careful to do it evenly, and to leave the surface solid and level, the reasons for which you will afterward discover in weeding and taking out plants to set in the field. This should be done in the spring, as soon as the ground will permit, say first of April, if the frost is out and the ground settled. The roll or spatter will cover the seed sufficiently without any other covering. To be able to sow the seed with the least trouble, mix it in thoroughly with wood-ashes or plaster, before sowing. To obtain plants earlier, you can mix your seed thoroughly in about a quart of light chip dirt from under your wood-shed; put it in some proper vessel, and wet to the consistence of soft putty, with water as warm as can be well borne by the hand. Set it on the mantle-shelf in the kitchen, not too near the stove or fire, but where it will keep warm. In the course of a week or ten days, the seed will have cracked the shell, and will show the small white germ or sprout. It should now be sowed broadcast very evenly, and treat as before described. If properly wet at first, it will need no more water to sprout the seed. Before sowing, pulverize the mass containing the seed, to facilitate the sowing. Having thus sown and rolled down your bed very nicely, it is well to have something to protect it from the encroachment of the fowls. For this purpose, spread a net of twine or a few brush over the surface, covering it so that they may not disturb the surface by scratching and wallowing. It may now be left till the weeds begin to make their appearance; these you will need to extract by the roots as soon as the plants can be distinguished; these last may be known by two very small nearly round leaves opening over flat on the ground. Now procure a plank or some substitute a little longer than your bed is wide, also two blocks 5 or 6 inches square, as long or longer than your plank is wide; place one on one side of the bed, the other on the opposite side; on these two blocks place your plank, and you will have a fine platform on which you can sit and weed any part, or all, of your bed, by moving it as occasion may require. To assist in pulling out the weeds, procure a moderately sharp-pointed knife, and with the same grasped in the hand with the thumb near the point, pinch out the weeds, being careful not to disturb the dirt any more than absolutely necessary. The process of weeding must be repeated as often as necessary, to keep the bed clean from weeds."

Obviously, no frost must be allowed to reach the seedbed when once sowing has taken place. To prevent this, and for another purpose to be described presently, Perry Hull advises the construction of a straw mat, as shown in Fig. 4, which is very light to handle, easily made, and

Fig. 4.

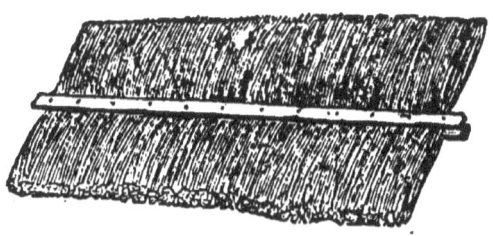

sufficiently strong to last one season. It is made "by laying a scantling (6 feet long, 1½ inches wide, ¾ inch thick) upon the barn floor; place a layer of good straight rye-straw upon it, so that the scantling will come about in the middle of the straw, then another layer with the tips the other way, that it may be of uniform thickness in all its parts (about 1½ inches thick). Place a similar scantling exactly over it, and with sixpenny nails, nail them tight; with an axe trim both edges straight, and to a width of 3 feet, and the mat is made. With these the beds should be covered every night, cold or warm; in the daytime they should be set up at the north side of the bed, at an angle of about 65 degrees, by driving crotches just inside of the bed, for the end of the scantling to rest in, the lower edge of the mat resting on the ground, outside the bed.

"The plants, as soon as they are out of the ground, which will be in a few days, require strict attention.

The beds should be made high enough, so that in fair weather a little water can be applied every night. After the fourth leaf appears, manure-water should be used. Place an old barrel near the beds, and throw into it ½ bushel of hen-manure, and fill with water; after it is well soaked, use ½ pailful of it, and fill up with clear water with the chill taken off. As the plants get larger, the strength of the infusion can be increased, being careful that it is not so strong as to turn the plants yellow. As soon as the plants are large enough to be readily taken hold of by the thumb and point of a knife, they should be thinned to about 144 per square foot, and kept free from weeds. This plan is decidedly preferable to raising under glass. It is less expensive, the plants are more hardy to set out in the field, are got fully as early, and a little carelessness on a hot day will not ruin the whole. It has been my method for the past 8 years, and during that time I have never failed to have good strong plants ready for the field between the 5th and 10th of June."

Mitjen, whose essay on tobacco-growing in Cuba has been already mentioned, recommends a system of shade frames borne on small tramway trucks, as illustrated in Fig. 5—(a) seed beds, raised above the surrounding level; (b) light pointed covers of thatch on a wooden frame, and provided with grooved wheels; (c) rails on which the frames run, facilitating their application or removal as the vicissitudes of the weather may demand.

Preparation of the Field.—Land intended to be planted with tobacco should receive several ploughings not less than 9 inches deep. As a rule, clay requires to be more deeply ploughed than sandy or loamy soil. It greatly conduces to success, if the land is allowed to lie fallow for several months before planting the crop, to admit of the proper preparation of the soil, by ploughing, rolling, harrowing, &c., and to allow the attainment of as fine a

FIG. 5.

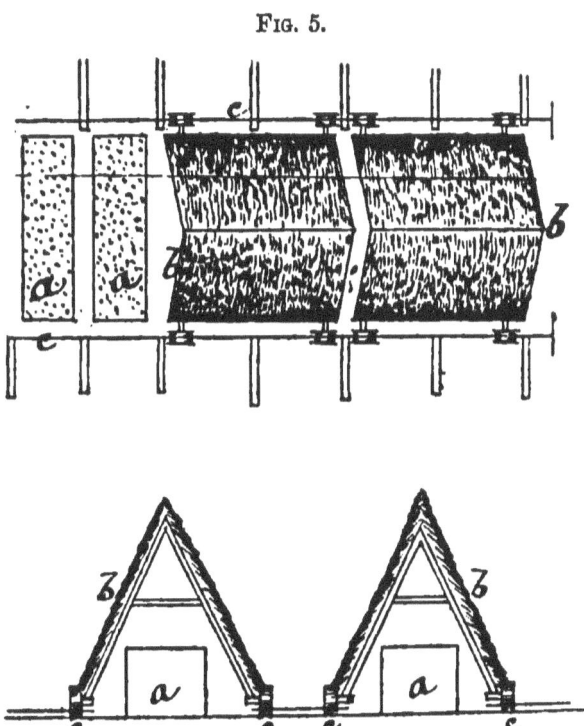

tilth as is usual in gardens. No crop will better repay the expense of proper preparation of the soil than tobacco; the fineness of the leaf and the aroma of the tobacco depend to a great degree upon this. The land should be ridged immediately before planting. The distance apart at which to make the ridges is governed by the quality of the soil and the sort of plant to be raised. With good soil, the ridges must be farther apart than in a poor one, because of producing larger leaves. The ridges should allow a passage between the rows, for the purpose of weeding, hoeing, suckering, &c., without breaking the leaves. In the lines, the plants may be 6 in.-1 ft. closer than the ridges. In some places, a plough is run at right angles across the ridges before planting, at the distance at which the plants have to stand in the lines, thus forming small hills on which the seedlings are planted.

Planting.—Planting should take place only in the evening (or even at night in India), unless the weather be cloudy, when it may be performed during the whole day. Some hours before commencing to transplant, the nursery should be thoroughly watered, to facilitate the removal of the plants, without tearing their roots. If the plants are of even size, so that all can be removed, the best plan is to take them out with a spade, or trowel, leaving a lump of soil on each. But in most cases, it will be necessary to take up each plant separately; this should be done very carefully, holding with the thumb and forefinger as near as possible to the roots, and drawing out the plants, if possible, with a little soil adhering to their roots. The plants are taken at once in a basket to the field for planting. An attendant going between two ridges places a plant on each hill, right and left. One attendant is sufficient for two planters, who follow immediately. The planting is nearly the same as with cabbages, but requires more care, the plants being more tender, and their roots and leaves springing nearly from the same point, they are more difficult to handle. The plants should be placed in a hollow made on each hill, which will serve as a reservoir for the water to be applied, and also afford some shade.

In India, the plants are watered immediately after planting; they should also by some means be shaded during the first few days, which can easily be done when only a small area is planted, but is rather difficult to manage on a large scale. In the latter case, the shade afforded by planting in a slight cavity must suffice. If the plants have been taken from the nursery with some soil adhering to their roots, and are kept sufficiently moist during the first few days, few of them will die. When the weather is dry, water should be applied at morning and evening, and after that time, once daily until the plants have taken root, after which, occasional waterings, varying with soil, weather, and kind of plant, must be given. In dry weather, and with a soil poor in humus, one watering every second or third day may be necessary, whereas with a soil rich in organic matter, and in a moist atmosphere, watering may be entirely dispensed with. During the first few days, the water is applied with a watering-pot, held very low, otherwise the soil would be washed from the plant-roots, and expose them to the direct rays of the sun, causing death. The arrangement of the plants in what is known as quincunx order, as shown in Fig. 6, is generally adopted.

This part of the operations connected with tobacco-growing is described at some length by Mitjen so far as the practice rules in Cuba. His translator remarks that " as soon as the land has been prepared, it should be furrowed at a distance of 1 yard between each two furrows. This operation should be simultaneous with the planting, and should be done, if possible, after 3 o'clock in the afternoon, and on cloudy days, so as to

Fig. 6.

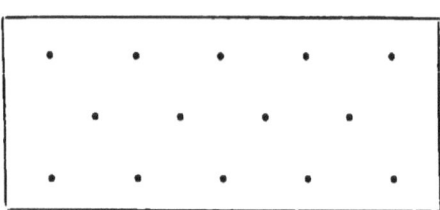

prevent the recently set plants from being scorched by the sun. The furrows should run more or less from north to south, as, by making them in this direction, the plants are less injured by the sun, or the strong winds which generally blow about the planting season. Immediately, and behind the man who is furrowing, another should follow, placing the plants at every ½ foot all along the furrow, and behind them another should at once set the plants, the first walking in the distance, or bank, and the other in the furrow. The one should open the land with his right hand, behind which, with his left, the other will place the plant, being careful neither to double the stalk nor the roots, and, letting the ground fall directly on the roots, should press it lightly on them with his hand. The plants should be buried half-way up the stalk, or, if the plant is small, it should be covered to where the leaves spread. Care should be taken that the plants have no *dry* mould sticking to their roots, and that no ground from the furrow falls in the *centre or*

CULTIVATION. 53

sprout, and when the planting is going on, the ground should not be too wet. The plants should be set on the side of the furrow, and on that side which is next the setting sun, so that the rising sun may strike upon them, and they may be somewhat protected from the rays of the afternoon sun.

" Generally the plants wither after being transplanted, but on the third or fourth day after they are set they begin to shoot up, and on the fifth day or the sixth, those that have not taken root can be distinguished. Then, and without loss of time, others should be supplied, this operation being repeated at the end of another 5 or 6 days, so that the whole field may be well filled with living plants. This is one of the most important operations for securing a good crop, because the fields will require as much cultivation and labour bestowed on them if they have vacant spots as if they were full and regularly planted, and, of course, the yield will be less, besides many other evils well known to practical *vegueros*.

"According to the best opinions admitted among *vegueros*, one man can take care of 12,000 tobacco plants, and prudence dictates that no more land should be planted than that which can be well attended to, as experience shows that in exceeding this number for each man, instead of proving advantageous to the planter, it is frequently the cause of considerable loss. Excessive planting produces, at once, an increase of labour, and if, unfortunately, a hard year should occur, occasioned by caterpillars or other causes, it almost always happens that the man who has only planted 12,000 plants, for each labourer he can command, produces four times as much tobacco, and of a better quality, than he who may have planted from 25,000 to 30,000 plants per labourer.

"When the plantations are out of proportion to the strength of the labour which can be counted on, all the work becomes slowly and badly done, and these faults most sensibly prejudice both the yield and the quality of the crop, and consequently the interest of the planter. Immediately after supplying the fields, the tobacco plants should be carefully inspected, almost daily, in order to exterminate the caterpillars of every kind that may be found, and this operation should *always* be made during the morning, because in the heat of the day the worms are accustomed to hide themselves from the sun, and the wind agitates the leaves too strongly to permit them to be handled without risk of being broken or torn, especially when they are somewhat large."

After-cultivation.—After the plants have once taken root, they grow rapidly They are hoed when about 6–9 in. high, and the soil is drawn from the furrows to raise the hills, maintaining a depression round the stems. If the soil is not very rich, a special manure should be applied at this stage of growth. The best manure generally will be nitre in a liquid state, which can be applied in the depression around the plants with a watering-pot. By applying it in solution and close to the plant, less is required than when spread over the whole field. Some weeks afterwards, another hoeing and heaping of earth round the plants will be necessary. It is most difficult to say the number of hoeings which may be required by a tobacco crop. The general rule to be followed is to keep the soil loose, friable, and free from weeds. The more organic matter the soil contains, the more will it remain loose and friable; the less organic matter, the more waterings will be required, which causes the soil to crust over, and to assume a close texture, and necessitates frequent hoeings. As long as the plants have not spread much, the hoeing may be done by a cultivator, followed by some men to perform the heaping. Insects which attack the tobacco must be carefully sought for and killed at once. They can easily be discovered in the mornings; if not killed, they may destroy the whole crop in a few days. Turkeys are invaluable for their grub-eating propensities.

Worms, in the American phraseology, here generally known as caterpillars, are the *bête noire* of the tobacco grower. The most common is highly destructive also to the potato and tomato foliage. The worm as it comes from the egg is so small as to be unobserved, but having an enormous appetite, it devours rapidly, and soon grows to a great size. When not feeding, it lifts up the head and fore-part of the body, and remains apparently lifeless. From its resemblance in this position to the Egyptian Sphinx, Linnæus gave the name *Sphinx* to the genus. The larva is of a light green colour, with whitish oblique stripes, and has a horn upon the rear end of the body. Though it is repulsive in appearance, it is perfectly harmless to touch, and may be picked off with the hands without fear. After it has reached its full size, it leaves the scene of its ravages and goes into the earth, where it throws off its skin and becomes a brown-coloured chrysalis. The curious projection, like a handle, at the end of the chrysalis, is a sheath which holds the tongue of

56   TOBACCO.

the future moth. The moth or perfect insect is fully 2 in. long in the body and the spread of its wings reaches

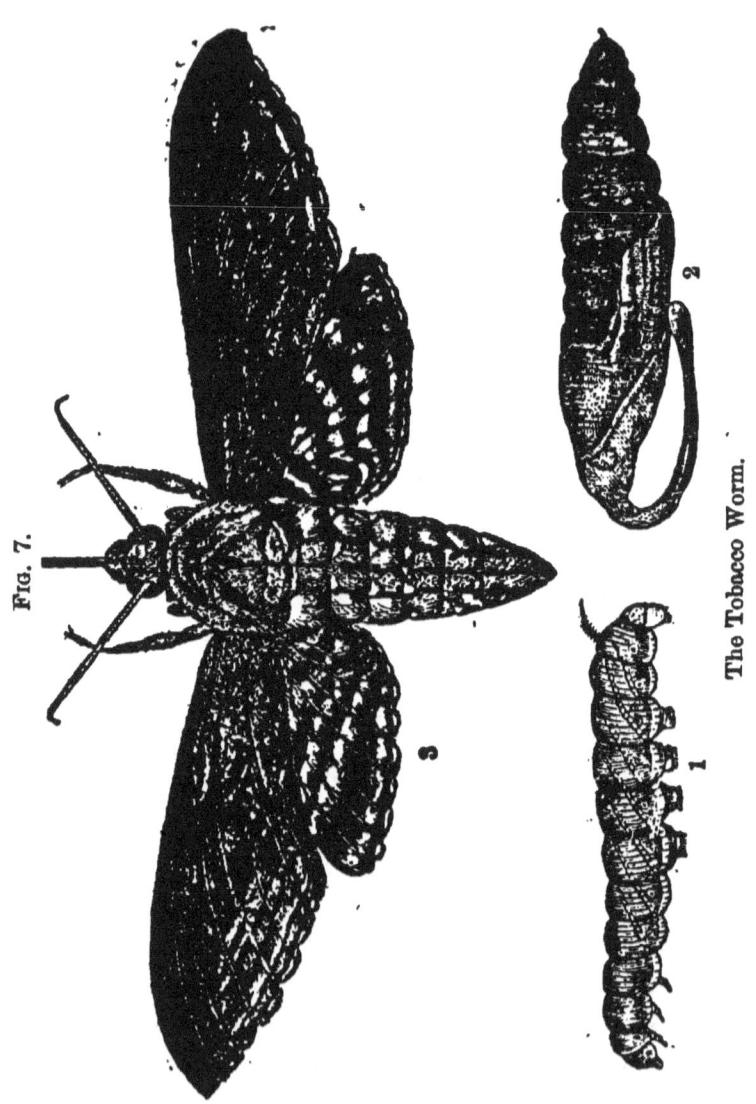

Fig. 7.   The Tobacco Worm.

5 in. It is of a grey colour, with orange-coloured spots on each side of the body. As there are five of these spots on each side, it is called *Sphinx quinque-maculatus*, or Five-spotted Sphinx. The moths may be seen towards night flitting about the flowers, from which they suck the juices by means of their remarkable tongue, which is 5-6 inches long. When the tongue is not in use, it is closely coiled up and hidden between the two feelers. From the manner of their flight and feeding, they are frequently mistaken for humming-birds, and are called " humming-bird moths," and " horn-blowers." The moths should always be destroyed if possible; by so doing we prevent the production of several hundreds of most destructive worms. Naturalists make one or two other species, which closely resemble the Five-spotted Moth, and are only distinguished by characters which would not be noticed except by the entomologist.

Judson Popenoe gives the following advice with regard to these pests. " As soon as worms appear, which is generally when the leaves are as big as a man's hand, go over the tobacco, looking carefully at every plant. The worms usually stay on the under side of the leaf; if you see a hole in the leaf, no matter how small, raise it up and you will generally find a worm under it. Worming can not be done too carefully. Miss one or two worms on a plant, and before you are aware of it the plant is nearly eaten up. When you find a worm, take hold of it with the thumb and forefinger, giving your thumb that peculiar twist which none but those who are practised in it know how to do, and put the proper amount of pressure on, and my word for it you will render his wormship harmless. Worming has to be continued until the tobacco is cut; the last worming to immediately precede cutting and housing."

Schneider remarks that "from the first starting of the tobacco plant, it has its enemies. First appears a cutworm that works in the soil and eats the roots off. Then comes a little caterpillar which enjoys itself on the young leaves, and lastly the beautiful and large tobacco-worm, which eats into the leaf, and in a short time leaves nothing but the leaf-stems and stalk. The only remedies against these enemies are the vigilance and industry of the planter—looking after them, digging up, picking, and destroying once or twice a day, or as often as there are any traces of them. Children, to whom premiums are offered, will be very successful in destroying them. A herd of turkeys, if given access to the tobacco-field, are a very valuable help. A negro from South Carolina told me a few days ago, that a solution of blue vitriol in water, sprinkled over the plants, will kill the worms. The remedy may be worth trying. Of course the solution must be made weak enough, so that it will not destroy the plants as well as the worms."

On the same subject, White recommends the planter on the "next, or at farthest, the second morning after having set your plants, go over to see that the worms do not eat up one-half of them. You can tell where they are and have been, by seeing a plant with a single leaf, and sometimes the whole plant eaten off and drawn down into the hole occupied by a large brown or black worm; you will see little ant-hills like, and round holes in the ground; by poking around a little in the dirt, you will find a worm very near the mouth of these little holes. Destroy it, and all you can find, and thus save your crop. This searching for worms must be kept up till they cease to do mischief. All plants missing in the field should be renewed from the bed at the first opportunity. The morning is the best time to find the worms, as they are near the surface of the ground; later, they retire into the ground to appear again near sundown, and work during the night and early morning."

Thomas describes tobacco worms as "hatched from eggs deposited by what is called the 'tobacco fly.' It is a large, dusky-brown, winged miller, nearly as large as a humming-bird. It lays its eggs on fair evenings and moonlight nights in July and August. It can be seen almost any clear evening, among what are called 'Jimson-weeds,' sucking the flowers. The eggs will hatch out in 24 hours, and the worms commence eating when less than $\frac{1}{2}$ inch long, and continue to eat till they attain the length of 4–5 inches. One worm, in 6 weeks, will destroy a plant so completely as to render it utterly valueless. This pest is vastly more numerous in some seasons than in others. Four years ago there were scarcely any; but for the last three years they have been destructively numerous. The worming of the crop, when they are numerous, is, by far, the most disagreeable and tedious labour attending it. Much of the value of the crop depends upon the care or inattention of performing this part of the work. The crop may have been planted in good time—ploughed, hoed, primed, suckered, topped, cut, and cured well; yet it may have been so riddled by worms as to be comparatively good for nothing in market;

hence, they must be picked off and destroyed, and that promptly."

Topping and Suckering.—The plants will commence to flower about two months after planting, when 2–7 feet high. When the flower-buds appear, they must be broken off, and with them the top and bottom leaves. By breaking off the flower-buds at an early date, the sap that would be used in the formation of these organs flows to the leaves, which thereby increase in size, and the outturn becomes much heavier than when the plant is allowed to flower. But it is generally admitted that the leaves lose much in aroma. To what extent the early removal of the flower-buds impairs the quality has not been properly investigated. It is very probable that the greater yield does not always compensate for the loss in quality. The bottom leaves are generally of inferior quality, small, torn, and dirty. The number of leaves to be left on the plant varies greatly, according to species, quality of soil, and method of cultivation. The minimum may be placed at 6, the maximum at 22. The only rule to be observed is to retain as many leaves as the plants are able to mature. Soon after the plants have been topped, suckers appear in the axils of the leaves; these should be broken off as soon as they come, at least they should not be allowed to grow longer than 4 inches. If the suckers are not removed soon after their appearance, the size of the leaves will be seriously impaired. After the plants are half-grown, great care must be taken when going through the lines, whether for the purposes of hoeing, watering, or suckering, &c., not to tear the leaves. In India, hoeing and suckering should be performed only when the leaves have lost part of their turgescence, attained at night. Insects, however, must be killed during the morning and evening; at other times, they are not easily found. Leaves which are torn are not fit for cigar-wrappers, and must often be thrown on the refuse heap as valueless, even if well developed and of good colour.

The plants commence to ripen about three months after being planted; this is indicated by the leaves assuming a marbled appearance, and a yellowish-green colour. The leaves also generally become gummy, and the tips bend downwards. It is considered that tobacco intended for snuff should have attained more maturity than tobacco for smoking. Nessler found that the less ripe leaves contained more carbonate of potash, and burnt consequently better, than the more ripe ones, but the total amount of potash was larger in the latter than in the former; cigars made from less ripe leaves kept the fire when lighted for a shorter time than those made from more ripe leaves.

In the words of Judson Popenoe, the " tobacco is ready to top when the button (as the blossom or top of the stalk is called) has put out sufficiently to be taken hold of, without injury to the top leaves. As tobacco is not regular in coming into blossom, it is the usual practice to let those stalks that blossom first, run a little beyond their time of topping, and then top all that is in button as you go. There is no particular height to top at, but as a general thing 16 to 18 leaves are left; judgment is necessary to determine where to top; if topped too high, 2 or 3 of the top leaves are so small as not to amount to much; if topped low, the tobacco spreads better; if just coming out in top, reach down among the top leaves, and with thumb and forefinger pinch the top or button off below 2 or 3 leaves; if well out in top, break off several inches down from the button and 4 or 5 leaves below it. As soon as the tobacco is topped, the suckers begin to grow; one shoots out from the stalk at the root of each leaf, on the upper side. When the top suckers are 3–4 inches long, the suckering should be done; with the right hand take hold of the top sucker, with the left take hold of the next, close to the stalk, and break them off, and so proceed, using both hands, stooping over the stalk, taking care not to injure the leaf. Break the suckers about half-way down the stalk, the balance being too short to need removing until the second suckering. In about 2 weeks from topping, the tobacco is ready to cut; now give it the last worming and suckering, breaking all suckers off down to the ground, and remove every worm, if you don't want your tobacco eaten in the sheds."

Another process, called "priming" by Schneider, is thus described by him. "The object of priming is to break off the leaves that come out too near the ground, which, when large, lie flat on it, and therefore rot or get dirty. This work should be done early, the sooner the better, so that the plant does not lose much strength by their growing. These leaves must not be torn off, especially not downward, because the plant would be injured, and instead of throwing the strength gained into the other leaves, it would be thrown away to heal the wound. The distance from the ground at which this priming should be done, depends upon the variety grown and upon the time at which the work is done: 4–6 inches is the right distance. This priming is not done by every one. One farmer may practise it, while his neighbour does not; but sorts the lower leaves separately, and sells them as so-called 'lugs,' for which he gets a little over half the price of the good upper leaves. Those who do not prime, must generally top lower, or they must risk that the whole plant, or at least the upper leaves, will not mature fully.

"Topping is done to throw the strength, which would go to develop seeds, into the leaves. It must, therefore, be done as early as the seed-buds show themselves, if not earlier. This work must be done, and the question is, how to do it. If there are but few leaves on the plant, even these will not ripen, if it is not topped; if there are many, then the grower has the choice either to break off the flower-stalk only or to take off one or more leaves also. This should be done in answer to the questions: 1st. Is there time enough to ripen even the upper leaves fully? and, 2nd, Are the plant and the soil strong enough to ripen all leaves, even the upper ones? The answers to these queries will decide the way of topping. If yes, he takes off the flower-stalk only; if no, he tops to 8, 10, 12, 14, or 16 leaves, according to his judgment, that is, he allows so many leaves to remain as will have a good fair chance of reaching maturity."

As Bishop remarks, cultivators are not agreed on the time and place for topping tobacco plants. "Some favour the plan of topping as soon as the blossom-buds appear, others prefer to wait until in blossom. I think there is no harm in letting the earliest plants bloom before being topped, but after once beginning, they should be broken off as soon as the buds begin to look yellow, and the latest plants as soon as the buds appear. A new beginner will be apt to top the plants too high. The object is to ripen and develop as many leaves as the plant can support; if topped too high, the top leaves are small, and when cured are nearly worthless, and the other leaves are not as large or heavy, whereas, if topped too low, then you lose one, two, or three leaves, which the plant might have supported. As a general rule, a plant just in blossom should be topped down to where the leaves are full 7 inches wide, leaving on the stalk from 15 to 18 leaves. This will leave the stalks about $2\frac{1}{2}$ feet high in good tobacco. Later in the season, top the plants sooner and lower. Let as many of the earliest plants as will be wanted remain for seed. One plant will furnish seed enough to put out 5 acres, at least. These should be wormed and suckered like the rest, only leaving the suckers above where you would ordinarily break it off, were you to top it. The piece should now be looked over every other day, to break off the suckers and catch the worms. This should be done as soon as the dew is off in the morning, and towards night, as the worms are eating then, and can be found more readily, while in the heat of the day they remain hid. Great care should be taken not to break off the leaves while going through it, as they are nearly all wasted before the crop is ripe. As soon as the top is broken off, the sap is thrown into the leaves, causing them to expand rapidly. In the meantime suckers will start out just above where each leaf joins the stalk; these must be broken off, or the growth of the leaf will be checked, as the sap will be thrown into these young sprouts. Those nearest the top will start soonest, and will require breaking off twice before the plant is ripe; those at the bottom must all be broken off. This is the hardest and slowest work of all. Not only will these suckers check the growth of the plants, but if allowed to grow will soon break or pry off the leaves, or cause them to grow out at right angles from the stalk, rendering them more liable to be broken off. It is a good plan to have a piece of corn on the north side of a piece of tobacco, or, at least, two or three rows, to shield the growing plants from winds."

Priming is defined by Thomas as "pulling off the bottom leaves to the number of 4 or 5," and he says that any plant large enough to be topped ought to be primed first. All conditions being favourable, he considers that in Ohio, a "tobacco plant will ripen in as many weeks, from the time of topping it, as there are leaves left on the stalk. Consequently, if the topping is done early, it can be topped high, if later, it must be done lower, and if still later, still lower. Planters differ very much at this point. Some will top as high as 16 leaves, others 10, and a great many at 8. My own opinion is, that a plant topped at 10 will weigh as much as one at 16, topped at the same time, and on the same kind of land. About a week after a plant has been topped the suckers will begin to grow. A sucker is only an auxiliary branch which shoots out at the junction of the leaves to the stalk. If not removed, they will grow, and bloom, and ripen seed, and in doing so they will 'suck' the parent-stem of much of its vitality. When the crop of suckers are about 1 inch long they can be pulled or rubbed off, and it should surely be done. In about a week or 10 days a second crop of them will appear. These must also be promptly removed, and then the third crop will show itself, which must be similarly treated. The longer they are permitted to remain on the plant, the more they retard its development, and delay its maturity."

CHAPTER III.

CURING.

GROWING tobacco is only half the battle. Having raised a crop to a state of perfection, the next object is to cure it for the market. This branch of the business demands fully as much care and skill as the purely agricultural part preceding it, and is perhaps equally influenced by the weather. The best crop ever grown may be completely spoiled by injudicious conduct during the drying, &c., while a growth of moderate quality may be made the most of by extra care and trouble.

Harvesting.—The leaf being matured, it should be harvested only after the dew is off the plants, and not on a rainy day. There are two modes of harvesting—gathering the leaves singly, and cutting down the whole plant. Gathering single leaves admits of removing them from the plant as they ripen; the bottom leaves are removed first, and the top ones are left some time longer, until they have attained full maturity. The cultivator is thereby enabled to gather his crop when it possesses the greatest value. This plan necessitates, however, a great amount of labour, and, in a hot climate, the single leaves are apt to dry so rapidly as not to attain a proper colour, unless stacked early in heaps. But stacking in heaps involves great risk of the leaves heating too much, and developing a bad flavour, whereby the tobacco loses more or less in value. For Indian circumstances generally, cutting the whole plants is better than gathering the leaves singly.

For cutting down the plants, a long knife or chopper is used. A man takes the plant with his left hand about 9 inches from the ground, and with the knife in his right hand, cuts through the stem of the plant just above the ground. If the plants are sufficiently "wilted," he may lay them on the ground and proceed to cut down others; if, however, they are so brittle as to cause the leaves to be injured by laying them down, he should give them to another person, to carry them at once under shade. During bright weather, the plants should not be allowed to lie exposed to the sun on the ground, or they will become sun-burnt, and lose in value. A temporary shed should be erected; it might be simply a light roof of palm-leaves or thatched straw, supported by poles; a large tree standing near will also serve the purpose. Under this shade, parallel rows of posts are put up, and on the posts, light poles or strong bamboos are fixed horizontally. The parallel lines should be about $4\frac{1}{2}$ feet apart and the horizontal poles about 4–5 feet from the ground, according to the height of the tobacco plants. Rods are cut in lengths of 5 feet, and laid over the parallel bars, so that they will project about 3 inches at each end. A very light and convenient shelter sometimes used for sun-drying in America, consists of rods laid crosswise, supported on four upright poles, and covered with a sloping roof of boards. The plants that have been cut are immediately brought into the shade, tied in pairs, and hung across the rods. They must not be hung so close as to press each other, and the rods should therefore be

6–12 inches apart. The framework should be so large as to allow of one day's cutting being hung. The plants are left thus for one day, during which time they will be wilted sufficiently to allow handling without tearing the leaves. In a very dry wind, mats or other cover should be laid against the plants most exposed to it, or their leaves will dry rapidly, shrivel up, and remain green. Next day the leaves are carted to the drying-shed. A cart supplied with a framework, in order that the plants may be hung as they were hung under the shade, is the best means. Perpendicular uprights at each corner of a cart or waggon are fixed together by horizontal poles. The plants may be hung so close as not to press heavily on each other, 200–400 being brought to the shed at one time.

As a general rule, Judson Popenoe thinks " tobacco should be cut in about 2 weeks from topping, at which time the leaves assume a spotted appearance and appear to have fulled up thicker; double up the leaf and press it together with thumb and finger, and, if ready to cut, the leaf where pressed will break crisp and short. Do not let your tobacco get over-ripe, or it will cure up yellow and spotted : it is better to cut too soon than too late. Take a hatchet or short corn-knife, grasp the stalk with the left hand, bend it well to the left, so as to expose the lower part of the stalk, strike with the knife just at the surface of the ground, let the stalk drop over on the ground without doubling the leaves under, and leave it to wilt. The usual practice is to worm and sucker while the dew is on in the morning, and as soon as the dew is off to commence cutting. There are some who advocate cutting in the afternoon, say 3 o'clock; let it wilt and lie out until the dew is off next day, and take it in before the sun gets hot enough to burn it. I prefer the first plan, because a heavy dew may fall on the tobacco, and next day be cloudy, leaving the tobacco wet and unpleasant to handle. After cutting, allow the tobacco to wilt long enough to make the leaves tough, so that they can be handled without tearing. Great care is now necessary to keep the tobacco from sun-burning; cutting should be commenced as soon as the dew is off, and all that is cut should be housed by 11 o'clock, unless it is cloudy; from 11 to 2 o'clock the direct rays of the sun on the tobacco, after it is cut, will burn the leaves in 20 minutes; after 2 P. M., as a general thing, there is no danger of such burning, the sun's rays not striking direct on the tobacco. Have a waggon at hand, with stiff boards, 12 feet long, laid on the running gears; as soon as the tobacco is wilted so that it can be handled without breaking, commence loading on both sides of the waggon on the front end, lapping the tobacco the same as loading fodder, keeping the butts out on both sides—build about 2 feet high, and so on until loaded."

Any one accustomed to the cultivation of the crop, says Bishop, " knows when it is ripe,—the veins of the leaves are swollen, the leaves begin to look spotted and feel thick and gummy. The ends of the leaves will crack on being doubled up. After it is ripe, the sooner it is cut the better, as it is liable to injury by frost or hail, and will not increase in weight as fast as the worms eat it, and the leaves get broken by catching them. The plants will generally ripen from the 1st to the 15th of September; they should not be cut immediately after a heavy rain unless in danger of frost, as a portion of the gum washes out, but should be allowed to stand 2-3 days. The cutting should not begin until the dew is off; a cloudy day is best, for when the sun shines hot, they will not have time to wilt sufficiently before they will sunburn, which may be known by the leaves turning white and looking puckered. Commence on one side of the piece, laying the plants all one way, in order to facilitate loading. The plants may, most of them, be broken off easily, by gently bending them over one way and another. Small plants, which will not break, may be sawed off with an old saw or cut with a hatchet. If the sun shines too hot, the plants should be turned over carefully to prevent burning. After lying an hour or two to wilt sufficiently, so as not to break by handling, they may be carted to the barn."

In the words of Schneider, "when the plant begins to yellow, it is time to put it away. It is cut off close to the ground, by turning up the bottom leaves and striking with a tobacco-knife, formed of an old scythe—such knives as are often used for cutting corn. Let it lie on the ground for a short time to wilt, and then carry it to the tobacco-house, when it may be put away in three different modes, by 'pegging,' 'spearing,' and 'splitting.' Pegging tobacco is the neatest way and best, yet the slowest. It is done by driving pegs about 6 inches long and ½ inch or less square into the stalk, about 4 inches from the big end of the stalk; and these pegs are driven in with a mallet, in a slanting direction, so as to hook on to the sticks in the house. It is then put on to a 'horse,' which, by a rope fixed to one corner, is pulled up in the house and there hung upon the sticks, which are regulated at proper distances. A 'tobacco-horse' is nothing more than three small sticks nailed together so as to form a triangle, each side being 3–4 feet long. Spearing is the plan I pursue; because it is neat enough and decidedly the quickest plan. A rough block, with a hole mortised in it, and a little fork a few inches from the hole for the tobacco-stick to rest upon, one end being in the hole and a spear on the other end of the stick, is all the apparatus required; the plant is then, with both hands, run over the spear and thus strung upon the sticks, which, when full, are taken to the house and hung up at once. There are 'dart-spears,' like the Indian dart, and 'round spears.' Either will do. 'Splitting' tobacco is admired by many, who contend that it cures brighter, quicker, and is less likely to 'house-burn' or injure from too thick hanging. This mode is pursued easily by simply splitting, with a knife made for the purpose, the plant from the top to within a few inches of the bottom, before it is cut down for housing."

Another planter observes that " when a plant begins to ripen, it will gradually assume a 'piebald' or spotted appearance. As the ripening advances, the spots will become more distinct and individualized. When the spots can be distinguished at the distance of 10 steps, and the leaves of the plant turn down, become stiff to the touch, and their ends curl under, the plant is ripe, and should be cut. From the moment it has arrived at maturity, it begins to decay. Remember that all the plants in your crop are to be hung after they are cut—

hung on something, and by something. Prepare a knife—a butcher-knife answers well—have it sharp—enter it at the top of the plant, where the top was broken off. Enter it centrally; press it downwards, dividing the stalk into two equal portions. Continue it downwards till within 5 inches of the ground. Withdraw the knife, and cut off the stalk close to the ground. The plant is now cut. Lay it on the ground with the lower end towards the sun. The plants should be placed in rows as they are cut, in order to facilitate the labour of gathering them. There is one caution to be heeded in cutting tobacco, and that is, do not let it be burnt or blistered by the heat of the sun. In some varieties of tobacco this will be effected in one hour; in others, not so soon. But this danger can be evaded in two ways: first, by cutting late in the evening; second, by throwing it in the shade, or covering it so as to weaken the power of the sun. Some varieties of tobacco will wilt (that is, become soft or limber) in 2 hours; others, in a longer time, according to the degree of sun-heat."

Bishop tells us that when "the plant begins to yellow or turn spotted, it is time to put it away. It is cut off close to the ground, turning up the leaves, and cutting off close to the roots, by a single stroke of a hatchet, or tobacco-knife, made of an old scythe, such as are used in cutting up corn. After cutting, let it lie on the ground a short time to wilt, when it may be handled without danger of tearing the leaves; it is then to be taken to the house to be 'hung.'"

The condition of the leaf, according to Pursley, may be judged in the following manner:—"When the tobacco is ripe, it has a yellow faded colour, and becomes brittle; the surface of the leaf is rough and ridged. By bending the leaf short between the fingers, it will break before it will double. The sticks to hang it on should be in readiness. The best mode of hanging or stringing is with a V-shaped spear, made of iron or steel. The spear has a socket, large to admit the end of the stick. The sticks should be sharpened at one end, to fit the socket; should be 4 feet 6 inches in length, 2 inches wide, and 1 inch thick. A stick of these dimensions will hold 8 plants. The tobacco should be cut off just below the bottom leaf, then turn the plant upside down, and let it remain so till the sun wilts it. When it is wilted it can be handled without breaking; then it should be taken up and laid in piles of 8 stalks each, placing the butts of the stalks towards the sun, to prevent it from sun-burning. When it is sun-burnt it turns black, and it cannot be cured any other colour than black, which ruins its sale. The sticks should be strewed along, one stick to a pile; place the spear on the end of the stick, and set the stick upright; then take up the tobacco, one stalk at a time, and thrust it on the stick, letting the spear pass through the stalk, about 6 inches from the butt end; then take the spear off and take up the stick, and shake the tobacco out straight, and set the stick up with the butts towards the sun."

Some tobacco-growers, remarks Pursley, "prefer splitting the stalk from the top down to within about 6 inches of the butt, then hang it on the sticks. But I cannot agree with them, for it is more difficult to handle, and is apt to slip off the stick, when moving it; besides, the tobacco cured in this manner is not so heavy as if it was speared. It dries out quicker by being split, but the substance evaporates instead of remaining in the leaf. I am not certain that it injures the taste of the tobacco, but I am certain that split tobacco is lighter than that which is speared. Some prefer hanging the tobacco on scaffolds in the field until it is ready to be put in the barn and cured by fire. But it is the safest to house it as soon as it is strung on the sticks. Scaffolding is done by placing poles on forks, about 4 feet apart, and 4–5 feet from the ground; then hang the tobacco between the poles, letting the ends of the sticks rest on the poles. This procedure is unsafe, for the rain may come and saturate the tobacco and wash off the gum, thus making it light and chaffy."

The maturity of tobacco is defined by Schneider as when the leaves, which have hitherto been green, on holding them "against the sun, show yellowish, reddish, or brownish spots, feel sticky, and when bent break off short and clean. Before this period sets in, the *drying-house* should be in good order. This house is built to give room for the free hanging up of the tobacco, so that it is protected from the sun, wind, and rain, and is allowed to dry by the free circulation of the air. Any building, therefore, will answer which has a good roof, boarded sides, and enough windows and air-holes (which can be closed at will) to keep up a mild circulation of air inside, and also to keep out strong and too quick drying winds. If the tobacco is grown on a large scale, the house should have large doorways to drive a waggon in and out. There must be sticks all over the house, either cross or lengthwise, and these sticks must be ready and in their places. Now the work of harvesting the crop is commenced on a clear or cloudy but not rainy day. The mature plants (those not ripe are left longer on the field if not too late in the season) are cut off near the ground, two of them tied together by the butt-ends and hung up in the field on riders, which rest on two forks fastened in the ground, and they are left there until evening to wilt; then they are brought to the drying-house and hung up. The tobacco is hung up on the upper sticks first, and the work continued downward; care is taken that the sticks are 6–8 inches apart, also that the plants are not too near together on the sticks, because the air should have free passage among the plants, and when they touch or rub against each other, unsightly spots are produced. The sticks must be pretty wide, so that the two plants which are tied together, and one of which hangs on each side, are held well apart. Later, when the tobacco has dried off somewhat, the sticks and plants may be moved a little nearer to each other; but the plants on the upper sticks must not touch those on the lower; they should be so arranged that one lower stick is just in the middle of the space between two upper ones."

Another method of harvesting is recommended by Schneider for those "who cultivate tobacco on a small scale, or who have hands and time enough. As all the leaves on the plant do not ripen at the same time, but the under leaves are always a little earlier than the upper ones, they may gather the crop in the leaf, that is, taking only the matured leaves from the stalk; this must be done daily, and so long as there are leaves on the stalk. In this way the crop will be harvested slower, and it will cost more, but the tobacco will be of more even quality and better. The leaves are strung on strings instead of being hung up on sticks, with the same care and precautions as recommended for hanging up the whole plants. After the leaves are off, the stalks must be cut off or pulled up, for they would still vegetate, and needlessly take away nourishment from the soil. No more tobacco, leaves or plants should be cut than can be taken to the drying-house and hung up the same day."

Perry Hull's instructions commence with a caution that the plant should never be cut while the dew is on the leaves; " but wait until it is off, say 10 o'clock, and what tobacco is cut from that time until 2 o'clock, if the day is hot, will need close attention. In short, the whole operation, from cutting in the field, to the hanging upon the poles in the barn, needs care, as a little carelessness or inattention will damage many dollars' worth. No hand should be allowed to handle it, who is unwilling to use care, and perform every operation just as directed, or else by breaking of leaves, or sticking fingers through them, &c., he may do more damage than his wages amount to. The plant to be cut should be taken by the left hand, not carelessly by the leaves, but carefully by the stalk, and as carefully leaned over, to give a chance to use the axe, which should have a handle about one foot long. Cut the plant with one blow, laying it carefully down, with the top to the sun; if it is laid otherwise, the leaf will burn before the main stalk of the leaf will wilt sufficiently to admit of handling. Even in that position, it may burn unless attended to, but not as soon. After lying until pretty well wilted, and before burning, turn it over and wilt the other side. When so wilted that the main stem has lost most of its brittleness, load as explained above; taking hold of the butt of the stalk, lay them carefully upon the arm, and again as carefully upon the load. If the day be very hot, use expedition in getting to the shed, else, if the distance be great, the load may heat, which will spoil the leaves for anything but fillers."

When the plants are carried into the shed, "if quite warm, they should be left only one plant deep upon the floor and scaffolds. If the day be cool, and they are to be hung up soon, they may lie much thicker. They should never be hung upon a pole less than 5 inches in width. If sawed pieces are used, saw them just that; if poles are used, see that they are about that; for if anything of less width is used, the plants will hang so close, that the chances of 'pole-burn' are greatly increased. They are fastened to the pole by a half hitch. (Their position is represented by Fig. 9 on p. 95.) It requires two hands to hang them, one to hand them, another to tie them. The poles should be about 18 inches apart, and the number hung upon a 12-foot pole will depend upon the size, from 24 to 30, so regulating them, that when thoroughly wilted, they will scarcely touch each other. If hung thicker than this, a little unfavourable weather will cause more or less pole-burn, sweat and mould. After the tobacco is hung, the building should be so thoroughly ventilated that there will be a circulation of air through every part. The ventilators should be kept open during all fair weather, until well cured down. During storms, shut the doors and exclude as much wet as possible; being cautious to give it a thorough ventilation again, as soon as the rain ceases. When it is cured enough to be husky in dry weather, exclude all hard winds, that will crack and damage the leaves. When the leaves are so much cured, that there is nothing about them green but the stem, a moderate quantity of wet weather will not injure it, but rather improve the colour; as the sap of the stalk works through the stems into the leaves, during moist weather until the stalk has been well frozen; after this takes place, the tobacco should be picked."

White estimates that in " the course of 2 or 3 weeks after topping, the plants will begin to ripen, which may be known by the change in colour of the leaf. It will look spotted with spots of lighter green, a yellowish green. When fully ripe the leaf may be folded together, and moderately pressed without breaking or cracking. Now is the time to begin to harvest it. All this is supposed to take place before there is any appearance of frost, as a very light frost often does great damage. All touched by it is ruined, and good for nothing. The crop must be cut and hung, even if not fully ripe, before any frosts occur. If there are strong appearances of a frost, you can secure the crop by cutting it down, and putting it either under your sheds, or by putting it in piles, not over 1 foot deep, in the field, and covering with straw. It is well to let it stand, if not fully ripe, as long as it can safely, for the cool nights have a tendency to thicken up the leaves. The cutting is best performed with a hay-knife, with a sharp, rounding point, in the following way: stand at the right-hand side of the plant or row; with the left hand grasp the stalk down 2 or 3 leaves from the top and lean it back on the row; now, with the point of your cutter held in the right hand 2-3 inches from the stalk, close to the root under the bottom leaf, with a sudden stroke or dab, sever the same from the root; lay it gently down back in a line with the row. Proceed in like manner to cut what you can take care of, and not get injured by sunburn. Have two rows of butts together, lying the same way for after-convenience. This cutting is done after the dew is off in the morning, or in the afternoon. Let it remain until the top side is somewhat wilted; then commence to turn it over. Step between the two rows with the butts lying toward you, and with each hand take a plant on either side; raise them from the ground, and by twisting the hands in or out, turn the plants, laying them either to the right or left, as most convenient, at right angles to their former position. Go through with the 2 rows, and you have the next 2 with the butts the other way; take these and lay the tips directly opposite those first turned, and you have an alley, with the butts of the plants of two rows on either side, which will be convenient to drive in to load. When wilted sufficient to be handled without breaking, if in the forenoon, you can load it from the rows as they lie; if in the afternoon, it is best to put in hakes, which is done by putting five plants at the bottom, and on these four, decreasing one on each layer, and terminating with one on the top; this will protect it from dew and wet. The best cart for hauling the tobacco is a one-horse waggon, geared long, with merely a platform resting on the axles. Such a cart can be driven between the rows and loaded from either side, having the butts of the plants uniformly one way, and laid crosswise on the platform. Great care should be used, in all the handling, not to bruise, break, or tear the leaves. Having cut all, excepting your seed-plants, strip all the leaves from these, and set a stake to each to tie it up to; let the stake be a foot taller than the plant; it will answer to keep a piece of old carpet from breaking down the stalk when you wish to cover it up on cold nights. Let the seed-plants stand till the pods or bolls are cured to a brown, and the seed is ripe; then cut off the top of the seed-stalk, and hang it up in some dry and safe place, where it will be ready to shell and use the next season; only the ripest and best pods should be used."

Libhart alludes to the existence of several ways of hanging cut tobacco plants, but specifies the two following as the best and shortest: "first, splitting and hanging it upon laths or poles and leaving it to partially cure in the field; secondly, nailing it to rails with lathing-nails, at once in the shed. The former method, for high northern latitudes, is by far the best, as it will cure in a much shorter time (and thus prevent the destruction of the crop by freezing in the shed), by the drying of the pith of the stalk, which is the main reservoir of moisture. It is performed as follows:—Have a chisel about 1 foot long and 3 inches broad, the sharp end not bevelled on one side, but coming to an edge by a gradual taper on both sides (a common tenon-saw will do pretty well); place the edge of the chisel in the centre of the stalk upon the end where it has been topped, and push it down, guiding it in its course so as not to break or cut off any leaves, to within 3–4 inches of the ground; the stalk may then be cut off with a hatchet, or with the chisel if it be made pretty strong. The splitting may be done in the morning when the leaves are too brittle to admit of the stalk being cut

G

down, and then when the sun has sufficiently wilted the leaves, the stalk may be cut and left to lie until it will bear handling without breaking the leaves. The lath being previously prepared, 4 feet in length and about 1 inch in thickness on one edge, and ½ inch on the other, and 2 inches broad (or poles cut in the forest will answer pretty well); then have trestles prepared high enough to allow the stalks to hang suspended without touching the ground, and set far enough apart in the field to admit of the lath reaching from one to another; now place the stalks of tobacco upon the lath (previously laid across the trestles), by slipping them over and down until they will hang perpendicular and 6–8 inches apart, so they will merely touch, without crowding too much. It may be left hanging thus exposed to the weather until the leaves are so wilted that the stalks hang apart without touching, and the lower leaves begin to dry, when it is taken off the trestles, each lath entire, and laid upon a waggon and hauled to the drying-shed."

Before the tobacco is ready for harvesting, Hudson suggests the preparation of " a supply of sticks for hanging. Sticks 4 feet long and 1 inch square are most convenient; 12 sticks to every 100 plants will be sufficient. For sun-curing, there should be a shed built at one or more convenient points of the patch. This may be done by placing posts in the ground to support the poles, as represented in Fig. 8. The poles *a* being for the support of the smaller poles *c*, upon which the tobacco-sticks are placed, and *b* for the cover, when necessary that it should be shedded."

Mitjen's translator gives the following account of the

Cuban practice. "Tobacco should be cut during the wane of the moon; and although most *vegueros* say that it is impossible to do this, because the leaves commence to ripen both during the new and the full moon, and would be over-ripe before its wane, we can, nevertheless, assert that we know persons who never cut their tobacco during the first quarter, or when rain has made it again green. These persons have never experienced any difficulty; rather, on the contrary, they are those who always obtain

Fig. 8.

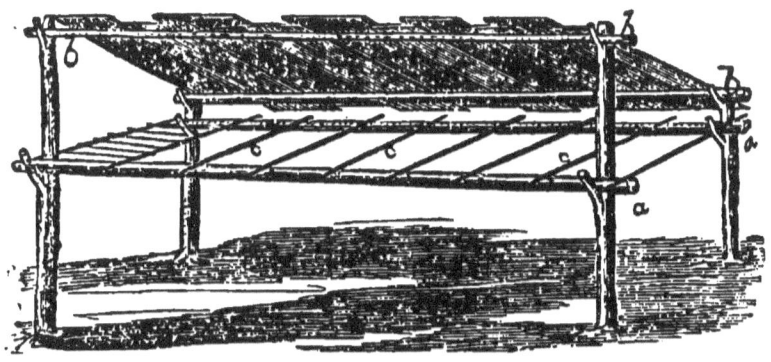

the best prices and the greatest money results. Cutting tobacco during the first quarter of the moon, or when vegetation is renewed in the leaf, is one of the principal reasons why the leaf becomes pricked with holes, and this very frequently even before it is taken from the plantation to the market. The system generally observed is, in cutting tobacco, to take off, at once, all those parts of the plants which may be really or apparently ripe, and to load up the poles indiscriminately, without any division between the pairs of leaves (*mancuernas*). This system is

G 2

highly prejudicial. The leaves of the same plant are not all of the same quality, neither do they all at the same time acquire the same degree of ripeness. Those of the crown, or the pairs at the top of the plant, immediately next the flower or seed, receive the sun direct on their upper surface, and are the first to ripen, whereas the lower ones, being shaded by the upper ones, remain still in an unripe state; moreover, the lower leaves at the foot of the plant, and even those of the fifth or fourth pairs (*mancuernas*), compared with those of the first, second, and third pairs, are inferior in quality, and, comparatively speaking, may be termed leaves without substance. The contact of these leaves with the upper ones frequently occasions putrid fermentation on the poles (*cujes*) and in the packs (this is vulgarly called *sahorno*), especially if there is much dampness in the atmosphere. When this misfortune happens in a tobacco curing-house all the weak leaves will be lost, and the strong ones will be so injured that the best quality of *capa* would turn to *tripa*, and that of bad consistency.

"The cause of this destruction, from which the *veguero* suffers more or less in the best of crops, may be easily explained. The curing of tobacco is nothing more than a series of fermentations. It ferments on the poles (*cujes*), ferments in the heaps (*pilon*), and ferments in the bales. All these fermentations are requisite for obtaining a good colour and smell, but it is better that each quality or consistency of tobacco should ferment apart. Tobacco of good strong quality, which is that produced by the upper leaves, naturally suffers a much stronger fermentation than the weak ones, because the former contain a larger proportion of juice; as the lower leaves have less substance, the fermentation is naturally weaker and lasts less time; but if the leaves are put in contact with those of a stronger quality, the fermentation would be kept up by the latter, and it would indispensably result that the weak ones would rot, and their contact be injurious to the stronger ones. But by separating, in the field, the leaves of different consistencies which each tobacco stalk produces, this evil is avoided, and the dry rot is rendered impossible, unless no care whatsoever is given in the curing-house. Therefore, the mode of reaping should be reformed. It is best to cut the tobacco when it is thoroughly ripe, and in the wane of the moon, making this operation in three sections or cuts, each of which should always be placed on separate poles, in separate rooms, heaps, and carefully picked.

"The first cut should consist only of the pair of crown leaves, and for the poles which they are hung on, a special corner in the curing-house should be set apart. After the first cutting, and 3 or 4 days of sun, the second and third pairs of leaves will be ripe, and may be cut at one and the same time, care being taken to place them on separate poles and rooms; and, lastly, 3 or 4 days after the second cutting, the remainder of the leaves may be gathered, but the last leaf near the ground should not be taken, as it has no consistency, and therefore no value as tobacco, and only serves to increase the work and give discredit to the class of tobacco.

"Tobacco should be cut during the hottest part of the day; each pair of leaves should be placed on the ground face downwards, so that the sun may strike on the under part of the leaf, and in this state it should be allowed to remain a sufficient length of time to wither, after which the pairs of leaves (*mancuernas*) should be picked up one by one, placed evenly on the arm, with the upper side of the leaf inwards, and each armful should be carried to and placed on the poles (*cujes*), which should be prepared beforehand near the spot where the tobacco is being cut. Two forked sticks should be placed strongly in the ground, and on these the pole should rest. After the tobacco leaves have been placed carefully on these poles and been allowed to wither, they should be carried to the curing-house before the sun has time to dry them. This operation must be performed by two labourers, who can carry each time two poles, placing the end of each on either shoulder, so that, in walking, the leaves on one pole may not cut against those on the other. These poles of leaves, when brought to the curing-house, should be fixed or hung by the points on the lowest stages, but so high that the points of the leaves do not touch the ground, and sufficiently apart one from the other that the leaves may not touch, because, being brought in from the field warmed by the sun, it is not judicious to allow them to touch. When the sun is not sufficiently strong to wither the cut leaves, reaping should not be continued. The tobacco should be so arranged on the poles that the pieces of stalk should gently touch one with the other, but without crowding." However, if the weather should be damp, and the leaves large, space should be left between the pairs.

Drying.—The drying-shed is prepared beforehand to receive the tobacco. When cultivating tobacco on a small scale, any shed will do, provided that it contains a sufficient number of doors and windows to admit of regulating the circulation of air. A roof made of straw seems to answer very well. The shed should be high enough to admit of hanging 3 rows of tobacco in it, one above the other. The bottom tier for the first row should be about 3–5 feet from the ground, according to the size of the plants, which should not touch the ground; the second tier should be 3–5 feet higher than the first; the third, 3–5 feet higher than the second; the whole being 10–17 feet high from the bottom of the shed to the highest tier. The tiers must be so arranged that the tobacco when hung on the upper tier should not touch that of the lower one, and that the rods on which the tobacco has been hung in the field fit exactly. The windows must face each other, and be placed between the tiers, so that the bottom part of the window is on the same level as the tier. When cultivating on a large scale, the same arrangements are made, but the building is higher, and is provided with a cellar, in which to place the tobacco for the purpose of stripping, &c.

The drying-shed being ready, the plants immediately on arrival at the shed are transferred from the conveyance, on the rods, to the lowest tier. No rule can be given as to the distance the rods should be placed from each other, as it varies according to the species of the plant, the degree of ripeness, and especially the state of the weather. The purpose of hanging the plant here on the lower tier is to cause the leaves to dry gradually, and assume a good yellow colour, and to create a slight fermentation in them, while allowing such a circulation of air between the plants as will facilitate the gradual escape of the moisture from them, and prevent the injurious development of ammonia and other combinations that give rise to bad flavour in the tobacco. How to attain this, exercises the judgment of the cultivator, who, by frequent examination of the plants, and by careful observation of the changes going on in the leaves, will soon find out the right way.

The rods should be placed closer together—(a) when the plants are much wilted on reaching the shed; (b) when the air is very dry, and the temperature is high; (c) when the leaves of the plant are very thin and contain little water. Plants which have the leaves closely arranged on the stems must be hung farther apart. When the air is very dry, and there is a strong breeze, the windows must be closed. If this is not sufficient, water may be poured on some heaps of sand, to create a moist atmosphere in the shed. When the stems of the plant are very thick, and consequently contain much sap, it is beneficial to open the windows, especially at morning and evening, for some hours, that the wind may pass over the butt-ends. As the windows are situated above the lowest tier, the leaves will not be much affected by it.

The leaves must be examined carefully every day; one plant may progress very well, whereas another close by may decompose too rapidly, and another too slowly. Although no change of weather occur, it may yet be necessary to alter the position of the rods, in order that each plant and leaf may receive air in such a degree as is most conducive to its proper decomposition. Any change in the weather necessitates different arrangements. The plant should remain on the lower tier until the leaves have turned yellow, which will take place within 6–10 days, according to circumstances; after this, they are hung on the upper tiers. There they should be more apart, each plant hanging free. When on the upper tiers, the tobacco may be said to be in the free-hang; and when on the lowest tier, in the close-hang. The object in hanging the plants more apart on the upper tier is to dry them more rapidly there, and for this purpose, the shutters may be opened, unless there be a strong dry wind. The light-yellow colour of the leaves should change into a dark yellow-golden or light-brown colour. After hanging on the upper tier for about a week, the veins of the leaves will be nearly dry, leaving only the midribs pliant. The drying of the leaf and the changing of its colour proceed gradually, commencing from the margin and proceeding to the midrib. At this time, the plants are hung closer together, the evaporation from the leaves being little, and the space and sticks being required. The plants hanging on two or three sticks may be hung on one stick. All the windows may be kept open from this time; the tobacco may also be brought into an open shed, or even hung outside exposed to the sun. In about a week more, the midribs will be entirely dried up, and the tobacco will be fit for stripping. In some climates, it may be necessary to facilitate the drying by the aid of artificial heat. For this purpose, heated air should be conducted into the drying-shed, without the fire, or the products of combustion, being admitted.

Pursley warns tobacco growers that the plant should not be exposed to the weather after it is cut, but should " be immediately conveyed to the barn and hung up. As soon as it gets about half yellowed, a slow fire should be started under it; if made too hot at first, the tobacco will turn black. About the second day the ends of the leaves will begin to curl up; then the fire should be gradually increased, till it heats the tobacco blood warm; it should be kept up so till the leaf is thoroughly cured. If this rule be strictly adhered to, the tobacco will be cured bright. The brighter it is cured the better it sells.

"Our barns are generally built of logs, some have frames. The barn should be made tight up to the tobacco, which should hang about 8 feet from the ground; above this leave cracks or air-holes, sufficient for free ventilation. A barn to hold $2\frac{1}{2}$ acres of tobacco, which is as much as one man can attend to, should be 24 feet square. It should have 5 tiers of poles, the lowest about 6 feet from the ground; these should extend across the barn, and be fastened at each end into the walls. The poles should be 4 feet apart, and the tiers directly one above another. The sticks which contain the tobacco should be placed within 8 inches of each other, on all the poles except the bottom ones, which should be left vacant directly over the fire. When tobacco is nearly cured, it very readily catches fire. If there be a wet spell of weather before the stalks are thoroughly dry, build a fire under the tobacco sufficiently hot to keep it dry. It should not get damp and pliant until the stalks are dry, then it may be allowed to get damp."

Libhart recommends that the shed "be constructed of timbers strong enough to resist storms, and boarded 'up and down.' About every 3 feet one board should be hinged, to readily open and shut. If it is intended to split and lath the tobacco, the inside of the shed must be divided by rails into widths to accommodate the lath, and likewise into tiers, one above the other, far enough apart to allow the stalks to hang from, well separate. The frame of rails and timbers inside the shed destined to sustain the weight of the tiers of tobacco (which, when green, is exceedingly heavy) should be strongly constructed, so as to preclude the possibility of breaking down, for if this should happen to the upper tier, in all probability the whole would be tumbled to the ground."

The housing of the crop proceeds, says Dennis, " as fast as it is cured up on the scaffold, or as the indications of rain make it necessary, care being taken not to bruise or tear it in hauling. The sticks of tobacco may be piled upon the waggon or cart, and hauled to the barn and hung up, commencing in the highest part of the building, and filling up as you go downwards. If the leaves are pretty well cured, you may hang it so as to touch, without crowding it; if not, there should be a little space between. If a cold, rainy spell comes on, you will need to introduce some means of artificial drying. A trench is sometimes dug, and a log or two of wood placed in it, and a fire made, taking care to remove the tobacco immediately over the fire, and avoiding much blaze. This is dangerous, and a better plan is to make a trench across the floor of the barn, of mason-work, covered with sheet-iron, and leading from a furnace outside the house on one side, to a chimney at a safe distance on the other. The colour and quality of tobacco may be improved by hanging it closely and curing by artificial heat, watching that it does not become 'funked,' or moulded, while curing; but the best plan for a beginner is to dry it safely, and make a sure crop, experimenting as he goes along, in order to improve the quality, as he may safely do so. When the stalk becomes dry and entirely cured, which will not usually be for some weeks, the crop is ready to 'strip.' The hanging tobacco yields to the influence of a rainy day or a foggy morning, and 'comes in case,' or softens, so it will not crumble. It must never be handled when dry. When it is just soft, not damp, or when it is barely so soft that it can be handled (if it is approaching that softened state), it may be taken down and taken off the sticks, and 'bulked,' by piling it alongside a partition, or by itself, with the butts of the stalks outward in every direction, and the tops or leaves in the centre. Several hundred pounds may be thus bulked down, and can be worked up while the hanging tobacco has gone out of case, and cannot be touched."

According to Bishop, it usually requires about 12 weeks to cure the plants thoroughly, that is, so that there is no more juice in the leaves or leaf-stems; it matters not if the main stalk is not dry, you need not expect it, and there will be green leaves that will not cure but freeze while green and are worthless. He calculates that to "hang an acre of good tobacco requires a building about 30 by 24 feet with 15-feet posts. Two girths should be framed into the posts on all sides of the building; one 5 feet above the sill, and the other 10 feet above, to rest the poles on, also to nail the covering boards to. This gives a space of 5 feet for each tier of plants. Have a beam run across the centre of the building, with a post in the middle with girths to correspond with those on the side, extending lengthwise through the middle of the building for the poles or rails, each 12 feet in length, to be laid upon; or if sticks are to be used (as hereafter described) lay rails or poles once in 4 feet for the sticks to rest upon. Place a ventilator upon the centre of the roof, and have one board in every 4 feet hung on hinges, to be opened or closed at pleasure. If made with a floor and a cellar underneath, to let down the tobacco into when ready stripped, it is all the better. We will now return to the crop, and commence hanging it. A common way of doing it is by tying with common twine. Tie the end of the string tightly around the butt of one plant, and by placing it against the side of the pole nearest you, put another plant on the opposite side and carry the string over and around it, placing the plants alternately on each side of the pole until filled, then fasten the string, place the pole in the right place (it should be nearly right before it is filled), and commence on the next one in like manner, having some one to hand the plants as wanted. As to how thick to hang it depends upon the size of the plants, but in good-sized tobacco about 9 inches on each side is close enough, that will be from 30–32 on each pole of 12 feet; place the poles 15–18 inches apart. Another method of hanging, much practised and approved by many, is to hang on slats or sticks sawed out 4 feet long, $1\frac{1}{4}$ inches wide, and $\frac{5}{8}$ inch thick. Chestnut timber is generally used here. The common lath answers very well for this purpose. An iron made something like a chisel is used to slip on to one end of the sticks, which are sharpened a little at one end to receive it. It is made about 8 inches long, wedge-shaped at the small end, and a socket $\frac{1}{2}$ inch by

1 inch to slip on to the sticks. When ready for use have a place fixed near where you unload, to hold one of these sticks out at right angles from a post and about 4 feet from the ground. Let the plants be handed you from the load and slip them on the stick, piercing the stalk about 6 inches from the butt; put 6 or 7 plants of medium size on each stick, thicker if smaller; when hung it will appear as in Fig. 9. As each stick is filled, it may be carried to its place in the barn. In getting them to the top of the barn, they may be handed up with a pitchfork, lifting them by the middle of the sticks. These sticks should be about 8 inches apart. I think a greater amount can be put into a given space by this method without danger of sweating, as it is more evenly distributed. The loose leaves that have been broken off while handling, may be cured by placing 4 or 5 together and securing to a small pole, in the same way as plants are hung with twine."

Hanging is done in the following manner:—" The 'hanger' stands in an erect position, having for a foothold the poles on the tier below the one which he is hanging; he has a ball of tobacco-twine (a twine made of flax, procurable at any seed-store) which for convenience is carried in the bosom of the loose blouse generally worn; he stands with the left side to the pole on which the tobacco is to be hung, left arm over it; the stalk of tobacco is handed to him by a boy whose duty it is to pass it to him; the stalk is then taken in the left hand and placed against the side of the pole, the butt projecting an inch or two, around which projection the twine is wound from left to right (the twine having previously been fastened to the pole); the next stalk is placed on the other side of the pole, just far enough along so that the leaves of the two stalks will not touch and 'pole-burn,' and so continue, the stalks being hung alternately on the sides of the pole, as seen in Fig. 9. After the house is filled, some put fires under the crop to hasten its

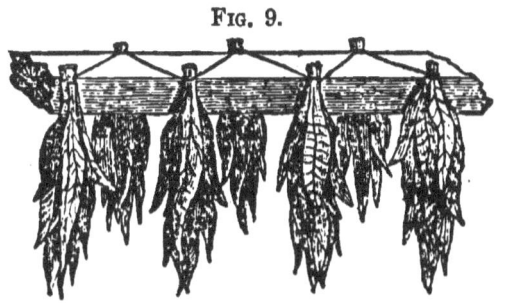

Fig. 9.

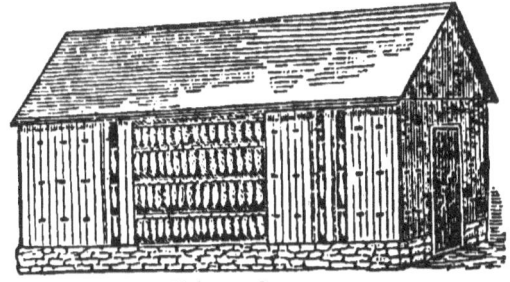

Fig. 10.

Tobacco-house.

drying; but it is found by experience that the practice is not a good one."

Bishop describes the common size of tobacco-house as about 100 feet long by 24 feet wide, posts 17 feet long, and built upon a wall 18 inches high; the buildings are framed with girths from bent to bent, for boarding up and down, the bents being 12 feet apart. The external appearance is illustrated in Fig. 10. "The boards for closing up the building should be 1 foot wide, and at intervals of about 5 feet a board should be hung with light strap hinges, to serve as a ventilator to admit light and dry air, and to exclude damp. These ventilators or doors must be closed on frosty nights, but in fair dry weather should remain open. The tobacco poles, the ends of which rest upon the bents, should be about

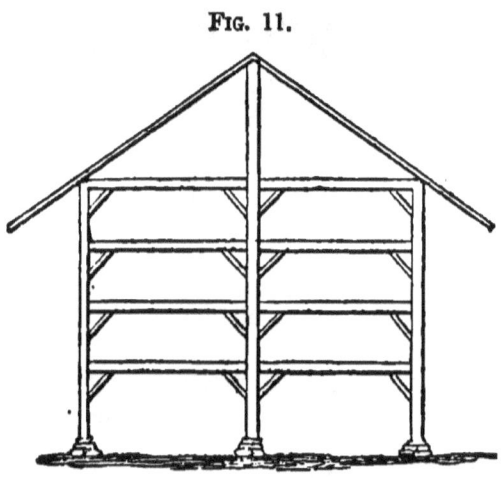

FIG. 11.

13 feet long, 2 inches thick by 6 inches wide, of some light timber, such as elm or basswood, and when hung with tobacco should be 8-10 inches apart. A large door should be placed at either end for ingress and egress. The poles, of which there should be 4 tiers, are laid from bent to bent, resting the ends of the cross beams in the bent, tiers 4 feet 4 inches apart." A sectional view of the barn is shown in Fig. 11.

White suggests that stables, sheds, and barn floors can be arranged "so as to hang up an acre or two by setting stanchions with holes mortised in them to hold rests for your poles about 4½ feet apart. Set such ones on either side with a very stout rail, one end in either post. Set these as often as you may need them, depending on the length of your poles. No poles should be so long as to sag very much when filled with plants. But for another reason I would build a house expressly for hanging and storing tobacco. Make it of good, liberal dimensions, 30 feet wide, by 40 or more in length; posts, 14 feet, with two tiers of girths for poles to rest on; one tier can hang on the beams, and another above on the purlin plates, thus hanging 4 tiers under the same roof. Ventilate by a ventilator in the roof, also by hanging every other board of the siding on hinges. For such a building, I would have a tight floor to the whole, and underneath a good walled cellar lighted with suitable windows, and chimney in one corner, with a stove, to keep fire in in very cold weather, to work by when stripping the tobacco. For poles to hang on, I would get, if possible, straight, slim, white pine staddles about 4–5 inches in diameter; shave the bark off smooth, and we have poles that will last and remain straight a lifetime, if kept housed.

"Having provided all required, even to the strong cotton or hemp twine for tying up the tobacco, have a good man to hand it to you. Commence by tying the end of your twine around the butt of a plant, about 2 inches from the end, in a slip or loose knot; place this plant at one side of the pole near the end, your hand carrying the twine over the pole; on the opposite side of the pole, about 6 inches along, place another plant, and with a single turn of the twine around it from before, round back, and by drawing it close, the plant is secure. Proceed thus till you have filled your pole; then with a knife, cut a notch in the pole and draw your twine through, and it is fast. You can now cut it off and commence another pole. Place the poles far enough apart to prevent the tobacco crowding; about 1 foot will do. In this manner you will have a row of plants hanging on each side of the pole about 1 foot apart. The man, in handing up, should take the plant by the butt, carefully from the pile or load, raise it up and gently shake it sideways, to shake off dirt and loosen the leaves when stuck together, and also adhering to the stalk; with the other hand, take hold about midways of the stalk and pass to the one tying up, enabling him to receive the plant in such a way as to not need to shift it in his hand, but to place it immediately into its position beside the pole. All leaves which are accidentally or otherwise broken from the plants, should be gathered up each day, and hung three or four in a bunch, the same way as the plants, or string them on a string; the latter is the best way—with a large needle-thread, a suitable cord, and on to this string the leaves one at a time, by running the needle through near the end of the stem. These can be hung by attaching the two ends to some suitable nail, and having it remain stretched. In this way they will cure very well.

"Having housed the whole of your crop, give it all the air you can, by opening doors, shutters, &c. Let them remain open during pleasant weather, remembering to close them in wet, damp weather, as well as nights; and also shading the crop so far as may be from the direct rays of the sun, to prevent blanching. When it has nearly cured, shut it up and let it remain till perfectly cured. This may be known by the stem of the leaves being dried up, so that no green sap will show itself. If you have hung in your stables and other places that you wish to use, it will be necessary to take it down and strip it at the first favourable opportunity, which is described farther along. The separate building elsewhere described is to be preferred, as it does not necessitate any immediate hurry in getting it down. In such it can be allowed to hang and freeze and thaw two or three times, which improves the colour and weight, and will give more leisure in stripping, &c. Watch a favourable time, when it rains and is damp, to open your buildings, and let in the damp air till the tobacco is damped, so that it can be handled without any danger of breaking the leaves. It need not get too damp, as in that case it is liable to injure in the pile before you can get it stripped. It will gain dampness from the stalk."

The Cuban tobacco planter, according to Davis, " would force the drying in wet weather and retard it in dry weather, as either extreme is injurious; the wet is injurious, as the leaves, when they change from the natural colour to a pale yellow and light brown, easily mildew; when dry, as before-named, it is taken down. Damp weather is best, so as not to break the leaves, which are immediately stripped from the stalks and sorted into as many grades as the market may require, from one to four and even more grades, as 'bright yellow, dull, seconds, and ground-leaves.' But I see no necessity for but three grades, as the over-ripe, the unripe, and the just ripe at cutting, and when properly dried they show their grade plain enough to sort. After being stripped and sorted, they are to be separately piled ('bulked' some say) in courses of leaves—2, 4, or 6 tiers of leaves, stems end out, and 3–4 feet high. The leaves should be kept straight in all these handlings. The heap should be made up each day separate, as it begins to make tobacco in 12 hours or so, by fermenting, which is variously called 'curing,' 'sweating,' 'conditioning,' &c. Soon as the heap begins to get warm it should be re-piled, putting the inner tier out so as to equalize the fermentation; some re-pile several times and some none; but the fermentation should be kept equal, and if covered with old sail-cloth it can be regulated. This fermenting is allowed to proceed for 4–6 weeks by careful manufacturers; as it is the process that makes the tobacco to suit the taste of tobacco-epicures it should be carefully done, yet many do it in a careless manner, and thus have an article so poor as to not find many lovers. At the end of the 4–6 weeks the Cuba grower would have one side of each leaf slightly moistened with the decoction of tobacco, which is made by letting some leaves rot in clean water, and then he would tie it up in hanks of 25 or 30 leaves, and hang one day for drying, then take it down and pack it in tight casks as being best. From these leaves he would make the best Cuba cigars. The Virginian grower would not wet his tobacco after it had fermented, but simply tie it in hanks so that 5 or 6 would weigh a pound, and then pack it in his hogsheads for market; and this, after it had lain from one to six months in the 'conditioning bulks.'"

Burton, translating from Mitjen, goes more fully into

the Cuban practice. He advises firstly that the "shoots and the sprouts should be put apart from the principal tobacco, with which it should never be mixed, neither in the heaps nor in the packages. The day after the tobacco has been cut and placed in the curing-houses, the poles should be pushed together, making thus a compact mass, with the object, that by means of the warmth, which this contact produces, the fermentation should commence, called *maduradero*. In this state it should remain 2 or 3 days, according to the consistency of the tobacco and the state of the atmosphere. By means of this first fermentation it acquires an equal and a yellowish colour: by the second or third day, at the latest, this colour should be uniform, and then without loss of time the poles should be spread apart, and given all the ventilation possible, so that fermentation may not continue, and the drying of the leaves may be facilitated—care being taken that they are not exposed to the dew, the sun, nor to sprinkling of water, should it rain. As the tobacco dries, the poles should be hung on higher pegs, so as to leave the lower ones unoccupied for the fresh leaves brought from the fields. This operation should be performed early in the morning whilst the leaves are flexible and soft; because later in the day they become crisper, and are more apt to tear.

"It is not judicious to allow the tobacco to dry too precipitately, by exposing it to a very strong current of air, because strong wind greatly injures its quality; many leaves break, and that silkiness of appearance is destroyed which good leaves should have, and which it is desirable to preserve. During heavy winds the doors of the drying-house should be kept closed; they should also be kept closed if there is much dampness in the atmosphere occasioned by heavy and continuous rain. Dampness causes mildew, which shows itself first in the points of the leaves, and is the commencement of the rot. Under these circumstances, and to check this evil, it is convenient to spread, or part the poles a little; and if the rains, or the excess of humidity continue, fires should be kindled and smoke made in the curing-houses, opening at the same time the doors and the windows, so as to facilitate the circulation of air whilst the smoking is going on.

"After the tobacco is thoroughly dry, it should be placed on the highest beams, or pegs, of the framework which support the poles, squeezing them compactly together. This must be done in the morning whilst the leaves are soft, and all this should be done with a view of protecting it from the effects of change in the atmosphere. The house should, after this, be kept closed, until it is time to make the heaps.

"The object of heaping up the tobacco is to produce a second fermentation, so as to equalize the colour of the leaf and wear out of it that excess of gluten or resinous matter which is natural to the plant; this fermentation makes the leaves more silky and ductile, and gives them a more agreeable flavour. The place for making the heaps should be prepared beforehand, in one or more of the rooms of the tobacco-house, by making a kind of box lined with *yaguas* (sheets of palm-tree bark) at the bottom and the sides, the base is a boarding on which should be placed a sufficient quantity of dry plantain leaves, which serve as a bed for the heaps.

"In the months of April or May, when the rainy season commences, the poles which are on the highest pegs of the scaffolding should be taken down and placed somewhat apart, one from the other, on the lower pegs. The doors of the house should be left open at night, so that the humidity from the atmosphere may enter, and when, in the morning, the tobacco is found to be soft and silky, it is fit to be placed in heaps. The pairs of leaves should then be collected in armfuls, with all the bits of stalks placed in one direction; the leaves that may be found doubled or crooked should be smoothed out, and each armful should be placed in layers in the heaps, placing the first layer at the bottom with all the woody pieces of the stalk touching the *yagua* which forms the sides of the case; other layers should be placed with the stalk reversed, and in this manner, crossing the leaves, the pile should be raised up level. When a pile has a sufficient height, another, and another, is made until the tobacco is finished or the case is full, so that each heap may form a compact mass of leaves protected by the pieces of stalk all round, which should never touch the leaves, but only touch each other. When the heaps have been thus made, they should be covered with dry plantain leaves, or palm skins, and, in front, by palm leaves.

"Tobacco should not be packed thus when it is too damp, because a very strong fermentation would ensue, which, if kept up longer than necessary, would pass to putrefaction. The tobacco only requires to be soft, or flexible, before packing, so as to produce a certain degree of heat, neither is it convenient to pack tobacco when too dry, for then it would not ferment at all, nor would any beneficial results be produced. When it has been packed sufficiently soft, it undergoes after the second or third day a degree of heat of 110° to 120° F. in the centre of the heap, and if it does not acquire this degree of heat it is because it has been packed too dry.

"We have already said that reaping or cutting tobacco should be performed in three distinct sections, preserving always a distinction, consequently the crown leaves should form one heap, or one set of heaps; the second and third pairs another, or others; the fourths and the fifths others; and lastly, the *capaduras* (second shoots from the same plants) others. This system, besides having the advantages which we have in another place described, greatly facilitates the sorting of the leaves, as the different qualities are from the first kept apart, and scarcely any other work remains to be done than that of taking out the broken leaves. Tobacco should be kept for at least 30 days in heaps, after which, sorting and choosing the leaves may commence, beginning first with the heaps of the inferior qualities."

Stripping.—Stripping may be performed at any time, provided the leaves, after being once properly dried, have again become pliable. For stripping, such a number of plants as will furnish work for several days are taken down on a morning, when the plants have absorbed some moisture, and have become elastic; they are put in a heap, and properly covered, to check evaporation. If, however, the night air should be so very dry that the leaves cannot absorb sufficient moisture to become pliable, a moist atmosphere can be created either by steam, or by pouring water on the floor, or by keeping vessels with water in the shed. If this cannot be done, the tobacco must remain hanging until there is damp weather. Under no condition should the tobacco be stripped when not pliant, that is if the leaves are so brittle that they would break when bent or rolled. The best arrangement is to keep the drying-shed and stripping-room separate, since the latter requires to be more moist than the former. A cellar under the drying-shed is best suited for stripping. It should be large enough to admit of the erection of a scaffold to receive the tobacco.

Pursley looks upon stripping as being labour suited to damp weather. He says, "the lugs, shipping, and manufacturing, which are worst, medium, and best qualities, should be separated at stripping. The 'lugs,' or worst quality, are found at the bottom of the plant; they are chaffy and light leaves, and should be stripped from the stalk and tied in bundles by themselves with all of the ragged, black, and injured leaves. The second quality, or 'shipping tobacco,' is a grade above the lugs; it is the red or brown tobacco; this should also be tied in separate bundles. The best, or 'manufacturing,' is the finest and brightest leaves, and should be put in bundles by itself. In stripping, the stems of the leaves should be broken off as close as possible to the stalk; this adds to the weight of the tobacco. In forming a bundle, the butts of the leaves should be placed evenly, and closely together, and pressed tightly in the hand; then a leaf should be folded to form a wrapper 2 inches in width; then wrap it tightly and smoothly around the butts of the leaves, winding it from the end down, about $2\frac{1}{2}$ inches, then open the bundle in the middle, and tuck the wrapper-leaf through the opening, and draw it snug, so that when the opening is closed the wrapper-leaf will remain; this forms a bundle which we call a 'hand of tobacco.' The hands should be strung on sticks, and hoisted up in the barn on the tier-poles; 18–20 hands may be put on each stick, at equal distances apart."

Libhart expresses his opinions on stripping in the following words. "At the setting in of a warm, drizzling, wet, foggy spell of weather, the shed must be opened on all sides to allow the damp atmosphere to pervade the whole interior; after the dry leaves have become damp enough to allow handling in any degree without breaking, the stalks must be taken off the lath or pulled down and laid in heaps about 18 inches or 2 feet high, and any desired length; if it is not intended to strip it immediately, it should be conveyed to a cellar or other apartment, where it will remain damp; it should not, however, be suffered to remain longer than 2 or 3 days in heaps, without examination, as there is sometimes sufficient moisture remaining in the stalks or frozen leaves to create heat and rot the good tobacco. If found to be heating, it should be changed about and aired and be stripped immediately. If found to be drying out, further evaporation may be checked by covering the heaps with damp straw or corn-fodder. Tobacco is usually stripped into two qualities, 'ground-leaf,' or 'fillers,' and 'wrappers'; the leaves that lie next the ground, generally from 2 to 4, are always more or less damaged by sand beaten on by the rain and other causes, hence they only command about half the price of the good tobacco or 'wrappers.' The ground-leaves are taken off first and tied up separately in bunches. With a bunch clasped in one hand, take a leaf and wrap it around (beginning at the end of the bunch), confining the end under the first turn, continue to wrap smoothly and neatly until about 3 inches of the leaf remains, then open the bunch in the middle and draw the remaining part of the leaf through. This forms a neat and compact 'hand,' that will bear a great deal of handling without coming open. After the ground-leaves have been removed, the good leaves are stripped off and tied up the same as the ground-leaves, with this exception: the leaves of each stalk should be tied in a bunch by themselves, to preserve a uniformity in colour and size, as tobacco is sold in the market according to colour and size, therefore if the leaves of a large and a small plant, or of a dark-coloured and a light one, be tied up together, it at once diminishes the appearance and value of the crop."

Dennis describes stripping as being "performed by holding the plant, top down, with the left hand, while with the right hand the leaves are pulled off, taking care to have the stems all even in the hand, so that the ends are together. When 10–15 leaves have thus been grasped by the right hand, change the handful to the left hand, and with the right, select a leaf and wrap it around the stems at the end, so as to bind them altogether and cover up the ends, then split the other leaves apart with the finger, and pull the end of your wrapping-leaf through, and you have a 'hand' of tobacco. A small 'hand' of leaves, uniform in size and colour, will be found the most desirable shape to tie it in, resembling Fig. 12. The bottom leaves of the plant, and all torn and defective leaves, should be tied up by themselves, and are known as 'lugs.' These 'hands' should be 'bulked' again, with the wrapped end out, and covered with straw, or anything that will retain the 'case,' and if subject to immediate sale, may be boxed up or hauled to market. If boxed, it should be put in tight boxes—if hauled, it should be kept covered until unloaded. Care must be taken to avoid 'high case'—extreme dampness or softness in bulking tobacco after it is stripped—as it may be 'funked' in bulk, and ruined; and it should not be packed in that condition when it is liable to remain long. It is a crop that is never off of hands."

Fig. 12.

Hand of Tobacco.

According to Perry Hull, stripping, or, as he terms it, "picking," should not take place till about December; "at least not until the *fat stems* (main stems of the leaves, which are not thoroughly cured at the butt-end) have mostly or all disappeared, which they will have done by that time, if the crop reached maturity before harvesting. The operations of picking and assorting are by many, who make only two classes or qualities of the tobacco, carried on at the same time. By far the preferable way is, especially if there is a very large crop to pick, to take off the leaves during damp or wet weather, tie them into bundles of 15-20 lb., with twine, and pack it away into cellars, or wherever it can be kept without drying up. It can then be assorted in any kind of weather, thus gaining considerable time, as two will pick and tie up in this way as much during one wet spell as 6 hands would, assorting and hanking up, at the same time. Another reason why the last practice is preferable is, that, by the former, the assorting can be but indifferently done; whereas, by the last, it can be done as carefully as desired. Tobacco should not be allowed to get too wet before picking; in fact, should not be allowed to get wet at all, so as to feel wet, only just damp enough to make the leaves pliable, so as to handle and pack without breaking or feeling husky. If allowed to get wet, before picking, it is next to impossible to get it dried to the proper state again so uniformly but that some of the leaves will still be too wet, while others will be dry enough to crack and break. So if the rains are long enough to get it too wet, which they often are, by all means let it remain upon the poles until the next wet spell."

Sorting.—Tobacco intended for smoking should be carefully sorted when stripped. There should be four sorts: 1st, large, equally good coloured, untorn leaves; 2nd, leaves of good size and colour, but torn; 3rd, leaves of inferior colour, and bottom leaves; 4th, refuse, shrivelled-up leaves, &c., to which may be added the suckers No. 1 leaves, when thin, elastic, and of good sorts, are mostly valued as wrappers (outside covers) for cigars, No. 2 may also be used as wrappers, but are less valued than No. 1; they are adapted for fillers and cut tobacco. The different sorts are kept separate. The best plan is to let the most intelligent man strip the leaves from the stem, and at once separate them according to quality. The leaves should then be made into hands, i. e. 10–20 leaves should be tied together by twisting a leaf round the end of the stalks, each sort being attended by a special man, to avoid mixing. The leaves of the first sort being large, 10–15 will be sufficient for a hand; more are required of the other sorts. When making the hands of the two first sorts, each leaf is taken separately, smoothened on a flat board, and left there while another is treated in the same way, continuing thus until a sufficient number is ready to make a hand. When the hand is ready, it is laid aside, and a weight is placed upon it to keep the leaves smooth.

To sell well, according to Perry Hull, tobacco " should be assorted into three classes or grades, Wrappers, Seconds, and Fillers. The wrappers will include the soundest, best-coloured leaves, the colour (a dark cinnamon) should be as uniform as possible; this quality should include nothing but what is fit for wrappers. The Seconds, which are used as binders for cigars, &c., will include the small top leaves, of which, if the tobacco was topped too high, there will be one or two to each plant—the bad colours, and those leaves somewhat damaged by worms and bad handling, but not so much so as to be ragged. The third class, or Fillers, will include the balance of the crop, bottom leaves, ragged leaves, &c. The tobacco should be done up into hanks of about $\frac{1}{3}$ lb. each, or about what can be encompassed by the thumb and fingers, winding at the butt with a pliable leaf, drawing the end through the hank to secure it."

The Cuban system of sorting is described at considerable length by Mitjen, whose remarks are interpreted by Burton as follows. The operation consists in "separating one from the other the different leaves, according to their strength and quality, and dividing the produce of the crop into various classes. These are, in practice, styled *Libra*, 1st quality; *Quebrado*, 2nd quality, broken; *Injuriado de primera; Injuriado de segunda, de tercera, de cuarta, de quinta, de sexta, de setima; Libra de pie*, and *capadura*.

"Under this classification it is presumed that attention has been bestowed, not only to the special quality of the leaf, but also to its size, and its state, whether whole or broken; but it is very seldom that exactness is found in this classification, because but very few persons possess the requisite skill which such a complicated mode of sorting requires. Moreover, by the abuse of mixing in one heap all kinds of leaves, frequently brought in from the fields all mixed together, the proper sorting of tobacco becomes a very complicated affair.

"This kind of classification and nomenclature is, moreover, absurd, and does not positively represent fixed qualities, under the denomination of which, prices might be arranged which would serve as a guide to the merchant as well as the grower. In a word, the names, with which the different qualities of tobacco are to-day distinguished, signify nothing, and it is ridiculous to be guided in business by them. Until this kind of classification and nomenclature is changed, it is impossible to quote the mercantile prices for the different qualities, because the name does not represent the quality; and this confusion tends greatly to the prejudice of the planter, and the merchant; and hinders attaining the perfection after which we should strive.

"We have shown that the practice of making a classification of seven *Injuriados* must not be taken as absolute. There are better modes of sorting in which a separation of 8, and even 9 *Injuriados* should be made, and others, and by far the greater proportion, in which only 5 *Injuriados* should be separated; so that the quality which, in one sorting, would appear under that of fifths—being the lowest of the crop—would be equal to eighths, or ninths, if picked more carefully; and the fifths, in a sorting, whose lowest class may be sevenths, is about equal in quality to that of thirds of other pickings, whose lowest class would be fifths, if both crops had produced equal kinds of tobacco.

"There is even more to confirm our opinion. Supposing two crops equal in all respects, and that each planter makes a separation of 7 *Injuriados*. This would not ensure that the intrinsic value of each respective quality would be equal; for each *Veguero* has his own particular mode of considering the different classes, and some make a much more careful sorting than others. In the supposed case it may happen, as it frequently does, that the *Veguero* A will take from his crop—which we will suppose to be one hundred packages—2 of the first, 3 of the second, 5 of the third, 8 of the fourth, 12 of the fifth, 30 of the sixth, and 40 of the seventh; whereas the *Veguero* B will take from his, 4 of the first, 6 of the second, 10 of the third, 16 of the fourth, 32 of the fifth, 21 of the sixth, and 11 of the seventh; and it would result, from the comparison of these two supposed pickings, that each of these classes of the *Vega* A would correspond to the immediate superior one of the *Vega* B, as will be shown on the following calculation:—

A.					B.			
			$	$				$ $
2 Bales,	1st .. at	120 = 240			4 Bales,	1st .. at	100 = 400
3 ,,	2nd .. ,,	100 = 300			6 ,,	2nd .. ,,	80 = 480
5 ,,	3rd .. ,,	80 = 400			10 ,,	3rd .. ,,	60 = 600
8 ,,	4th .. ,,	60 = 480			16 ,,	4th .. ,,	40 = 640
12 ,,	5th .. ,,	40 = 480			32 ,,	5th .. ,,	25 = 800
30 ,,	6th .. ,,	25 = 750			21 ,,	6th .. ,,	20 = 420
40 ,,	7th .. ,,	20 = 800			11 ,,	7th .. ,,	10 = 110
100		$3450			100		$3450

"Here it may be seen that the second of A is worth as much as the first of B, the third of A as much as the second of B, and so successively in the other classes; and as it is of importance that names should represent fixed objects, and that each quality should represent a relative value, we think that the sortings and the classifications deserve a reform, which would undoubtedly bring with it advantages to the planter, to the merchant, the manufacturer, and the consumer.

"The reform in the sortings should take its origin from a reform in the plantátion or field, and principally in the manner of cutting. By observing a methodical and well-calculated system, each one of the operations prepares and facilitates the execution of the succeeding one. In its proper place, we have recommended that the tobacco planter should not attempt to plant more than 12,000 plants for each labourer employed, so that all the plants may receive proper cultivation and attention. If all these plants are equally well taken care of, if the land has been properly prepared with manure, and all have had the same advantage of season, it is a necessary consequence that the fruit will be equally good. If afterwards the cutting or cropping is made in 3 sections, preserving always the separation we have recommended, we shall have, naturally, not a capricious assortment of leaves, but one in the order established by nature.

"None will, we think, question the fact that the pairs of leaves on one stalk must be equal in quality to those cut from an adjoining stalk, that is to say, all the crown leaves must be of the same quality, all the second also, and so successively. This admitted, we have the separation of qualities made, almost, in the field, and it only remains to separate the sizes, and the sound leaves from the torn ones, an operation which any person can make; and thus it will be unnecessary to employ those workmen who style themselves sorters, who are supposed to have an exact knowledge of the properties of each leaf. The sortings ought, therefore, to be made by classes, or by bales, each containing the separate qualities beginning with the bale of *capaduras* and *mamones*, which may be mixed together in the same bale. Of this quality, however, not more than two classes should be made, which may be called suckers and sprouts; and in the class called sprouts, the sound and larger leaves of good consistency should be placed. The result would be a *tripa* of good quality, and, after throwing away all those that are really without substance, the remainder would form the second class, and would make a useful *tripa*, although inferior to the former.

"When these are made, the next bales should be made of tobacco chosen from the inferior class of leaves, of which 3 classes ought to be made, and called *sano, quebrado,* and *desecho de tercera*. In the first class of these, which we will call third quality, should be placed all the sound leaves which have any consistency; and this would form a weak *capa*, equal to that which is now called clear fifths, *quinta limpia*, and this might be called *sano de tercera*. The second class should contain the torn or broken leaves of good consistency, but not so much broken or injured as to merit only the name of shavings, as the leaves which are very much torn, or small pieces of leaves, are called. This class would be called *quebrado de tercera*, and might be used for inferior *tripa*. The last class of this quality, after throwing away all the useless leaves, would be called *desecho*.

"After this, and in the same order as the preceding, three classes should be made from the sortings for the heaps of bad seconds and thirds, and called *sano, quebrado,* and *tripa* of the second class. The first of these should contain all the sound leaves, and should be called *sano de segunda*, second-class sound. The second should be composed of the damaged leaves, but good for making *capa*, and should be called second-class broken; and the third, which will be the most broken, should be called second-class *tripa*.

"Finally, the picking, or sorting for the pile of pairs of crown leaves should be made; and of this quality there should also be three classes, which will be denominated '*sano,*' '*quebrado,*' and '*tripa de corona,*' observing always the same order as was done for the piles or heaps of seconds and thirds.

"Sorting carried on in this order is so simplified that we do not doubt it might be done in one-third the time taken under the present system; and the labour of the re-sorters would be dispensed with, which most of the *vegueros* have now to employ and pay, as many of them do not consider themselves sufficiently expert in the matter to classify their own tobacco. This classification and nomenclature represent exact qualities to which a relative value can be fixed, and may serve as a base for mercantile transactions.

"The manufacturer will not have to contend with bales of mixed tobacco containing all the different classes which the *vega* may have produced; and he will find this division very convenient to determine the time when each class may be used without having any loss from finding in them leaves that are not seasoned, whilst others of the same bale, and perhaps of the same *manojo*, may have become deteriorated from having remained too long in fermentation. The manufacturer will, without any great trouble, be able to make the assortment for strong and weak *tripa* according to the quality of *capa* which is going to be used, a most essential point in cigar making, and thus he will be able to make cigars with all perfection. All these advantages will result from adopting the reform in the manner of sorting which we propose. And, in spite of its simplicity, it is much more positive and extensive, as it will be composed of four qualities subdivided into eleven classes. The consumer, too, will have the advantage of being able to procure cigars manufactured completely of the quality which he prefers, and the contents of each box, or each set of boxes, will be all equal both in flavour and colour, which, under the present system, it is difficult to find. The classes will be styled:—

First quality	{ 1st class Sound crown. 2nd ,, Broken ,, 3rd ,, Stuffing ,,
Second quality	{ 1st class Sound seconds. 2nd ,, Broken ,, 3rd ,, Stuffing ,,
Third quality	{ 1st class Sound thirds. 2nd ,, Broken ,, 3rd ,, Stuffing ,,

Fourth quality, 1st and 2nd Suckers and sprouts.

"It is scarcely necessary to add that, according to the preceding system of sorting, only 3 divisions, cases, or rooms, with *yaguas*, will be required for depositing the respective qualities which the workmen may be assorting, until sufficient quantity has been collected in each to commence the seasoning or painting, *betumeo, enmannillado*, or *engavillado, manojo*, and *enterciadura*.

"In all kinds of sortings, the fragments of broken leaves, too small to use for cigars, should be collected, sponged, and with them packages made of *picadura*. This should be preserved, and the following year it will be useful for making *betun*. Wash the tobacco, or rather sponge it, with a solution made from these pieces of good leaves, and not with a solution made from stalks and trash of new tobacco, as some do. The wash (*betun*) has the same effect on tobacco that yeast has on bread. It is the agent employed to produce a strong and quick fermentation, from which results that strong and agreeable aroma that may be observed in old tobacco which has been well *betumeado* (sponged with tobacco infusion). This infusion, made with fresh tobacco, is not bad if made carefully, but we consider that made with old tobacco is the best, because it instantly imparts an agreeable odour to the leaves on which it is used; and, instead of the infusion which is generally used, it would be cleaner and better, if a strong decoction was made from *picadura*—the small pieces of leaves of good tobacco—and used after it had become cold, or on the day after the boiling is made.

"If the wash is made by infusion, at least two jugs should be used to make it in, and it should be only used on the third or fourth day, renewing it as often as it appears to pass into a state of putrid fermentation, in which state it is of no use, and on which account two deposits are necessary, so that one at least may always be in a fit state to use, whilst the other is acquiring the necessary strength and a transparent golden colour, in which state it is fit for use.

"Each tobacco leaf should be dyed separately, and not, as some do, after it has been made up into *gavillas*—small bundles tied at one end of the leaf. It is very important that all the leaves should equally receive the benefit, and this is impossible when several are tied together. The good system of dyeing is used by all practical *vegueros;* to save labour some do it otherwise, to the great injury of the aroma and quality, and no small risk of the tobacco becoming spotted, and full of holes; for tobacco invariably commences to show these spots and small holes near the heads of the *gavilla*, where the dye has not been able to penetrate owing to the manner in which the leaves are tied. Each leaf ought, therefore, to be dyed separately, as the most intelligent people do. The leaves should be placed separately in rows on a bench, having all the heads in one line; then the dye should be applied by means of a sponge, which should be soaked in the dye or infusion, and squeezed, so that a dampness only will be communicated to the leaf.

" In passing the sponge over the leaf, it should be drawn from the head or thick part near the stalk, down the large vein to the point, so that the thick vein down the centre of the leaf may receive the heaviest part of the infusion, from which the dye pushes along the transversal veins, and all parts derive benefit from it.

" After dyeing the first layer on the bench, another one is placed above this, keeping always the leaves in the same direction; and this operation is repeated, and each layer is sponged, until the pile from which they are taken is exhausted. As this new pile of dyed leaves gradually increases in height, it should be gently pressed down with the hand, and, when finished, should be covered over with green plantain leaves. This operation should be done in the morning, and by nightfall the tobacco will have acquired the necessary softness, and soaked up the infusion, so that the leaves, although very flexible, will have no signs of excess in moisture. If they have, they should be spread to dry somewhat, because, when the bundles of leaves are being tied up, they should not be excessively wet, as the result would probably be so strong a fermentation that it would degenerate into a putrid one. The leaves should have a soft silkiness, but should have no positive signs of water on them after they have been dyed.

"When the tobacco is in a good state of softness, the next operation is the '*cabeceo*.' This operation consists in uniting the leaves by the heads—putting them perfectly even, and joining together a uniform number of each class. The leaves should be collected in the palm of the left hand, drawing gently the right hand over all the length of each leaf from the head to the point, and tying them at the heads with a piece of *yagua* or vine, or, as most people do, by binding one of the leaves round the head of the bundle. This operation is generally made in the evening, and the following morning they should be placed in the bales, as it injures the tobacco to allow it to dry in *manojos* before putting it into bales, for, if too dry, fermentation is retarded, or is incomplete in the bales.

"We have described the manner of washing or dyeing, in making the *gavillas*, and tying them in bundles as the most practical *vegueros* do. In this part we should not, we think, advise any innovation, except that of using old seasoned tobacco instead of fresh for making the infusion, and substituting a decoction made by boiling, instead of an infusion in cold water. But we strongly advise a reform in the sorting and the classification; and a fixed number of each class of leaves should be put in each *gavilla*, as a basis from which to start all calculations for mercantile transactions. We believe, therefore, it would be convenient to fix, after the following order,

CURING. 121

the number of leaves which each head '*gavilla*' should contain:—

First quality	Sound	25	leaves to each *gavilla*
	Broken or torn	30	,, ,,
	For stuffing	40	,, ,,
Second quality	Sound	30	,, ,,
	Broken or torn	35	,, ,,
	Stuffing	43	,, ,,
Third quality	Sound	40	,, ,,
	Broken or torn	45	,, ,,
	Desecho		These three classes may be added without counting the number of leaves,
Fourth quality	Suckers		
	Sprouts		

but making the heads (*gavillas*) of a regular uniform size; and the *manojos* and bales of about the same size as those of 'sound' and 'broken' of the third quality, the latter weighing 100-125 lb.

"By following strictly this method, and by establishing these quantities and qualities, as a basis for all contracts, any defects found might easily be obviated; and very exact calculations might be made of the number of cigars each bale would yield, after having examined its special condition; and its real value might be estimated either by bales or bundles, or by weight."

Bulking.—Bulking means placing the tobacco-leaves in heaps for the purpose of heating, in order to develop colour and flavour; this is carried out in various ways, nearly all involving great labour and risk, as in most instances tobacco loses more or less in value during the process called "curing." The more care is taken in raising the crop, the less attention the tobacco requires in the shed. With a good kind of tobacco, grown on light, friable soil, treated as described, little care will be needed, after the leaves are dried and stripped. By the drying process, the leaves will have undergone a slow fermentation, which makes it unnecessary to watch or guide a regular fermentation afterwards, hence bulking and fermenting, as generally understood, are not required.

After being made into hands, the tobacco is put into heaps (bulked) before it again dries. Every evening, the tobacco that has been stripped during the day is bulked; but if the weather be very dry, it must be bulked as soon as a certain number of hands is ready. The heaps should be made 4–8 feet square and 4–8 feet high; all the stalks are outside, and the whole is covered by mats, &c., to check evaporation. The drier the tobacco, the larger must the heaps be made, to encourage a slight fermentation. The extent of the fermentation can be easily controlled. If the colour of the leaves is not uniform, or if it is desired to give them a browner colour, the heaps must be made large, and a somewhat moist atmosphere is required in the storing-room. This will cause fermentation to set in after a short time, and the heat to rise after some days, so much so that rebulking is required, which is done by putting the top leaves of the old heap at the bottom of the new one. Under such circumstances, the heap must be frequently examined during the few first weeks, to prevent overheating. It is advisable to rebulk the tobacco also, even when not much heated, after the first fourteen days, and again a month later, to ascertain the exact state in which it is. Sometimes the tobacco becomes mouldy; this occurs especially with tobacco which has been manured with chlorides, which cause it to become more hygroscopic than when manured otherwise. If this occurs, the mould must be brushed off, and, if necessary, the tobacco be dried. The tobacco may now remain heaped in the store-room until there is a chance for sale. It must be remembered, however, that the best time for selling varies very much. Some tobacco is fit for smoking a few weeks after drying, whereas others may burn very badly at that time, yet become a good burning article after being stored for several months.

After assorting, Perry Hull advises that the tobacco " be corded up awhile, in a dry place, that the butts may be thoroughly cured before packing in the cases. The pile is made with the butts out, and tips interlapping in the middle, at every other course, at the ends turning the butts toward the end. Get upon the pile upon the knees, take hold of the butt of a hank with one hand, drawing the leaves at the tip together with the other, and placing it upon the pile in that position, immediately putting the knee upon it. After the pile is finished, it should be covered over with boards, to keep it from drying up, and a few days before packing into the cases, should be well weighted down, which will save a great deal of pressing at that time. Such a pile should be made only about 2½–3 feet high, and then closely watched to prevent a premature sweat, which often, if the weather be mild, will take place in such a pile, which will not be sufficient to render the tobacco fit for working, but which, if not intercepted at the commencement, will be sufficient to prevent a proper sweat afterwards. Check, therefore, the first symptoms of heat in such a pile, by opening the pile, and repacking it, shaking out the hanks and giving them time to cool off."

Bowie gives a caution that the tobacco " should not be too moist or ' high,' as it is termed, when put in stalk bulk, or it will get warm, the leaves stick to the stalk, get a bad smell, and change colour; besides, if left too long, it will rot. To bulk tobacco requires judgment and neatness. Two logs should be laid parallel to each other, about 30 inches apart, and the space between them filled with sticks for the purpose of keeping the tobacco from the dampness of the ground. The bundles are then taken one at a time, spread out and smoothed down, which is most conveniently done by putting it against the breast and stroking the leaves downward smooth and straight with the right hand. It is then passed, two bundles at a time, to the man bulking. He takes them and lays them down and presses them with his hands; they are laid, two at a time, in a straight line—the broad part of the bundles slightly projecting over the next two— and two rows of bundles are put in a bulk, both rows carried on together, the heads being on the outside, and the tails just lapping one over the other in regular succession. The bulk, when carried up to a convenient height, should have a few sticks laid across to keep it in place. It must often be examined, and if getting warm it ought to be immediately changed and laid down in another bulk of less height, and not pressed as it is laid down; this is called 'wind-rowing'; being loose and open, it admits the air between the rows of bundles, hence the term. The next process in this troublesome, but beautiful crop, is to 'condition' it for 'packing.' The 'bright,' 'yellow,' and 'second' tobacco will condition, but most generally in such bulks as I have just described, but it is best to hang up the 'dull' as soon almost as stripped. If the bright or second do not dry thoroughly in the bulks, that should also be hung up in the house to become well dried. To properly hang up tobacco to condition, small-sized sticks should be procured, and each one nicely smoothed with the drawing-knife, and kept for that purpose. After it has once been perfectly dry, either hanging up or in bulks—so dry that the heads are easily knocked off, and the shoulders of the bundles crack upon pressure like pipe-stems—it should be taken down, or if in bulks, removed, the first soft, moist spell of weather, as soon as it is soft and yielding enough, as it will become too dry to handle without crumbling or breaking, and it must be put in 4 or 6 row bulks of any convenient length and height, the higher the better, laid down close, so that as little of the leaves or shoulders as possible be exposed on the outside of the bulk. When completed put sticks and logs of wood, &c., on the top so as to weigh it down. Here it will keep sweet and in nice order for packing at any time, no matter what the weather be, if it was conditioned properly, it will not change a particle while in the condition-bulk."

Packing.—Tobacco in America is commonly packed in barrels, the layers being at right angles to each other alternately, and the butt-ends being always towards the outside. The usual size is about 4 feet 6 inches deep, 3 feet 6 inches in diameter at one end, and 3 feet 4 inches at the other, to enable the contents to be uncovered for examination without disturbing the mass. The packing is effected under considerable hydraulic pressure. Elsewhere all kinds of packages are employed, and their weights are very various.

In Bishop's opinion the best size for boxes is the following:—" 3 feet 6 inches long, 2 feet 4 inches wide, 2 feet 6 inches in depth, manufactured from planed pine boards, 1 inch in thickness, with standards 2 inches square, inside at each corner to nail to. Having thus your boxes prepared, and the tobacco in good condition, the first soft, mild day that comes proceed to packing; the bundles or 'hands' of tobacco must be taken from the bulk and laid in courses in the box, laying the butts of the 'hands' to the outside of the box, allowing the ends to lap over each other, and endeavouring to keep the centre of the box a little higher than the edges—these courses to be packed as solid as possible by the hand. If any of the bundles are 'soft' or have an ill smell, they must be exposed to the fire or sun until sweet and dry before being packed. When the box is nearly full, a false cover (just large enough to slip inside the box) must be placed on the tobacco, and pressed as heavily as possible with the lever or screw power; remove the pressure and re-fill, pressure finally being applied to the real cover, which may then be tacked down. A box of the size I have mentioned, when filled, should contain about 400 lb. of tobacco, and thus packed, will keep for years."

Another planter considers that parcels of "less than 1500 lb. may be carried to market almost in any way; but more than that should be 'prized' in hogsheads. Several farmers might combine their crops for prizing.

CURING.

As to the size, form, and materials of the hogsheads. In Virginia, the size of the hogsheads is prescribed by law. They must be made of seasoned pine or poplar. They must be 4 feet 6 inches long; 3 feet 6 inches in diameter, at one end, and 3 feet 4 inches at the other. This difference of diameter is to allow the tobacco to be inspected. This may be something new to persons of the North, therefore I will explain the mode of inspecting tobacco in the hogshead. An inspector is appointed by law to inspect or examine the tobacco prized in hogsheads. His first step is, to place the hogshead big end upward. He then removes the lining, and takes out the head. He next inverts the position of the hogshead, that is, puts the little end up, and raises it entirely from the tobacco. The mass of prized tobacco stands before him without a covering. The outside may be all right, but his sworn duty is to examine it through and through, as well as round and round. For this purpose he drives an iron bar to the middle, near the top of the mass, prises up and takes out a handful of bundles. He repeats that operation on two other points of the mass. He then inspects or examines the parcels extracted, and rates the whole hogshead according to their quality. The hogshead is replaced and made secure. The hogsheads and the samples taken from them bear corresponding marks, and the former is sold by the latter. The staves of the hogshead must not be wider than 5, nor narrower than 3 inches, $\frac{5}{8}$ inch thick, and dressed on the inside. The heading must be seasoned pine or poplar, and 1 inch thick, with 8 hoops. Such a hogshead will well answer in other States as well as in Virginia.

"Weigh out, say 300 lb. It takes two hands to do this work, one inside the hogshead and the other out. One is called the 'packer,' the other the 'waiter.' The packer so arranges the bundles, in placing them, as to make 4 courses in one layer. Repeat the layers until the 300 lb. are packed. The weight (lever-power) is then applied. After 6 hours, put in 200 lb. more and apply the weight; 6 hours, and so on, until 1300–1500 lb. have been put in. The softer the tobacco, the more of it can be put in a hogshead. If the tobacco is of the first quality, 1500 lb. is enough. But if lower qualities, 1800 lb. can be put in. The finer the quality the less weight it can bear without injury; and *vice versâ*. Having prized the crop, it is ready for market."

According to Pursley, a hogshead "4 feet in length, and 3 feet in diameter, is the medium size; 1000 lb. is considered a full hogshead; but one of the above dimensions can hold 1500 lb. by hard pressing; but this blackens the tobacco, and injures the sale of it. Packing in the hogshead is done by first laying a course or layer of bundles straight across the bottom, keeping the butts even and close together; then fill up on each side of the centre course, placing the butts against the staves; then the butts of the hands that lie against the hogshead should be covered up with 2 or 3 others, pressed closely down. The next centre course should be laid across the first, and done in the same manner as before, and so on, crossing each course in succession, until the hogshead is two-thirds full; when the press should be applied till the tobacco is pressed down to within $1\frac{1}{2}$ foot of the bottom of the hogshead. The press should remain on an hour or more, in order that the tobacco may settle together ; then the press should be raised, and the packing resumed as before, till the tobacco is within 1½ foot of the top; then the press should again be applied till the tobacco is pressed half-way down the hogshead; the same proportion should be observed until the hogshead is full. Then put the head in, and it is ready for market."

Perry Hull would have packing-cases " made of cheap pine lumber, 3 feet 8 inches long by 2 feet 6 inches wide and high, outside measurement; they should be made tight and strong; there should be corner-pieces nailed in 1½ inch square, nailing to them well from both ways. The tobacco is packed in, with the butts towards each end ; taking hold of the butt with one hand, the tip with the other, and giving the hank a slight twist, lay it in the case in that position. A lever or screw can be used to do the pressing, whichever is the most convenient. From 360 lb. to 380 is the proper weight for packing; though if the tobacco is very dry, 400 lb. will probably not sweat too hard; and if quite wet (which it never should be), 350 may.

"After being packed, the tobacco should never be kept in a damp cellar; a good tight barn or other outbuilding, where the cases can stand on a floor, is the best place. The crop usually passes from the hands of growers, into those of speculators and dealers, before the sweating season. The first symptoms of sweating appear about as soon as settled warm weather comes, usually the fore part of May ; it then commences to grow warm, and 'wet' to appearance, which increases for about 3 weeks, when it reaches its culminating point and commences to cool off.

K

One unaccustomed to the crop, upon examining it at this period, would be sure to think it was rotting, but if not too damp when packed, there is no danger. Sometimes, if a case is known to be too wet, the lids can be started, to give a little vent to the steam and gases which are generated, and this is about all that can be done for it; and it is far safer to see that the proper condition is secured before packing, than to do even this. The weight will commence to decrease about as soon as the heat commences, and it has been ascertained by weighing at the various stages, that more than half of the shrinkage is accomplished by the time that the sweat has reached its culminating point. About 10 per cent. is allowed for the shrinkage of a crop, in just the right state when packed; if wetter, it will shrink as high as 12-13 per cent., and if very dry, it may shrink less than 10 per cent. The different grades usually bring about the following prices: Wrappers, 14 cents per lb.; Seconds, 7-8 cents; Fillers, 3-4 cents. The proportion of the different grades in a good crop should be, Wrappers, three-fifths, and Seconds and Fillers, each one-fifth."

Judson Popenoe thinks boxes "should be made 30 inches square by 42 inches in length outside; saw the endboards 28 inches long, nail them to two $1\frac{1}{4}$-inch square slats so that the head will be 28 inches square; when two heads are made, nail the sides of the box to the heads so as to come even with the outside of the head, the sides being 28 inches wide; then nail the bottom on firmly; the top can be nailed slightly until after the tobacco is packed, when it can be nailed firm. Set your box by the side of the bulk, and let one hand get in the box and another pass the tobacco to him, one hand at a time, taking care not to shake it out, but put in the box as it comes from bulk, with the butt of the hand next the end of the box. Place close and press with the knee firmly; lay alternate courses at each end, and if the tobacco is not long enough to lap sufficiently to fill the centre, put a few hands crosswise in the centre. When the box is full, place it under a lever; have a follower, which is a cover made of inch boards, nailed to two pieces of scantling and made to fit inside of the box; lay this on the tobacco, and build with blocks of scantling on it of a sufficient height for the lever to be clear of the box when pressed. Press down firmly with a strong lever, and, while kneeing in another box full, let the lever remain, so that the tobacco gets set in the box. When ready, take the lever off and fill up as before, about 6 inches higher than the box; press it below the top of the box, take off your lever and nail on the top as quickly as possible. Some use tobacco-presses for packing, which are perhaps more convenient; they are of various patterns, but a lever saves the expense of a press and is in the reach of all. If tobacco is sold at the shed, it should be sold before packing, being easier examined in bulk than box."

Mitjen is of opinion that, "except in cases where the extraordinary size of the leaves will not permit it, all the bales should be made up of 80 '*manojos*'; but in the former case 60 of the first classes of the first quality will be sufficient. The fixed number of 80 *manojos* is convenient for making calculations. We have already said that the day following that on which the *manojos* were tied up, they should be packed in bales, so as not to allow them time to dry too much. Bearing this in mind, the dyeing and tying up of the *manojos* should not be commenced until there is a sufficient quantity of assorted leaves to make a bale or bales; should there be a surplus of *manojos* after the bales are made up, they should be kept protected from the air, until another set of bales is about to be made up.

"We do not think it is necessary to further explain the manner of placing the *yaguas*, in order to make the bales, but it is expedient to state that 3 layers of *manojos* should not be put in one bale, because it makes a bad shape, and the tierces or bales appear much smaller than they really are. The bales should be made of 2 layers, having the heads of the *manojos* placed towards the outside. When the first layer of one of the heads of the bale is placed, the heads of the other layer should be so arranged that they will be about half-way over the points of the others; and if the tobacco is very small, to each row of *manojos* may be laid crossways, two *manojos* with their heads touching the *yaguas*, so that the tobacco placed in the bale may form a compact even mass, impervious to the air. The same should be done in the other rows, care being taken that the bale is made somewhat thicker in the middle, and never have a hollow there,—a sure sign of loose packing, —and into which the air finds its way, preventing fermentation, proper curing, as well as aroma—the tobacco becoming dry too soon. After the bales are tied up, they should be placed in the sun or wind until the humidity of the *yagua* is dry. They should then be placed on boards in the storehouse, putting them two and two, one on the other; and after eight days they should be moved, placing them below those which had been above, so that they may ferment and be equally pressed."

For pressing tobacco into the hogshead, Hudson suggests that "a hole be mortised in a tree, in which the end of the lever can be inserted, passing over the hogshead, and working by a tree or post, in which should be pins at intervals of 8-10 inches, by which a small lever may be

FIG. 13.

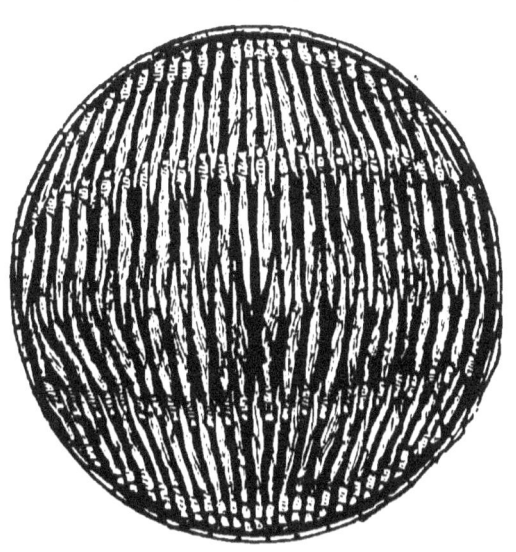

used to force the first lever down on the tobacco ; 50-100 lb. may be placed in the hogshead and firmly pressed a few hours, and as much added again, and so on. Fig. 13 will serve to represent the manner in which the hands (or ties) may be placed in the hogshead—filling the middle first, then the outer edges—placing the tops toward the centre, and observing to keep the centre and edges full."

Improving.—It is sometimes the custom to subject the

tobacco-leaves to some sort of improvement. There is no doubt that, by proper application of ingredients, the value of tobacco may be much enhanced. The most costly tobacco often commands a high price, not so much on account of its inherent flavour, as from that given to it artificially. In most instances, the best course to be adopted is to leave the improvement of the leaves to the manufacturer. Many ingredients are employed to improve smoking-tobacco. They tend:—1, to make the tobacco more elastic and flexible; 2, to remove the coarse flavour; 3, to add a particular flavour; 4, to improve the burning quality; 5, to improve the colour. To make the tobacco more flexible and pliant, the leaves are macerated in, or sprinkled with, a solution of sugar. In hot countries, this process is often necessary, to give tobacco such an elasticity as to fit it for handling, especially when intended for wrappers. To remove the coarse flavour, it is often macerated in water, or in very dilute hydrochl ric acid. In Holland, 4–8 oz. of hydrochloric acid, diluted with 25–30 measures of water, is applied to 100 lb. of tobacco. The coarser the flavour of the tobacco, the stronger is the solution used. The time of maceration varies between $\frac{1}{2}$ and 1 hour. Sometimes tobacco is steeped in a mixture of sugar solution and diluted hydrochloric acid. To extract the fatty matter, it is macerated in alcohol or spirit of wine. To give a fine flavour, numerous substances are employed, some of which are kept secret. The following ingredients are mostly in use:—Water, cognac, vanilla, sugar, rose-wood, cassia, clove, benzoin, citron oil, rose-wood oil, amber, thyme, lavender, raisins, sassafras-wood, saltpetre, orange, and many others. The burning quality is improved by macerating in or sprinkling with solutions of carbonate of potash, acetate of potash, acetate of lime, or saltpetre, &c. Badly-burning cigars inserted for a moment in such solutions are much improved. Tobacco treated with acetate of lime yields a very white ash. The colour is sometimes improved by fumigating the leaves with sulphur, and by the application of ochre and saffron.

Although it may be said that fine tobaccos generally do not require any impregnation with foreign matter for the sake of flavour, yet the manufacturer frequently endeavours to give the leaf a particular aroma. An inferior tobacco, however, which often would not find a market, is sometimes so much improved by artificial means, as to compete successfully with the genuine fine article. It is said that in Germany indigenous tobacco is often so much "improved" that the cigars made from it, after being covered with a fine tobacco leaf, are sold as genuine Havanas. A special preparation of tobacco for snuff is seldom attempted by the cultivator. With reference to the preparation of tobacco for export, the sorting of the leaf is of the utmost importance ; only first and second sorts should be exported. It would be well to remove the midribs, whereby the cost of transport and customs duty would be greatly reduced.

The value of a cigar depends, not only on the intrinsic value of the leaf, but to a great extent on the mode of manufacture. Thus, the raw material may be of good quality, but if the maker does not classify the leaves properly, or if he rolls his cigars too hard, which must vary according to the qualities of the leaves, the cigar will burn badly. The best-burning leaves must always be used for wrappers. If this should be neglected, the inside of the cigar burns faster than the covering, the air has no access to the burning parts, and the empyreumatical substances are volatilized without being decomposed. Such cigars therefore make much smoke, and smell badly.

CHAPTER IV.

PRODUCTION AND COMMERCE.

DETAILS concerning the different modes of cultivating and curing, and of the extent of the production and commerce in tobacco in the various countries, will best be given in the alphabetical order of the countries.

Afghanistan.—The tobacco grown at Kandahar is celebrated in all the neighbouring states for its mild and agreeable flavour, and is largely exported to Hindustan and Bokhara. Three kinds are grown, viz. :—Kandahari, Balkhi, and Mansurabadi. Of these, the last named is the most esteemed, and fetches the highest price, viz. 6 lb. for 2s.-4s. The Kandahari sells for a little less than half this price, and the Balkhi for a little more. The Mansurabadi is not much exported, being mostly consumed in the country. The cultivation is conducted with great care, and the same plants yield two crops of leaves in the year. Of these, the first, which is called *sargul*, is the best, the leaves having a mild and sweet flavour; it is mostly consumed by the wealthy classes, or exported. The second crop is called *mundhai*: the leaves have a tough and fibrous texture, and a strong acrid taste; it is usually smoked by the poor people, and is also made into snuff. The plants are raised from seed in small beds, prepared for the purpose by careful manuring with wood-ashes and stable-refuse mixed together. From these nurseries, the young plants are transplanted into the fields, previously prepared for their reception, the earth being laid out in regular ridges and furrows. The plants are fixed into the sides of these little ridges, and watered by means of the intervening furrows. Often the young plants, packed in moist clay, and bound up in straw, are conveyed to distant parts of the country; but the produce of these, it is said, does not equal that of the plants reared at Kandahar. About six weeks after transplanting, that is, about May–June, the first crop is reaped, the whole plant being cut away about 6 inches from the ground, and only some 5 or 6 of the lowest leaves being left. Each plant, as cut, is laid on the ridge, and here each side is alternately exposed for a night and a day to the effects of the dew and sun, by which their green colour becomes brown. After this, they are collected in large heaps in a corner of the field, and covered over with mats, or a layer of straw, &c., and allowed to remain so for 8–10 days, during which the stems shrivel, and give up their moisture to the leaves. At the end of this time, the heaps are conveyed away into the villages, where the stalks are separated from the leaves, the latter are then dried in the shade and tightly packed in bundles about 14 inches square, and in this shape are sold by the grower. After the first crop is gathered, the ground is turned with a spade, well manured, and freely irrigated. In due course, the old stems shoot up and produce fresh leaves, and in six weeks or two months, the second crop is cut. Sometimes, though seldom, a third crop is realized, but the quality of this tobacco is very inferior, and it is only fit for making snuff.

Africa.—The tobacco-plant extends throughout Central

and East Africa, wherever the equinoctial rains fall. It is cultivated to some extent in the Bondei of Usambara, but seems to be the special product of the Handei district, whence considerable quantities are sent to Pangani for export. Usambara also exports to Zanzibar stiff, thin, round cakes, which have been pounded in wooden mortars, and neatly packed in plaintain-leaves. It is dark and well-flavoured. The Cape of Good Hope, in 1865, had 933 *morgen* (of 2·116 acres) under tobacco, yielding 1,632,746 lb.; in 1875, 1243 *morgen* afforded 3,060,241 lb. Tobacco is grown considerably in Oudtshorn and other districts of the Cape Colony, and on the warmer farms in the Transvaal, but to the greatest extent on the coast. The supply is already sufficient for local demands, and tobacco promises to become a staple of South African agricultural industry.

A recent writer on this portion of the British colonies says, "tobacco, though cultivated as an article of commerce for export, has not met with much success, as the passion for the weed has become deeply rooted in the natives of the coast and interior, so that it is cultivated by them in many parts of the province for their own consumption, and forms a regular article of sale and barter amongst themselves." The tobacco leaf is dried very carelessly by the natives, and is made up in a peculiar way, as follows:—It is first plaited, and when the plait has reached a length of 3–4 feet, it is wound up in the form of a spiral. Gradually drying in this shape, it preserves its form without any binding, and it is unwound and cut off in short pieces when required for use or sale. This mode of preparation is invariable among the Makua and Yao, between the Roouma and Zambesi. Consul O'Neill says that "were the natives instructed in some simple method of drying and pressing the leaf, the valuable product would be probably brought down by them in considerable quantities, affording, as it would do, a larger margin for profit than does the culture of oil seeds, and it might become a regular article of colonial manufacture and export."

Tobacco-growing is a very important industry in Algeria. The culture and manufacture are quite free, but the French Government buys all the best produce, for manufacture and sale by the State factory in Paris. The cultivation continues to increase, and is highly remunerative where the land is capable of irrigation. In 1876–7, the 1889 Europeans engaged in it cultivated 2471 *hectares* (of $2\frac{1}{2}$ acres), and produced 2,782,500 *kilo.* (of 2·2 lb.); the 8021 natives cultivated 4154 *hectares*, which yielded 1,889,124 *kilo.* The year 1877–8 was less favourable, and the area decreased by 425 *hectares*. Still worse results were expected in 1878–9, owing to scarcity of water. The kind most grown is called *chebli*. The produce per *hectare* of fine and *chebli* is estimated at 6–8 *quintals*; the other kinds give 10–12. The exports in 1877 and 1878 respectively were as follows:—Manufactured, 121,090 *kilo.*, and 124,117 *kilo.*; unmanufactured, 3,445,441 *kilo.* and 1,509,266 *kilo.* In 1879, 1087 Europeans planted 3180 *hectares*, and gathered 1,226,181 *kilo.*; 11,079 natives planted 6584 *hectares*, and produced 1,384,802 *kilo.*; the exports were 2,481,218 *kilo.* unmanufactured, and 146,345 *kilo.* manufactured.

The figures for 1883 were:—1240 European planters

cultivated 2278 *hectares* and produced 2,250,671 *kilo.*, whilst 8735 native planters cultivated 6416 *hectares* and produced 2,977,067 *kilo.*, the total product being 5,227,738 *kilo*. This does not differ to any great extent from the result of the previous year. Tobacco is capable of being produced in much greater quantity, says the British Consul, but the market is limited. The colonists themselves and the Government appear to be the only purchasers.

Australia.—In the year ending 31st March, 1879, New South Wales had 835 acres under tobacco, and the crop amounted to 7932 cwt. In the same year, Victoria cultivated 1936 acres, which yielded 15,662 cwt., valued at 43,853*l*. Queensland grew 36 acres of tobacco in 1879.

Austro-Hungary.—The manufacture and sale of tobacco is a Government monopoly in the Austro-Hungarian empire, and the revenue thus derived is the most lucrative item of the indirect income of the State. The only tobacco-growing provinces of Austria are Galicia and Bukowina, producing about 4 million *kilo.* from 2900 *hectares*; and South Tyrol, where 290 *hectares* yield almost 4 million *kilo.* of green tobacco. The respective approximate values of the two products are $18\frac{1}{3}$ *florin* (of 1*s*. $11\frac{1}{2}d$.) and $4\frac{2}{3}$ *florin* per 100 *kilo*. The chief supplies are furnished by Hungary, which was once so noted for its tobacco, but the industry is now completely crippled by the fiscal regulations. The area (in acres) under cultivation fluctuates remarkably; in 1860, it was $679\frac{1}{4}$; in 1865, 68,141; in 1869, $843\frac{3}{4}$; in 1875, 26,817; in 1879, 7316. The total areas (in acres) under cultivation in the whole empire in

1876, 1877, and 1878 respectively were, 144,493, 148,126, 143,447; the yields in *kilo.*, 46,033,163, 44,164,038, 40,978,540; and the yield (in *kilo.*) per *joch* (of 1·43 acre), 445, 426, 408. Fiume, in 1877, exported by sea 2862 cwt. of manufactured tobacco; and by land, 31,200 cwt. of leaf, and 53,712 cwt. of manufactured. In 1879, it shipped 9900 *kilo.* of leaf tobacco direct to England. In 1883, the tobacco harvest was 26,560 metrical centners (about equivalent to cwts.), being 1595 in advance of 1882. The total exports of raw tobacco were 55,842 metrical centners in 1883, and 74,475 in 1884. The port of Fiume shipped 613 tons of tobacco leaf in 1883, of which 189,300 *kilo.* value 75,720 florins, went to Gibraltar. In 1884, the shipments from Fiume were 1673 tons.

Borneo.—Tobacco is grown in small quantities by the Dyaks and people of Bruni; but they are unskilful in its manufacture, though the flavour of the product of Bruni is much esteemed by Europeans. Under skilful management, and by introducing a better kind if necessary, it might become as profitable to this island as it now is to the neighbouring ones of the Philippines, Java, &c. The Dyaks might be more readily induced to cultivate this plant, the nature of which they know, than plants which are strange to them. More recently it is announced that plantations have been commenced in British North Borneo, and samples of the leaf sent to Europe have been favourably reported on. The exports from Sarawak in 1884 were valued at 2020 dollars to foreign ports, and 34,257 dollars in coasting vessels, making a total of 36,277 dollars. In the same year, British North Borneo shipped 2113 dollars' worth; and Sandakan, 1537 dollars' worth.

Bourbon.—Efforts are being made to successfully introduce tobacco into the rotation of crops on the sugar estates, with the object of supplying the article to the French *régie* or Government monopoly, which buys annually upwards of 40 million francs' worth of tobacco in the islands of Cuba, Java, and other colonies. The results hitherto obtained are not unsatisfactory, and this article may shortly acquire importance among Bourbon products. The exports in 1884 were 10,185 *kilo.*, value 61,110 *fr.*

Brazil.—In Brazil, tobacco is chiefly cultivated in the provinces of Bahia, Minas, Sao Paulo, and Para. The town of Purificaçao, in Bahia, is the centre of an important district. The cultivation is increasing, and greater care is being taken in the preparation. The common up-country method is to pick the leaves from the stalks, dry them under the hut-roofs, remove the midribs, and spread them in superposed layers, amounting to 2–8 lb., for rolling together and binding with bark strips. These rolls are bound very tightly with cord, and left for several days, when the cord is replaced by strips of *jacitára*, the split stem of a climbing palm (*Desmoncus sp. div.*), and have a stick-like form 1½ inch in diameter. They are sold in *masas* of 4–6 feet in length, but the tobacco is not considered good till it has fermented for 5–6 months, when it is hard and black, and shaved off as required for pipes, cigarettes, and cigars, the last made with wrappers of *tauari* bark (*Couratari guianensis*). The Tapajos tobacco is considered the finest in the Amazon valley. The export of tobacco from Bahia in 1877–8 was 17,272,678 *kilo.*, and in 1878–9, 18,149,201 *kilo.*, almost the whole being to Germany. Santos, in 1878–9, shipped 381,310 *kilo.* Bahia sends away immense numbers of cigars coastwise. Maceio exported 4336*l*. worth in 1876, but none in 1879.

Some interesting particulars are given in the last report of the United States Consul-General at Rio de Janeiro, as to the cultivation and manufacture of tobacco in Brazil. It appears that the cultivation began about the year 1600, in the province of Bahia, and from thence extended to all the other districts along the coast. Among the localities earliest known for their tobacco production was the lake district of Pernambuco, now the province of Alagoas, where an excellent quality was produced, which commanded very high prices. During the following century the cultivation increased so rapidly in Alagoas and Bahia, that at the commencement of the succeeding century, the average annual export had reached 2857 tons from the latter, and 285 tons from the former province. The earliest export statistics available for the whole empire, are for the year 1839-40, in which the export amounted to 295,966 *arrobas*, the *arroba* being equivalent to about 32 lb.; and the value exceeded 65,000*l*. For the next thirteen years, the exports averaged 8,000,000 lb. annually, with a value steadily increasing. During each of the years 1853-55, the amount exported was 22,000,000 lb., of the total value each year of 200,000*l*. In 1879-80, the export was 50,000,000 lb., of the value 659,000*l*.; in 1880-81, 44,000,000 lb., of the value of 650,000*l*., and in 1881-82, 52,000,000 lb., of the value of 680,000*l*. Though the principal tobacco-producing province of the empire is Bahia, tobacco of good quality is grown in every part of Brazil, from the Amazon to the Rio Grande frontier. Some localities in the province of Amazonas have long been known for the excellent quality of their tobacco, while in the Rio market one of the brands most esteemed comes from the province of Goyaz. The local consumption of tobacco is very great, and principally in smoking. Bahia tobacco used to be largely exported in rolls, weighing 8 *arrobas*, or 256 lb. each; of late years, however, large quantities of the leaves in bales are exported to Hamburg. Cigar factories are established in all large cities throughout the tobacco-growing regions, which give employment to a large number of men, women, and children. The methods employed in the cultivation and preparation of the plant are very much the same as they were nearly 200 years ago. The labour employed is that of slaves, to whom are assigned special descriptions of work. In former times curing tobacco in rolls required much constant labour, the ropes composing each roll being unwound, twisted, and re-wound during a period varying from 10 to 15 days. The Brazilian tobacco is generally characterized by its strength and dark colour, particularly in Bahia. In that province the practice is to manure heavily, which occasions a very rank growth and strong flavour. In Minas Geraes the tobacco is somewhat milder, and some advance has lately been made in a few localities towards improved processes of curing. This seed may be germinated in any season of the year, but the months of June, July, and August are generally preferred for planting, because germination and transplanting are brought into or near the rainy season. Tobacco plants planted in this season are considered the best growers, and produce the largest leaves. Those, however, which are germinated in the dry season, and sustained by irrigation, grow with

L

greater vigour, and possess a finer aroma. The land selected for the plants is cleared, and the surface worked with the hoe, after which it is marked off into parallel rows about 3 feet apart, according to locality and the size of the mature plants. In transplanting, the young plants are set from 2 to 3 feet apart, and are manured heavily in the pits opened for them. Great care is necessary for a time to protect the shoots from the sun, and to irrigate plentifully when the transplanting occurs in a dry season. The work of cultivation and keeping down the weeds is performed entirely with the hoe, and only two or three times during the season. In gathering in the crops, planters wait until the plants are fully matured, this being determined by doubling and breaking one of the top leaves. In Bahia and other Brazilian provinces the lower leaf is often picked by itself, and in a few days the next, and so on as long as the plant will develop the lower leaves into what is classed first quality. These leaves are hung up two and two, under cover and across poles, 24 hours after picking and sweating. When it is intended to twist the leaves into ropes, they are left hanging about 2 days, when they are taken down, carefully freed from the heavy parts of the midrib, doubled in halves, and laid away for the rope twister. This operation requires considerable dexterity, and is generally entrusted to the best slave on the plantation. The operation requires a rude windlass, which is slowly turned in winding the rope, which is twisted by hand. A boy is usually employed entirely to hand leaves to the twister. These ropes are unwound and re-wound once or twice a day, for a period of 10–15 days, according to the weather, and are twisted a little harder each time. In curing, the tobacco grows darker and darker, until it becomes jet black. The juices exuding from the rolls are carefully caught and preserved until the last winding, when, mixed with lard, syrup, and various aromatic herbs, they are used to pass the rope through, previous to the final winding. The last step is to cut the cured ropes in certain lengths, and to re-wind them upon light wooden sticks, about 2 feet in length, the winding being very compact and regular. The rolls are then covered with leather or strong canvas, when they are ready for market. Formerly, these rolls were made to weigh 8 *arrobas*, or 256 lb., though rolls of 3 *arrobas* were made for the home markets. At the present day the weights vary according to the locality. The large exportation of tobacco in leaf has considerably changed the character of tobacco-growing in Bahia, the process of curing and packing the leaf being simpler than the old process of manufacturing *rolos*. Tobacco-growing is heavily protected and taxed in Brazil, nearly all the provinces imposing separate protective taxes, in addition to those imposed by the Government. Besides these, the municipalities are permitted to levy taxes on the article. The present export tax on tobacco, in Brazil, amounts to as much as 18 per cent.

The local market quotations are thus given:—

		s. d.	s. d.		
Patentes	6808–8170 *real*	(=12 2-	14 7)	per 10 *kilo.*	(= 22 lb.)
Santo Amaro, assorted		(3 7-	5 8)	,,	,,
Alagrinhas..	2791–5106..	(5 0-	8 2)	,,	,,
São Felix	3745–4425	(6 8-	7 10¼)	,,	,,

The Bahia export in 1883–4 was 15,644,010 *kilo.*, value 400,246*l.*

Canary Islands.—With the declining importance of cochineal, tobacco-growing is gaining ground, and the quality of the article has been much improved, while factories for drying and preparing the leaf have been established in various localities. The exports for the year 1883–4 were:—27 lb., value 8*l.*, to France; 2268 cwt., value 9809*l.*, to Spain; 1753 lb., value 375*l.*, to Germany; and 939 lb., value 189*l.*, to West Coast of Africa.

China.—The chief tobacco-growing provinces of China are Chihli, Hopih, Hoonan, Szechuen, and Shingking. The use of tobacco is wide-spread and common, and considerable local trade is carried on in it. The exports from Amoy were 2573 *piculs* (of 133⅓ lb.), value 13,561*l.*, in 1877; and 3994½ *piculs*, value 17,936*l.*, in 1878. Wenchow exported 27¾ *piculs* of leaf in 1878, and 321½ in 1879. The exports and re-exports from Hankow in 1878 were 65,070¾ *piculs* of leaf, and 46,241¾ of prepared. In 1879, Hankow exported and re-exported 63,180 *piculs* prepared, value 311,754*l.*, and 58,094 of leaf, value 118,534*l.* There is an immense supply from the provinces, and the leaf is fine in colour, texture, and fragrance, but though sent to America and England for cigar-making, the trade has not been remunerative. It is now used in cigarettes and various cut mixtures as "Turkish," but when better known, will be smoked on its own merits. Canton exported 1730¾ *piculs* in 1877, 1742¾ in 1878, and 2397 in 1879. The exports of leaf from Ningpo were 407 *piculs* in 1874, 571 in 1875, 211 in 1876, 530 in 1877, 378 in 1878, and 165 in 1879. Kiungchow exported 449¼ *piculs* of leaf in 1878; and 85½ *piculs*, value 136*l.*, in 1879. Kiukiang exported 28,120½ *piculs* of leaf, value 85,678*l*., in 1878; and 14,659 of leaf, and 802 of stalk, in 1879.

Chinkiang imported 13,328 *piculs* of leaf, and 1914 of prepared, in 1879. Macao receives tobacco from the Hokshan district, and prepares it for exportation to Java, the Straits, and California, the annual export being about 10,000 *piculs*. The Newchwang imports of prepared native tobacco were 8052 *piculs* in 1877, 8354 in 1878, and 6630 in 1879. Shanghai, in 1879, imported 58,460 *piculs* of native leaf, 79,081½ of prepared, and 1187½ of stalk; and exported and re-exported 31,541 of leaf, and 29,672¼ of prepared. Taiwan imported 3017¼ *piculs* of prepared native in 1879. Tientsin exported 1047⅓ *piculs* native tobacco in 1878, and 693½ in 1879. Tobacco is grown in the hilly districts near Wuhu; the leaves are gathered in October, and sun-dried on wicker-work frames. The exports in 1879 were 597½ *piculs* of leaf, and 742 of prepared.

Cochin-China.—The culture of tobacco is extending in Cochin-China, and it is even said that a considerable quantity is exported to China, but it improves little in quality. The area reported to be under tobacco cultivation in 1878 (including coffee) was 2361 acres.

Costa Rica.—The free cultivation of tobacco was stopped in January 1884, and its free sale only permitted till December 31, 1885.

Ecuador.—The tobacco crop of Ecuador for 1879 was not so large as usual, owing to an unfavourable season. Esmeraldas, the most northerly port, and whence nearly all the tobacco shipments are made, despatched about 3000 *quintals* in 1879. Guayaquil exported 150 *quintals* in

1877, none in 1878, and 10 in 1879. In 1883, the exports from Guayaquil were 1374 *quintals*, value 5496*l.*; in 1884, only 96 *quintals*, 192*l.*

Fiji.—The Fiji Islands are well adapted to tobacco culture. The natives produce a good deal, which nearly approaches the American leaf. With careful curing, it would find a market in England. The native product is rolled, which prevents its being made into cigars. Samples of leaf-tobacco in hands, raised from foreign seeds, exhibited very unequal qualities, and a tendency to revert to American forms, the Havana returning to the Virginian type. Cut up for smoking, they were deficient in flavour, but were considered satisfactory as a first experiment.

France.—The area occupied by tobacco in France in 1873 was 14,858 *hectares* (of $2\frac{1}{2}$ acres), yielding at the rate of 12 *quintals* (of $220\frac{1}{2}$ lb.). The amount of land authorized to grow tobacco in Pas de Calais in 1879 was 2100 acres, and the quantity furnished to the Government was 3,659,636 lb., the prices (per *kilo.*) paid by the Government being 1 *fr.* 45*c.* for 1sts, 1 *fr.* 12*c.* for 2nds, 88*c.* for 3rds, and 10–66*c.* for other inferior qualities. The number of plants grown per acre is about 17,000. The department Nord affords rather more than Pas de Calais.

By the Imperial decrees of December 29th, 1810, and January 12th, 1811, it was ordained that the purchase of tobacco in leaf and the fabrication and sale, whether wholesale or retail, of manufactures of tobacco, should be exclusively confined to the Administration of Indirect Taxes (Régie des Droits Unis) in all the departments of

France. At present the Régie has in operation 16 large manufactories, 27 "magasins de culture," and 4 "magasins de transit." It employs over 19,000 workpeople, of whom about 80 per cent. are women and girls. The usual daily earnings are, for men, from 2s. 7d. to 3s. 11d., and for women, from 1s. 2d. to 2s. 4d. For faithful or exemplary services, the workpeople receive annually rewards, varying in amounts from 15s. to 20l. Mr. Scidmore, the United States Consular Agent in Paris, gives the following description of the manner in which the operations of the Régie are carried on. At the beginning of each year the Minister of Finance designates the number of hectares upon which, and the departments within which, the cultivation of tobacco may be undertaken during the following season. The last ministerial decree upon this subject confines the privilege to the departments of the Alpes Maritimes, Bouches du Rhône, Dordogne, Gironde, Ille-et-Vilaine, Landes, Lot-et-Garonne, Meurthe-et-Moselle, Nord, Pas de Calais, Puy de Dôme, Hautes-Pyrénées, Haute-Saône, Savoie, Haute Savoie, and Var. In the month of October or November, an agent of the Régie proceeds to the communes among which the prefects have apportioned the allotments, and receives the declaration of every proprietor desiring to profit by the authorization. A Commission, composed of the prefect, of the director of indirect taxes, a superior agent of cultivation, a member of the council general, and of a member of the council of the arrondissement, not being planters, then examine the declarations, and admit, reduce, or reject them. After a planter is accorded permission to cultivate, he is subjected to close official supervision, and to numerous stringent regulations concerning details as to the prohibition to sow any other seed than that furnished to him by the administration, the mode of planting, &c.; and, in addition to the surveillance as to these matters, two official inventories are taken of the growing crop—the first to ascertain the extent of land under cultivation and the number of plants, the second to determine the number of leaves for which the planter will be held accountable. When the tobacco has been gathered in a manner described by regulations of minute detail, the planter takes it to the magazine of the Régie, where it is subjected to the inspection of a commission of five disinterested experts, who separate the leaves into three portions, according to quality; the planter is then paid for each portion in accordance with the tariff of prices promulgated by the Minister of Finance. Foreign tobacco is obtained through contract with private parties, after published proposals by the Minister of Finance through the French Consular Corps abroad, and through a special government agency established at Havana. At present a little over one-third of the tobacco purchased by the Régie is of French growth; over one-half consists of foreign leaf, mostly obtained from the United States, and the remainder is made up by importations of cigars from Havana and Manilla, and by cigarettes and miscellaneous productions of various countries, and by custom-house seizures. The magazines distributed throughout the country are of two sorts, "magasins de transit" for foreign tobacco, and "magasins de culture" for indigenous tobacco. In the "magasins de transit" the foreign leaves have not to submit to any other manipulation than the sampling of packages, after which they are forwarded to the factories in such quantities as may be demanded. With the indigenous tobacco the course is different; this when received from the hands of the French grower is usually very imperfectly dried, and has to be subjected to a curing process. After the bundles are thoroughly thrashed, they are put in heaps according to maturity, and fermented in a temperature as high as 30° to 40° Centigrade. This maturation lasts from six to nine months, depending upon the locality, and the condition of the leaves as received, and is interrupted from time to time by the operation of shaking and turning in order to prevent too great fermentation. When this fermentation is concluded, those leaves containing less than twenty per cent. of water are ready to be packed. At this point certain of the leaves undergo a stemming process; they are then packed by hydraulic pressure in bales and hogsheads weighing from 400 to 500 *kilo.* each, and in this state they remain stored in the magazine for some months to acquire further ripeness. It is usually 15–18 months after they are gathered that the leaves are considered to be in a fit condition to be sent to the manufactory. Upon arrival at the manufactory, the packages are sorted and emptied; the leaves are spread out in large bins or receive a preparatory wetting with water containing 10 per cent. of sea salt, in order to produce flexibility and prevent powdering. This process occupies 24 hours. Then follows the sorting according to quality, and the distribution to the various workrooms for composition.

When intended for the manufacture of snuff, the leaves

are put into machines and chopped into strips of the width of a finger; they are then moistened with pure water or tobacco juice of various strengths, the necessary quantity and quality of which is determined by chemical analysis. These strips are then piled up in masses containing from 35,000 to 40,000 kilogrammes, in rooms where a high and even temperature is maintained by steam-pipes and ventilators. Here they remain to ferment during a month or six weeks, when they are dried, ground into powder, and sifted. This powder then receives a wetting, is packed in stout wooden bins, in quantities ranging from 25,000 to 30,000 *kilo.*, and so remain to ferment for several months. During the course of the final fermentation, the powder is tested and moved from one bin to another from time to time, in order to ensure a successful issue of the process. When the samples taken from the bins indicate maturity, the snuff is packed in barrels and casks, and is ready for the market. For the manufacture of smoking-tobacco, the leaves, after the stemming process, receive their first moistening, which lasts 24 hours. They are then neatly arranged, with their edges parallel, and are taken to the chopping machines; the machines in use at the Régie are capable of chopping 220 lb. per hour, the knives being renewed twice during that time. The tobacco, on leaving the choppers, contains about 25 per cent. of humidity, and is immediately conveyed into one end of a revolving drying cylinder, heated to a uniform temperature of 203° Fahrenheit, from the opposite end of which it issues, at the expiration of fifteen minutes, in a dried state and freed from albumen. It is then put through a second cylinder, similar in construction to the last, but which subjects the tobacco to a strong draught of cold air to eliminate all dust and heat. The tobacco is then packed in well-aired bins, where it remains from four to six weeks, after which it is carefully overhauled by hand to remove the pieces of stems and foreign matter that may have escaped notice in the previous operations. It is then put up in packages, varying in weight from 40 grammes upwards. These packages are surrounded with a paper band, upon which are printed the Government tax stamp, the date of manufacture, the weight, the price, and the letter " H," followed by figures. The last mark signifies the amount of humidity contained in the tobacco at the time it was put into the packets. Consul Scidmore says that in no instance since its inauguration has there been a year without enormous profits to the tobacco monopoly in France, and in a table appended to his report, it appears that from the date of its foundation (1811) to the end of 1878, the net total gain to the French Government amounted to 287,703,881*l*.

The following table from a recent report shows that the consumption of tobacco in France has been steadily increasing:—

Year.	Population.	Amount consumed.	Amount per Head.
		Kilogrammes.	Grammes.
1815	29,250,000	8,981,403	307
1826	31,673,853	11,595,084	366
1831	32,731,256	11,071,088	338
1841	34,018,715	16,461,934	484
1851	35,546,919	19,718,089	555
1864	37,133,424	28,019,803	755
1866	37,807,203	30,627,663	810
1872	35,844,414	27,031,000	754
1876	36,643,087	31,188,846	851

The amount consumed in the different departments varies very much. Snuff-taking is most practised in Oise, Seine Inférieure, Eure, and Eure-et-Loir, at the maximum rate of 375 *grm.* per head; and least in the departments of Doubs, Pyrénées Orientales, Nord, Haut Rhin, and Haute Savoie, where the average is but 100 *grm.* In smoking, however, there is rather a reverse order of things, the Nord, Haut-Rhin, and Pas de Calais consuming at the rate of 2 *kilo.* per head, while the minimum is found in Haute Savoie, Cantal, Corrèze, Creuse, Aveyron, Dordogne, Lot, and Lozère. Ten departments only consume tobacco above the average, while 70 are actually below it. If all France smoked the same quantity as do the people of Nord, Haut-Rhin, and Pas de Calais, the consumption for the whole country would be 73,286,174 *kilo.* instead of 31,000,000; and *vice versâ* it would be only 6,265,968 *kilo.* if calculated according to the average of Lozère, which is only at the rate of 171 *grm.* per head.

The department of the Nord, in 1884, had 449 *hectares* (of 2·47 acres) under tobacco, the yield of which was 1,168,206 *kilo.*

Germany.—The total area of land engaged in growing tobacco in Germany in 1878 was about 44,520 acres; nearly two-thirds of this total was distributed among Rhenish Bavaria, Baden, S. Hesse, and Alsace-Lorraine. The total consumption of tobacco in the German empire in that year was 2,196,000 cwt. The home production was 596,776 cwt., the remainder being imported.

The aggregate area of land cultivated with tobacco in the States of the German Customs Union did not vary considerably during ten years, being 21,509 *hectares* in 1863, and 20,918 in 1872, to which must be added the newly annexed provinces of Alsace and Lorraine, which bring up the total to 24,745 *hectares*. It appears that, with particular regard to the year 1872, the cultivation was carried on in 4067 different localities, by 94,916 taxable growers, and by 83,675 smaller growers, whose production, owing to its limited extent, was exempt from taxation. By far the larger number were small growers, the area cultivated by each not exceeding an average of 10 *ares*. In Prussia the aggregate of land cultivated during the year 1871 amounted to 5925 *hectares*, or 26 per cent. of the entire territory of the kingdom; the aggregate yield of the harvest in the same year was 198,890 *centners*. It appears that the extent of tobacco-growing land has, during the last fifty years, been gradually diminishing in Prussia, and that accordingly the expectations entertained in the beginning of that period of a great future development of this branch of agriculture have not been realized. The reasons for the gradual decline are considered to be, on the one hand, the growing competition of the South German growers, and the increase in the importations of American tobacco; on the other hand, the fact that the cultivation of beetroot for sugar, and of potatoes for distilling purposes, has proved to be a more profitable business than tobacco production. It has, moreover, been found by many years' experience, that whilst the quality of the tobacco cultivated in most parts of Prussia is not such as to enable the growers to compete successfully with the importers of foreign, particularly North American sorts, the labour attending its cultivation and its preparation for the market, as well as the uncertainty of only an average crop, are out of proportion, as a rule, to the average profits arising therefrom. The cultivation of the plant has consequently gradually become restricted chiefly to those districts of the country where either the soil is peculiarly adapted for the purpose, or where it is carried on for the private use of the producer.

In Bavaria, as is well known, tobacco is cultivated very extensively, particularly in the Palatinate and in Franconia, viz. the districts around Nüremberg and Erlangen. The area of land in 1871 was 4721 *hectares*, which produced 144,153 *centners*. In Saxony but little tobacco is grown, the total area planted therewith in 1871 not having exceeded 6 *hectares*, upon which 130 *centners* were produced. Although in parts of Wirtemberg the soil and climate are said to be very favourable to the growth of the plant, the area of land cultivated is, upon the whole, a very limited one, and did not exceed 178 *hectares*. The yield of the harvest is given at 5571 *centners*. In the year 1858 the extent of production in Wirtemberg is stated to have been four times as great as it is at present. The Grand Duchy of Baden has at all times been the chief tobacco-growing part of Germany, and as far back as the end of the seventeenth century special laws for regulating the cultivation, preparation, and warehousing of this article were in force. The great importance accordingly attaching to this branch of agriculture and industry for so large a proportion of the inhabitants of Baden, renders it but natural that any project of increasing the tobacco tax should meet with very strong opposition amongst most classes of the Grand Duchy. The most prominent tobacco-growing districts of Baden are those of Carlsruhe, Mannheim, Heidelberg, Badenburg, Schwitzingen, and Lahr; the quality of the plant grown in these parts being a very inferior one. The produce of the districts mentioned is therefore applied chiefly to the manufacture of "cigar-wrappers," and is exported in considerable quantities to Bremen, Hamburg, Switzerland, Holland, and even to America, for the use of the cigar-makers. The prices of the best kinds of Baden tobacco are consequently also, on an average, much higher than those realized by other German growers. The area in Hesse was 979 *hectares*, the chief district being around the town of Darmstadt; the production was 31,311 *centners*. The most prominent amongst the Thuringian States as regards tobacco production, is the Duchy of Saxe-Menningen; the land cultivated in 1871 in all of them put together was 202 *hectares*, the yield of the harvest in that year having been 4806 *centners*. In the two German states of Mecklenburg, 6106 *centners* were raised from 165 *hectares* of land. The most important district is that of Neu-Brandenburg, in Mecklenburgh-Strelitz. Only a small extent of land, viz. 69 *hectares*, is used for tobacco in the Duchy of Brunswick, the same being situated near the town of Helmstadt; the amount raised was 2391 *centners*.

In the recently acquired provinces of Alsace-Lorraine, tobacco cultivation has been extensively carried on for many years, more especially in the country around Strasburg, Mülhausen, Schirmeck, and Münster, and to a smaller extent near Metz and Thionville. The aggregate area of land cultivated in 1871 in both provinces is given at 3159 *hectares*, upon which 115,518 *centners* of tobacco were raised. According to the statistics and information furnished by Consul Ward, the quantity of tobacco produced in Germany in the year 1871 amounted to 713,845 *centners*, the whole being estimated in value at 60,284,210 dols., or about 9,042,613*l*. sterling.

A Consular report of March 31, 1885, remarks that one of the most prominent branches of agriculture in Baden is that of tobacco, of which about 300,000 to 350,000 cwt. annually are grown, whereof large quantities are exported. Owing to the comparatively high tax on production of $22\frac{1}{2}$ marks per 50 *kilo.*, the grower has been forced to seek a more rational system of cultivation, and a more careful treatment of the plant and the curing of the leaf. Government pays particular attention to this culture. A Commission has been appointed for the purpose of studying and investigating the treatment of tobacco in Holland, and the results are to be adopted and propagated, so far as the climate admits.

It is very doubtful whether the labours of the Commission will greatly influence the farmers, who are of a very conservative disposition; moreover, there is a greater obstacle to struggle against, namely, their desire to increase the quantity of the production, and with it their income, without regard to the question of deterioration of the quality of tobacco; the peasantry, like other classes, participates in the desire to better its material condition.

The surface of land occupied by tobacco plantations represented in 1883 for the whole of the empire the considerable figure of 22,068 *hectares*; this year a reduction is to be noted, as official reports bring the total to 21,108 *hectares* only.

The Grand Duchy of Baden participated in the above figures with 7788 *hectares* for 1883, and 7647 *hectares* for 1884.

Notwithstanding this difference, the result of the crop will not essentially be smaller (as regards the weight of the total), the new produce proving heavier in weight and in substance. While in 1883 the hectare produced about 1900 *kilo.*, it is supposed that for 1884 it will yield from 1800 to 2000 *kilo.* These figures tend to prove that the 1884 tobacco is richer in quality, and consequently more durable, and less capable of treatment than that of the preceding years; although the quality is somewhat inferior to that of 1882 and 1883 it may fairly be considered as good.

The subjoined remarks deal with the tobacco trade of Bremen. The number of casks of Kentucky tobacco sold in 1884 fell considerably below that disposed of in 1883. This is explainable by the circumstance that lugs and cuttings were altogether wanting. The prices of leaf on the whole remained steady, except in October and November, when they soon regained their firmness through no more supplies from America being expected, owing to the continued demand for strong tobacco in that country. Business in Virginia tobacco also suffered from the want of inferior qualities. Prices, considered high from the beginning, showed even a rising tendency at the end of the season. Transactions in Maryland and scrubs exceeded the average of the last five years. Ohio and Bay suffered, as hitherto, from the protection afforded to home growths. Operations in stems were, considering the depression in trade, not unsatisfactory.

A good business was done in almost all descriptions of tobacco in serons, chests, bales, and baskets, and sales surpassed those of previous years.

The subjoined table presents a comparison of the transactions in the various sorts of tobacco during the last two years:—

Description of Tobacco.	Description of Packing.	Imports.		Sales.	
		1883.	1884.	1883.	1884.
Kentucky	Casks	20,828	12,084	20,012	12,514
Virginia	,,	3,937	5,250	4,848	5,196
Maryland	,,	4,929	5,615	4,579	5,811
Scrubs	,,	383	1,363	383	1,027
Ohio	,,	581	1,155	566	1,174
Bay	,,	101	136	234	134
Stems	,,	5,013	7,332	8,163	5,403
Havana	Serons	16,127	15,027	13,121	11,967
Cuba and Yara	,,	22,467	22,259	29,297	17,383
St. Domingo	,,	83,836	59,665	58,121	44,065
Seed-leaf	Chests	17,070	18,723	77,000	18,203
Porto Rico	Bales	1,133	300	1,137	2,210
Esmeralda	,,	705	549	776	599
Columbia	Serons and bales	11,862	21,041	14,032	22,659
Varnias	Leaves and rolls	922	2,065	3,174	2,065
Brazil, in leaves	Bales	131,982	185,061	139,397	189,246
Paraguay	,,	2,672	2,601	2,879	2,819
Rio Grande	,,	4,571	..	10,199	1,340
Manilla	,,	50	77	21	106
Mexican	,,	..	10	..	10
Turkish and Greek	,,	6,155	6,825	8,235	8,105
Other varieties	,,	1,496	2,017	1,441	3,357

Good qualities of Havana fetched adequate prices. The demand for Cuba, Yara, Carmen, and Domingo was brisk;

Brazilian and Felix found ready buyers, owing to the last good crop, the prices rising towards the close of the year. The stock of Porto Rico was realized at a low figure. In seed-leaf Pennsylvania plants were chiefly imported, and, being of a good quality, were for the most part promptly disposed of. Much inclination was shown for Turkish tobacco, and the same remark applies to business in Paraguay, of which the supplies might have been greater. Chinese tobacco, very brisk at first on account of its fine quality, later on fell off again considerably.

The value of the tobacco consumed in Germany in 1878 is calculated to have been 353 million marks, or 17,650,000*l.* sterling, the total return to the revenue being 26,383,966 marks, or 1,319,198*l.* The quantity consumed in that empire in the year is stated at 2,196,000 cwt., or rather more than 100,000 tons. Of this quantity 582,600 cwt., or upwards of 29,000 tons, were consumed in the form of cigars. Reckoning a hundred cigars to a pound in weight, the number of cigars consumed in Germany in 1878 would be upwards of seven thousand millions, which would give two cigars a day all the year round to ten million smokers. But besides cigars the Germans smoked in the year 1,327,200 cwt., or upwards of 60,000 tons of tobacco more or less manufactured. In the form of snuff they took 160,600 cwt., or 8000 tons, in the course of the year, while in the way of chewing-tobacco they limited themselves to the moderate quantity of 14,200 cwt., or about 700 tons. Rather more than one-third of the total weight of tobacco consumed was grown within the limits of Germany, the quantity so produced in 1878 being 596,776 cwt., while the imports amounted to 1,768,855 cwt. of tobacco leaves,

4827 cwt. of roll tobacco, 14,170 cwt. of cigars, 8321 cwt. of stems for snuffs, 513 cwt. of snuff, and 101 cwt. of chewing-tobacco. The total area of land engaged in growing the plant in 1878 was 18,016 *hectares*, or about 44,520 acres. Two-thirds of that quantity was grown in Rhenish Bavaria, Baden, South Hesse, and Alsace-Lorraine, in which districts 11,623 *hectares* were employed in the cultivation of the plant.

Great Britain.—The proposal to re-establish tobacco culture in the United Kingdom has called for the following sensible article in the *Planters' Gazette.*

"The question of growing tobacco in the United Kingdom is not so simple as patriotic Irishmen and enthusiasts of acclimatization might think. Tobacco has been classed, like tea and coffee, as among those necessaries of life which could not be grown with any advantage in the United Kingdom, and might therefore be freely taxed for revenue purposes. It is, indeed, true that a passable herb may be grown and called tobacco, in many parts of the United Kingdom, but the fact has been generally recognized that competition with more tropical countries is practically fruitless, and therefore to be abandoned. It is easily to be understood that so aromatic a crop, monopolizing so many of the best and rarest qualities of the soil, would require high manuring; and that, just as is the case of any other crop—such as hops, or even wheat—one could get nothing of the special excellence of the herb required but what one has previously put into the soil. But, to be profitable, the plant requires good heat as well as good soil. This, therefore, is the whole economical question, and upon that the matter mainly hinges. The claim to grow real tobacco in England or Ireland is based upon the allegation that the herb can be grown at a profit. The best evidence furnished to the House of Commons on Monday evening on this point was that of Lord Harris, who affirmed boldly that Ireland and parts of England were prepared to enter into a fair competition with the recognized productive colonies. The Government, and with them, Lord Iddesleigh, are in favour of an experiment largely granting all that is asked, and carefully observing the result. Then, when the British tobacco comes upon the ordinary market, let it be taxed as any other similar product would be. The Government could not view with anything but dismay the prospect of a fall in revenue; and there is no question, therefore, that the home-grown tobacco must pay duty to the full. The *crux* of the question is how such duty can be enforced without an army of revenue officers, whose practical duties would bear no reasonable proportion to their probable cost. Our own impression is that tobacco can never be grown in these islands on any large scale to compete with the growers within the tropics, and that the expense of collecting revenue would be out of all proportion to the amount collected. At the same time, it ill becomes us as a Free-trading nation to shut out any class of our own countrymen, by duties distinctly prohibitive, from following a branch of agriculture which they think they could make profitable. It is against our principle to offer a bounty on the forced cultivation of exotics, such as tobacco undoubtedly is when grown in these islands, but it would be still worse to maintain, on merely pedantic grounds, a prohibitive import on a crop which many men think the smaller tenants could produce to the great advantage of their holdings. We are by no means sanguine of their success; but that is no reason why they should not try."

Greece.—The production of tobacco in Greece is about 4 million *okes* (of 2¾ lb.) annually. Patras, in 1878, exported 300 tons to Holland, Austria, and Turkey, at a value of 25–30*l*. a ton. The values of the exports from Syra, in 1879, were 3503*l*. to Great Britain, 2325*l*. to Turkey, 88*l*. to the Danubian Principalities, 236*l*. to France, 554*l*. to Austria, 436*l*. to Egypt, 1605*l*. to Russia; and in 1878, 1528*l*. to Turkey, 1875*l*. to Great Britain, 93*l*. to the Danubian Principalities, 441*l*. to Austria, 334*l*. to France, 266*l*. to Russia, 39*l*. to Egypt.

In 1884, Nauplia exported 13,000*l*. worth of tobacco; and Calamata, 2400*l*. worth. The value at Patras was 45*s*. per cwt. Syra imported 439*l*. worth of tobacco and 305*l*. worth of tumbeki from Turkey; but exported 10,459*l*. worth of tobacco to Turkey, 697*l*. worth to Great Britain, 17,723*l*. worth to Egypt, 200*l*. worth to Russia, 120*l*. worth to Roumania, 2963*l*. worth to Italy, 1176*l*. worth to France, and 200*l*. worth to Austria.

Holland.—There were 4117 acres under tobacco in Holland in 1878, which produced 3,132,875 *kilo*. The imports of tobacco into Holland in 1878 were as follows:—Maryland, 5249, Kentucky, 500, and Virginian, 107 hogsheads; Java, 87,998, seed-leaf, 100, Sumatra, 33,671 packages. In 1876 and 1877, there were 5900 and 8993 packages respectively from Rio Grande. The exports of leaf from Holland in 1879 were 3,900,000 *kilo*.

COMPARATIVE STATEMENT OF THE IMPORTS OF THE VARIOUS KINDS
OF TOBACCO DURING THE FIVE YEARS 1879-83.

	Maryland.	Virginia and Kentucky.	Java.	Seed-leaf.	Brazil.	Sumatra.
	Hhds.	Hhds.	Packages.	Packages.	Packages.	Packages.
In 1879	7,234	85	102,791	192	1,548	44,477
1880	4,775	147	34,037	1,007	339	52,151
1881	2,989	151	81,225	454	1,098	59,468
1882	3,405	26	103,384	905	Nil.	73,444
1883	4,240	976	30,975	2,500	675	10,111

India.—An immense area is occupied in producing tobacco in India. In Madras, Dindigul is the great tobacco district, and cheroots are manufactured at Trichinopoli. The islands in the delta of the Godavari also yield *lunka* tobacco, the climate being suitable, and the plants being raised on rather poor, light soil, highly manured and well watered. Manilla seeds have been tried on the lower Palnai Hills, but the Wynaad has proved to be the best locality. In Bombay, the Kaira and Khandesh tobaccos are superior; altogether over 40,000 acres were under the crop in this presidency in 1871-2, and the exports were 3 million lb. Shiraz and Manilla seeds yield good plants in Gujrat and Khandesh. The total areas under tobacco in 1871-2 were thus returned:—Bengal, about 300,000 acres; Punjab, over 90,000; Oudh, 69,500; Rungpore, 60,000 (affording the so-called "Burma cheroots"); Central Provinces, 55,000; Tirhoot, 40,000; Cooch Behar, 24,000; Mysore, 20,000; Dinagepore, 20,000; Purneah, 20,000; Behar, 18,500; Burma, 13,000; Monghyr, 9-10,000; Nuddea, 9-10,000. The best tobacco districts are said to be Sandoway and the island of Cheduba, in

Arracan; Rungpore, in Bengal; and Bhilsa, in the Central Provinces. The results of many analyses of South Indian tobaccos show that their ash seldom contains more than 5-6 per cent. of carbonate of potash, while American range from 20-40 per cent., indicating the poverty of the Indian soils in this important ingredient. It might, however, be supplied at moderate cost in the shape of saltpetre, which is actually exported largely from the tobacco-growing districts.

The bulk of the Indian tobacco exported consists of leaf, the kinds chiefly shipped being the "Bispah" and "Poolah" varieties of the Rungpore kind; the quantities of cigars and other manufactured tobacco exported are very small. The exports in lb. for the four years 1875-79 were:—

	1875-76.	1876-77.	1877-78.	1878-79.
Unmanufactured	22,861,711	10,508,720	10,594,604	13,279,158
Manufactured:				
Cigars	152,189	190,136	189,742	196,759
Other sorts ..	232,720	205,033	317,887	247,743
Total ..	23,246,620	10,903,889	11,102,233	13,723,660

On the other hand, a considerable quantity of manufactured tobacco, averaging over 1½ million lb. yearly, is imported, showing that India is still merely a producer of raw material, and is dependent upon other countries for the manufactured article in a condition fit for consumption. Even as regards the raw material, India might do a great deal more than at present, for there would be a large and constant demand on the continent of Europe for Indian leaf, if it could be obtained of somewhat better quality. The French and Italian tobacco departments are prepared to take Indian tobacco in large quantities, if it can be supplied of a quality suited to their purposes; and there would also be an extensive demand from Austria and Germany. Although the shipments consist mainly of leaf tobacco, and that not of good quality, tobacco manufacture is now making a promising beginning. In the enterprise being carried on at Ghazipore, in the North-West Provinces, and at Poosah, in Bengal, both the cultivation and manufacture are under the supervision of skilled American growers and curers. Some of this tobacco sent to the *Administration des Tabacs* in Paris has been very favourably reported on. The factory at Ghazipore is now turning out about 500 lb. a day of all classes, the greater part being black cavendish and honeydew, for the army. The machinery is capable of turning out 3500 lb. a day, as soon as sufficient hands have been trained.

Hitherto no Indian tobacco has realized any valuation approaching that of American. The average price of the American "shipping tobacco" is 5–6d. a lb., higher classes of bright leaf from Virginia realize as much as 7–13d. a lb., while the price of Indian tobacco has generally been 1–2d. a lb. But the 15,000 lb. of Poosah leaf from the 1877 crop reached England when American shipping leaf was at 4–5d. a lb., or 25 per cent. below the normal rate. The consignment was, moreover, packed in rather damp order, and contained a quantity of moisture which caused it to be assessed under the highest rate of the new tariff, which imposes 3s. 10d. duty when the moisture is over 10 per cent., against 3*s*. 6*d*. under 10 per cent. This made a difference in the value, estimated at 1*d*. a lb. The price obtained was 3¾*d*., which would have been 4¾*d*. had the tobacco been drier, and the sale has been followed by orders of large shipments.

The high prices, too, realized for the best samples of the 1876 and 1877 crops, indicate that Indian leaf can be turned out equal to the best shipping tobacco from America. A tierce of strips from the 1876-77 crop from Ghazipore sold for 7*d*. a lb., and the greater part of the rest for 5*d*. or more, while a portion of the Poosah leaf of 1877-78 was valued at 5*d*. when the market was 25 per cent. below normal rates. These facts seem to guarantee future success, since the quantity of the higher classes can be largely increased, and a greater portion of the crop be brought to the same higher level. The chief point to be ascertained was whether a sufficiently high level could be attained at all. It has been attained. The cured leaf of 1878 is very much superior to any hitherto turned out, especially that from Ghazipore. A new market is not unlikely to open in France. The French Government have already asked for a consignment for trial of 1000-1500 lb.

The reason why the manufacture of smoking-tobacco for Indian consumption has occupied so large a share in the operations is, that the Indian market, though small, pays far more handsome profits than the English market.

The price paid for reasonably good American manufactured tobacco in India ranges from one to three *rupees* a lb. Ghazipore and Poosah tobacco is sold at half that price, at a much higher profit than can be obtained by sending cured leaf to England.

While Indian cured leaf can find a sale in the English market at prices which will enable it to compete there with American cured leaf, Indian manufactured leaf is proved to compete successfully with American manufactured leaf in India itself, with a fair prospect of success in a similar competition in the colonies. It may be stated in general terms that 4*d*. a lb. for cured leaf in England, and 6-10 *annas* for manufactured leaf in India, will secure sufficient or even handsome profits. The opening for profits will perhaps be better understood if it is explained that 1*d*. a lb. represents an asset of about 5*l*. an acre. The one great advantage which India has over America is cheap labour. It is now proved that the leaf is, for all practical purposes, as good as the American leaf, and there is hardly any doubt that America cannot afford to send home leaf at the price at which India can sell.

The exports of tobacco from British India during the years 1874-5 to 1878-9 have been as follows:—

		1875.	1876.	1877.	1878.	1879.
Unmanufactured	lb.	33,411,504	22,861,711	10,508,720	10,594,604	13,279,158
Manufactured.	lb.	425,040	384,909	395,169	507,629	444,502
	No.	2,999,940	..	..	..	..

The following letter from the manager of the Poosah tobacco farms, Tirhoot, describes the system of growing and curing now adopted in India.

"Preparation of Soil.—Tobacco land should be well-drained upland which has lain fallow some time or that has had some light crop in it; this land should be well manured with well-rotted manure. We plough our lands twice monthly. Just before the time for transplanting the soil is ploughed up and well pulverized by a henger or beam of wood drawn by bullocks over the upturned soil so as to bend it and to break up any lumps of earth. The soil should be sufficiently dry for this purpose so as not to cake and harden.

"Seed-beds.—These should be made up in a suitable situation, that is, protected from the afternoon sun, having some building or grove of trees on the west side. The seed-beds should be raised some six inches off the ground and have trenches dug all round so as to carry off any superfluous moisture, the beds should be well worked with a kodalie and good, rotted manure well worked in. After pulverizing the soil and levelling it, pick off any stones or other rubbish and it will be ready for sowing the seed. The size of the bed should be about 4 feet by 15 feet; this is more convenient than square beds, as it enables the plants to be attended to without risk of destroying them by trampling on them.

"Sowing the Seed.—The seed is sown broadcast with the hand, mixed with some sand or ashes so as to sow evenly; care should be taken not to sow too thickly. About one chittak of seed ought to be found sufficient for one of these beds which would furnish enough plants for one beegah of land. After having sown and if there is a hot sun, it would be advisable to cover the beds with light mats. This seed should germinate in seven or ten days at least.

American seed does; Sumatra takes much longer. The plants may require watering, which should be done with a watering-can with a rose, when the plants are well up and large. Only water seed-beds in the evening. As soon as the seedlings have leaves of the size of a penny, they are capable of bearing transplanting. Before taking up the seedling to transplant, water the beds well an hour beforehand; this is done to loosen the earth about the roots so that the plants may be taken up without injury. To take up the seedlings they should be seized by the under side of the two largest leaves by the finger and thumb, having one leaf on each side, not by the stem, then pull up gently, taking care not to break the leaves. They may then be placed in an open basket. When the basket is full it should be covered with a cloth if the sun is hot, and the seedlings slightly sprinkled with water and then carried off to transplant. The seedlings are planted out in rows 3 feet by 2 feet apart, for which purpose a knotted cord is used, the knots being 3 feet apart. This cord is drawn by two men—one at each end. Across the field or portion of the field at a distance of 2 feet from the outer edge, the cord is drawn out and then trampled upon by coolies. The knots leave an impression in the soil where the seedlings have to be planted. The cord is then raised and put down again at another distance of 2 feet from the first, and so on till sufficient land has been marked off. This work can be done during the day, and the transplanting in the evening.

" Transplanting.—Transplanting should be done in the evening if there is any sun; in cloudy weather it can be done all the day long. Rainy weather is most suitable as it dispenses with watering and the plants settle better. A boy takes a basket of seedlings and walks up the row, dropping a plant here and there where the marks have been made; he is followed by a man who makes a hole with a *kurpie*, into which he places a seedling, and then presses the soil around the roots firmly with his fingers, and then goes on with the rest. As transplanting can hardly be done here without watering, a boy carrying a can without a rose follows the man who is transplanting, and waters each plant he comes across; but, as I mentioned above, if the transplanting could be done in rainy weather, the watering would be unnecessary. When growing the young plants require some attention. After the plants have been planted a week or so, weather permitting, it is advisable to loosen and open the soil around them with a kurpie, and also to eradicate weeds which may appear. Later on a kodalie may be used to work the earth between the rows. As soon as the plants have made growth and begin to throw out flower or seed-heads, which will take place in about eight weeks or so, they should be topped, viz. the flower heads should be broken off before they flower in this way. The stem on which the head was found should be seized about two to three feet from the ground and snapped clean off by the hand or fingers. This topping will cause the plant to throw out heavy leaves. The higher up the stem is broken off, so will the leaves of the plant become thinner and smaller. We generally leave about ten to twelve leaves to each plant. After topping, numerous suckers and offshoots will spring up; these should be promptly broken off as soon as they appear, as they take a lot of nourishment from the plant. The plant ripens in about three months. We cut here in January, and none but ripe plants should be cut.

"How to Cut Ripe Plants.—A tobacco plant is known to be ripe if the leaf cracks when taken between finger and thumb and pressed, and also when the leaves present a swollen appearance and have a heavy look. The stem when cut is full of sap, very thin rind on edge, the leaves are carved over and look mottled, the ribs of the plant get brittle, and are easily broken off; when fully ripe, the plant is cut at one stroke close to the ground. The best instrument to cut the plant with is a kurpie. When cut, the plant is allowed to hang over on its side and wilt or droop in the sun. This wilting takes from one to two hours according to the strength of the sun. When sufficiently wilted (which is known when the plants look drooping and the ribs can be bent slightly without breaking) the plants are placed in a cart and taken to the curing-house. Plants should not be cut in rainy or cloudy weather, as it is obvious the sun would not be hot enough to wilt were the weather cloudy, and the rain washes off the gum and thereby decreases the weight of the plant. Plants should not be cut after the rain unless the gum has returned to the leaves, which is known by their sticky, gummy feeling."

The results of many analyses of the tobacco of South India show that the ashes of these tobaccos seldom contain more than 5 or 6 per cent. of potash carbonate, while the ashes of American tobacco contain from 20 to 40 per cent., proving the poverty of Indian tobacco soils in this important plant-food—a plant-food, however, easily obtainable in the shape of saltpetre, and at a moderate cost. But, though saltpetre is largely exported from the tobacco-growing districts, it is never employed as a manure for tobacco.

Italy.—Tobacco is cultivated in Italy in the provinces of Ancona, Benevento, Terra di Lavoro, Principato Citeriore, Terra d'Otranto, Umbria, Vicenza, and Sardinia. The area and produce in the following years were :—in 1870, 9544 acres, 67,192 cwt. ; 1872, 12,256 acres, 82,349 cwt.; 1874, 8202 acres, 90,300 cwt. The exports from Naples in 1879 were 2006 *kilo.*, value 401*l.*

The British Consul at Cagliari reports that the cultivation of tobacco is only carried on in the district of Sassari, and in the plains of Sassari, Portotorres, Nurra, Sorso, and Sennori. No positive data on this branch of industry can be had, it having been exclusively carried on till 1883 by a private company, called the Regía Cointeressata. Without fear of being wrong, it may be calculated that the tobacco cultivators reach the number of 100, who employ during the period of five months from 600 to 700 labourers; the plantation varies from 4,000,000 to 5,000,000 plants, producing a harvest from 2000 to 2500 *quintals* of tobacco leaves, at a value of about 125,000 *lire.*

Japan.—Japanese tobacco is well known in the London market, but it is often in a soft condition, and then scarcely saleable. More care is needed in drying it before packing.

Java.—Tobacco, termed by the natives *tombáku*, or *sáta*, is an article of very general cultivation in Java, but is only extensively raised for exportation in the central districts of Kedu and Banyumas. As it requires a soil of the richest mould, but at the same time not subject to inundations, these districts hold out peculiar advantages to the tobacco-planter, not to be found on the low lands. For internal consumption, small quantities are raised in convenient spots everywhere. In Kedu, tobacco forms, after rice, by far the most important article of cultivation, and, in consequence of the fitness of the soil, the plant grows to the height of 8-10 feet, on lands not previously dressed or manured, with a luxuriance seldom witnessed in India. Cultivated here alternately with rice, only one crop of either is obtained within the year; but after the harvest of the rice, or the gathering of the tobacco leaves, the land is allowed to remain fallow, till the season again arrives for preparing it to receive the other. The young plant is not raised within the district, but procured from the high lands in the vicinity, principally from the district of Kalibéber, on the slope of the mountain Diéng or Práhu, where it is raised and sold by the hundred to the cultivators of the adjoining districts. The transplantation takes place in June, and the plant is at its full growth in October. The exports in the year 1877-8 were 212,500 *piculs* to Holland, and 213 to Singapore; in 1878-9, they were 248,566 *piculs* to Holland, and 872 to Singapore. The value of the export to Holland in 1879 was stated at 1,250,000*l*. The exports in 1884 were 140,351 *piculs* to Holland, and 2490 to Great Britain.

New Zealand.—This colony has not yet figured as a tobacco grower, but the duty on locally produced tobacco is only 1*s*. a lb., and this is expected to stimulate the home industry.

Nicaragua.—It appears that the total exports of tobacco

were 13,787 lb., value 4830 dollars, in 1883, but only 300 lb., value 240 dollars, in 1884. At present it is a Government monopoly.

Paraguay.—Consul Baker, of Buenos Ayres, states that one of the most valuable crops of Paraguay is tobacco; in 1829, its production amounted to only 2,675,000 lb., while in 1860, the crop amounted to 15,000,000 lb.; but the war with the allies almost ruined this source of wealth. It has, however, somewhat recovered its importance, the exports alone last year amounting to 8,975,000 lb. A large proportion of the crop is annually worked up into cigars, a branch of industry which is almost entirely in the hands of the women. The tobacco planted in Paraguay originally came from Havana, with the exception of a particular kind which is called in Paraguay, blue tobacco, *peti-hoby*, the origin of which is unknown. The favourite leaf is a yellow tobacco, *peti-para*, grown chiefly in Villa Rica, which possesses about 6 per cent. of nicotine.

Persia.—The whole of the eastern coast of the Black Sea, i. e. Mingrelia, Lazistan, Abkhasia, and Circassia, is admirably suited for tobacco cultivation. The country between Poti and Súkhúm Kalé contains admirable sites for tobacco plantations, labour for which can be got from Trebizond. A great demand for tobacco of good quality exists in the country, and a practical planter should do well. A quantity of coarse, badly-cured tobacco, of no commercial value, is produced in Imeritia and Georgia. Great success has attended the culture in Ghilan. The first seed introduced was from Samsoun; since then Yenija seed has been tried, and some parcels attained the standard of the best Turkish tobacco. It can be produced at about

20s. a *pood* (of 36 lb.), giving a profit of 22s. a cwt. Hitherto the cultivation has been confined to the plains, where both soil and atmosphere are damp, but it might be worth trying the hill-skirts. About 2000 cwt. were produced in 1878. The exports of tobacco, the produce of Ghilan, from Resht to Russia, were valued at 4615*l*. in 1878, and 6154*l*. in 1879. The values (in rupees) of the exports in 1879 were 13,000 from Bushire, 73,500 from Lingah, and 35,000 from Bahrein.

At the time when I wrote the article on tobacco in Spons' Encyclopædia, the true source and history of an article called "tumbeki" was still in doubt. From researches made at the instigation of my friend E. Morell Holmes, F.L.S., the Curator of the Pharmaceutical Society's Museum, it is now clear that it is a Persian tobacco, and as such calls for mention here. The following paragraph reproduces what I said on the subject in Spons' Encyclopædia.

"Tumbeki.—This word, under a multitude of forms, is the common name in several Eastern languages (Bengali, Hindustani, Telugu, Sunda, Javanese, Malayan, Persian, Guzerati, Deccan) for ordinary tobacco. But in Asia Minor, it is applied to a narcotic leaf which is spoken of as distinct from tobacco, and is separately classified in the Consular Returns. Botanical authorities are at variance as to the plant which affords it, some attributing it to a *Lobelia*, while others consider it a kind of tobacco. The latter appears to be the more correct supposition. The flower resembles the tobacco in being trumpet-shaped; the leaf is broader, larger, and rounder than that of the tobacco raised in Turkey, and is also wrinkled like the inner leaf of the cabbage. The plant is raised from seed in nurseries, and when it has 4 or 5 leaves, is planted out in April in the prepared field, and watered sparingly. It is 'set' in a day or two, and is then hoed occasionally to free it from weeds. After inflorescence, and when the plant is sufficiently 'cooked,' it is cut down, or pulled up bodily, and re-set in the ground till the leaves are wilted. These leaves are dried, and, after exposure to the dew, are pressed heavily, when they undergo a kind of fermentation which develops the aroma. It is exceedingly narcotic: so much so, that it is usually steeped in water before use, and placed in the pipe (a *naryhilé* or water-pipe) while still wet. The exports of this article (the produce of Persia) from the port of Trebizonde are considerable:—In 1877, they were 13,342 bales (of 1¾ cwt.), value 106,736l., to Turkey; in 1878, 11,571 bales, 92,568l., to Turkey; in 1879, 9659 bales, 77,272l., to Turkey, and 866 bales, 6928l., to Greece. Aleppo, in 1878, sent 4 tons, value 320l., to Turkey, and 11 tons, 880l., to Egypt. The exports of the article, the produce of the interior of Persia, from Resht to Russia, were valued at 5000l. in 1877, and 3846l. in 1878."

It will be interesting to compare this with Holmes' paper read before the Pharmaceutical Society on February 10, 1886:—

"Tumbeki is the name under which an article of regular commerce between Persia and Turkey is mentioned in the consular reports, especially in that for Trebizonde.

"Two or three years ago an inquiry was made at this institution concerning the nature and botanical source of umbeki, and the only information I was then able to give was that in the 'Treasury of Botany' tumbeky is stated to be the narcotic leaf of a species of lobelia.

"From its frequent occurrence in the Blue Books in the same list with tobacco, and from the large quantities mentioned as an export from Trebizonde, my correspondent suggested that it was probably something used for smoking like tobacco. In the hope that tumbeki might prove to be some drug possessing important narcotic or possible medicinal properties, I wrote to Mr. A. Biliotti, Consul at Trebizonde, for information. In reply, he forwarded samples of tumbeki of different growths and qualities. This proved on examination to be unquestionably some kind of tobacco, and being puzzled to know why it figured in the Blue Books as a distinct article, I asked Mr. Thomas Christy, F.L.S., to make inquiries for me in Persia. He received the following note through Mr. Zanni, the well-known chemist at Constantinople, from whom I received the following information :—

"'There are three qualities of the teymbeki, all derived from the *Nicotiana persica*.

"'1. Shiraz teymbeki, valued at twenty gold piastres per oke.*

"'2. Kechan teymbeki, valued at ten gold piastres.

"'3. Teheran teymbeki, equal in value to No. 2.

"'The Shiraz is the best quality, the leaves are four decimetres long and half a decimetre wide. The leaves of the two other qualities are not so large. The quantity of alkaloid in the leaves of teymbeki is more than in the leaves of *Nicotiana Tabacum*; it is much used in Constantinople, but more so in Egypt, Syria, and particularly in

* The oke equals ten kilogrames ; a piastre, 2½d.

Persia. Teymbeki is smoked in a special apparatus known as the narghileh.* The apparatus is found in every coffee-house and even in a great number of private houses. It resembles somewhat the wash bottle used in laboratories for washing filters with distilled water, but is often made of metal. The teymbeki is placed in a small reservoir on the top of the flask and burns in contact with a piece of incandescent charcoal. The vapour is drawn through the tube, which passes to the bottom of the water and collects above it, whence it is inhaled through the longer tube.† It is in fact a water-pipe.'

"Having ascertained then that tumbeki was a species of tobacco, I sought for further confirmation of the statement that it is the produce of *N. persica*, and wrote on the subject to Professor Hausknecht, who is well known as one of the best authorities on the botany of Persia. He kindly replied as follows:—

"'Tumbeki is the produce of *Nicotiana rustica*, and is almost exclusively used for the water-pipes called kalian or narghileh. The plant is cultivated throughout the whole of Persia, especially in Ispahan and Shiraz, whence the best kind comes.'

"But the statement of M. Zanni that tumbeki contains more alkaloid than tobacco, and that of Professor Hausknecht that tumbeki is the produce of *N. rustica*, seemed to conflict with the statements in books that *N. rustica* is less active than *N. Tabacum*.

* So called from its resemblance in shape to a *narghil* or coconut.
† A full and interesting account of the forms and uses of the varieties of the kalian and narghileh is given in the 'Land of the Lion and the Sun,' p. 29.

"In the 'Commercial Report,' No. 25, 1883, p. 1056, under 'Smyrna,' Consul Dennis confirms M. Zauni's statement concerning tumbeki. He says:—'It is much stronger than ordinary tobacco, and cannot be smoked in the usual way, therefore it is exclusively used for the narghili.' He also adds that a large quantity is consumed in the district of Smyrna, but much is also re-exported to Egypt and other parts of Turkey. It is imported from Persia, both through Trebizonde and Bushire on the Persian Gulf.

"Mr. J. B. Fraser, in his work on Persia (1826), remarks, 'The tobacco smoked in the kalian is called tumbaku in distinction to tootoon, or that smoked in pipes or cigarettes. It is sold in the leaf, which is packed dry in layers, and is preserved in bags sewn up in raw hide. It improves by age, but is quite unsmokable the first year. The best comes from Jaroum, south of Shiraz.'

"In an interesting article in 'Harper's Magazine' (January 1886, p. 224) on the 'Domestic and Court Customs of Persia,' the writer remarks concerning tumbeki:—'The kaliân or water pipe differs from the Turkish narghileh by having a short straight stem. In it is smoked the tobacco called tumbakee—a species grown only in Persia. That of Shiraz is very delicate in flavour and is the best. The tumbakee must be first soaked in water and squeezed like a sponge or it will cause vertigo. A live coal, made from the root of the vine, is placed on the tobacco, and the smoke is drawn through the water with a gentle inhaling, depositing the oil in its passage through the water.'

"In De Candolle's 'Prodromus,' vol. xii., pt. 1, p. 567,

it is stated under *Nicotiana persica*, that it yields the celebrated tobacco of Shiraz. This species closely resembles *N. Tabacum* in the form of its leaves, which are, however, rather acute than acuminate; but the flowers are different both in shape and colour. In *N. Tabacum* the stem leaves are sessile, and the corolla is funnel-shaped or inflated below the limb, and is of a pinkish-red colour; in *N. persica*, the tube of the corolla is club-shaped and the limb more spreading; the colour is white inside and greenish outside. When in blossom, therefore, the two plants are easily distinguished. *N. rustica*, on the other hand, has *stalked* cordate leaves and a short yellowish corolla, with the tube and limb both short.

"The leaves of tumbeki which I have received from Trebizonde and Constantinople both correspond with *N. persica* in character, but not with *N. rustica*, since they have no trace of a petiole. So far as it is possible to ascertain therefore, in the absence of flowers, the weight of evidence is in favour of tumbeki being the produce of *N. persica*. In order to ascertain the correctness of the statement that tumbeki is stronger than tobacco, I handed some specimen to Messrs. E. J. Eastes and W. H. Ince for chemical examination, which they kindly undertook at my request."

Following is the report of these gentlemen on the chemistry of the subject:—

"Four samples of tumbeki were brought under our notice by Mr. Holmes, Curator of the Museum of the Pharmaceutical Society, being of interest on account of their reported greater strength in nicotine as compared with tobacco. The following are the results of our investigations. We may state that so far as we have been able to ascertain no previous researches have been undertaken on the subject.

"Preliminary Examination.—The presence of an alkaloid was demonstrated on the addition of the usual reagents to the acid infusion.

"Isolation of Alkaloid for Physical Examination.—The powdered tumbeki was placed in a retort with milk of lime and steam passed through it till the distillate was no longer alkaline. Alkaloid in abundance was found in the distillate, which had a distinct odour of nicotine. The distillate was then extracted with ether, and the ether slowly driven off. The residue obtained was a light straw coloured oily liquid of powerful odour, giving off irritating fumes when heated.

"Estimation of Nicotine.—In the estimation of nicotine much difficulty was experienced, owing to imperfect knowledge of the alkaloid, and to the imperfect methods recommended in various papers on the subject. The only method we found reliable was by using a standard solution of Mayer's reagent, obtained by mixing 13·546 grams of mercuric chloride in solution with 49·8 grams of potassic iodide, in solution, and adding water to make 1 litre.* One c.c. of this solution represents ·003945 grams of nicotine, the precipitate having the formula $C_{10}H_{16}N_2I_2 . HgI_2$.

"The method we adopted of working with this solution was as follows:—One or more grams of dried and powdered tumbeki were treated with diluted sulphuric

* Dragendorff, 'Chemische Werthbestimmung starkwirkender Droguen,' § 63, p. 52 *et seq.*

acid (2·5 per cent.) for several hours on a water-bath, filtered, and the leaves washed with hot 1 per cent. acid till the filtrate was colourless.

"The filtrate was then either evaporated to a low bulk and extracted with alcohol, to get rid of albuminous matters which interfered with the reaction, or neutralized with sodic hydrate and the alkaloid extracted with chloroform, the chloroformic solution being shaken with diluted sulphuric acid as in the ordinary methods of alkaloid extraction.

"The objection to the first method is that the alcohol has to be driven off before the Mayer's reagent can be added, which is troublesome and lengthens the process.

"The solution of the alkaloid in excess of sulphuric acid having been obtained, Mayer's reagent was carefully added till no more precipitation was observed, the end of the reaction being ascertained when on filtering some of the nicotine solution into a watch-glass and adding a drop of the reagent, no precipitate was formed. With careful manipulation concordant results were obtained.

"Other methods tried were as follows:

"Volumetric method.—Ten or more grams of powdered tumbeki were distilled with a solution of sodic or potassic hydrate, the distillate being passed into a known volume of decinormal standard solution of sulphuric acid, and the amount of acid neutralized by the nicotine was determined by a standard decinormal solution of soda and the nicotine calculated.

"By this method the results obtained were invariably too high owing to an appreciable quantity of ammonium salts contained in the leaves. Dr. Kissling * has also noticed the high percentages obtained by this method of estimating nicotine.

"Kosutány treats the leaves with milk of lime till all the ammonia is driven off, and then extracts with water; shakes the aqueous solution with petroleum ether and proceeds as before.

"This method was not found to give good results, for though the ammonium salts do not interfere with the reaction, yet the petroleum ether does not extract the whole of the alkaloid, and thus a low percentage is obtained.

"Extraction by Ammoniacal Ether.—This consists in extracting the powdered leaves in an upright extractor, by an ethereal solution of ammonia, and either driving off the ether and weighing the residue as nicotine; or volumetrically estimating the residue by decinormal solution of sulphuric acid, or precipitating the alkaloid by platinum perchloride. In either case, whichever way the residue is estimated, the results are too high, owing to the difficulty of entirely getting rid of the ammonia.

"The following are the percentages of nicotine in the tumbeki:—

'*Ispahan.*'—I. By Mayer's Reagent.

A. (midrib) .. .. 8·156 per cent.
B. (leaf).. .. .. 5·508 ,, ,,
C. (leaf and midrib) .. .. .. 5·589 ,, ,,
D. (leaf) .. .. 5·3865 ,, ,,

5·4945 per cent. average.

---

* The 'Analyst,' January 1886, p. 16; 'Chem. Zeit.,' ix., 1886.

II. By Volumetric Method.

By working on 10 grams = 7·2 per cent.
By working on 50 grams = 7;228 ,, ,,

'Hidjaz.'—I. By Mayer's Reagent.

A. (leaf and midrib) .. .. .. 2·025 per cent.
B. (leaf and midrib) .. .. .. 2·268 ,, ,,
C. (leaf and midrib) .. .. .. 2·028 ,, ,,
D. (leaf and midrib) .. .. .. 1·863 ,, ,,

2·046 per cent. average.

II. By Volumetric Process.

A. .. .. 2·37 per cent.

III. By Ethereal Solution of Ammonia.

3·6 per cent.

'Kechan.'—By Mayer's Solution.

A. (leaf and midrib).. .. .. 2·835 per cent.
B. (leaf and midrib).. .. .. 3·0375 ,, ,,
C. (leaf and midrib).. .. .. 2·85525 ,, ,,

2·90925 per cent. average.

'Shiraz.'—By Mayer's Solution.

A. (leaf and midrib) .. .. .. 5·8725 per cent.
B. (leaf and midrib) .. .. .. 5·7975 ,, ,,

5·835 per cent. average.

"Estimation of Saccharoid Matter; calculated as cane sugar.—The fermentation process was the one adopted, not that we consider it by any means a good one, but because it was the only one practicable. Fehling's solution was inadmissible, owing to the precipitation of colouring and other matters, and the polariscope gave no indication. The objections to the fermentation process are due to the small amount of alcohol produced in the relatively large bulk of liquid. This renders the solution liable to acetification, and the ultimate distillate obtained is very weak in spirit, making it extremely difficult to obtain the correct specific gravity; the specific gravities obtained were always between ·998 and unity.

"We worked as follows:—200 grains of dried tumbeki were exhausted by repeated infusion in boiling water. The filtered liquid when cool was mixed with 100 grains of German yeast and allowed to stand three days in a warm place to ferment.

"About one-third was then distilled, the distillate being redistilled and three successive fractions of 500 fluid grains collected, the alcohol in each being estimated; the third portion contained little if any spirit.

"It being stated that basic acetate of lead removes saccharoid matter from the kindred plant tobacco; we tried its action on the infusion of tumbeki.

"At the onset it was found impossible to thoroughly wash the bulky precipitate caused by the lead; so, to ensure a definite result, sufficient basic acetate of lead was added to the infusion of 200 grains of tumbeki and the whole made up to 30 fluid ounces with distilled water and well mixed. An aliquot part (20 fluid ounces) was then filtered off, excess of lead removed by sulphuretted hydrogen, the sulphide filtered out, the solution boiled to drive off the sulphuretted hydrogen and the infusion, when cool, was fermented in the usual way. But acetic acid was necessarily present from the decomposition of the lead salt by the sulphuretted hydrogen, and this on distilling would tend to raise the specific gravity. To remedy this, slaked lime, or preferably potassic hydrate, was added before redistilling, but considering that from one to three per cent. of ammoniacal salt is contained in the original tumbeki, it is probable that some might still remain and by the action of the fixed alkali furnish a trace of free ammonia which would lower the specific gravity, and thus apparently raise the percentage of alcohol. As far as we can judge basic acetate of lead does not seem to remove fermentable matter from infusion of tumbeki.

	I.		II.	
		Pb treatment.		Pb treatment.
Ispahan ..	2·64	2·67	—	2·35
Hidjaz ..	3·00	2·8	2·7	—
Kechan ..	5·58	5·33	—	—
Shiraz ..	3·48	3·88	3·23	3·1

"Ash.—The following bases and acids were uniformly found in the ashes:—Sodium, potassium, lithium, magnesium, calcium, iron, aluminium, silica, chlorine, phosphoric acid, sulphuric acid, carbonic acid.

GENERAL TABLE OF RESULTS.

	Ispahan.	Hidjaz.	Kechan.	Shiraz.
Nicotine	5·4945	2·046	2·909	5·835
Saccharoid matter	2·64	2·85	5·58	3·355
Saccharoid matter after Pb treatment	2·51	2·80	5·33	3·49
Soluble in water	42·0	42·3	39·9	55·6
Insoluble in water	58·0	57·7	60·1	44·4
Ash	22·0	28·5	28·5	26·15

"The foregoing work has been carried out in the laboratories of the Pharmaceutical Society."

Philippines.—The soil and climate of the Philippines are eminently suited to tobacco culture; but the unjust Spanish monopoly cripples the industry, and it is declining. Next to the Cuban (Vuelta abajo) and a few prime Turkish sorts, Manilla tobacco is admitted to be the best. Most of the Philippines produce it. According to the quality of the produce, the provinces rank as follows:—(1) Cayagan and Ysabel, (2) Ygorrotes, (3) Island of Mindanáo, (4) Bisayas, (5) New Ecija. On the average, over 400 million cigars, and a quantity of tobacco sufficient to bring up the total weight to 56,000 cwt., are annually exported. The advantage of the plantations in Cayagan lies in the annual deposit of alluvial matters by the overflowing of the large streams. The cultivation in Bisayas promises to become extinct, whereas if the natives were free to sell in the best market, the industry would increase immensely. The yield of the Cebu district in 1878 was 8780 *quintals*, the whole of which went to the cigar factories of Cadiz and Alicante. The exports from Manilla were:—in 1877 17,526,700 lb. tobacco, value 525,801*l.*; 87,007,000 cigars, value 243,619*l.*; 1878, 15,630,400 lb. tobacco, value 468,918*l.*; 136,835,000 cigars, value 383,136*l.*; 1879, 9971 *quintals* (of 101½ lb.) tobacco leaf to Great Britain, and 74,490 *quintals* to Spain; cigars, 10,571,000 to Great Britain, 6,557,000 to Australia, 44,586,000 to the Straits Settlements and India, 25,861,000 to China and Japan, 693,000 to the United States, 100,000 to California, 1,521,000 to Spain and the Continent; the total values amounted to 480,263*l*. The exports of tobacco from Yloilo were 25,454 *piculs* (of 133⅓ lb.) in 1878, and 20,600 *quintals* (of 101½ lb.) in 1879, all to Spain.

Roumania.—Tobacco was extensively cultivated at one time, with success, near Macin and in other parts; but the monopoly has greatly affected the condition of the industry.

Russia.—As regards the production of tobacco, Russia ranks second among continental countries, but the consumption is less per head than in other lands. Consul Stanton says that smoking began in the latter part of the sixteenth century, and the habit steadily increased, notwithstanding the fact that it was punished by the knout, slitting of the nostrils, and banishment to Siberia. It is most extensively cultivated in Tshernigoff, Poltava, Bessarabia, and Samara. In Poland, the production is not large, and is mainly confined to the vicinity of Warsaw. It is chiefly cultivated by the peasants and is often their only occupation.

In 1883, Riga exported 70,722 *pouds* of leaf tobacco, valued at 194,486 *rubles*. Sevastopol shipped 59 *pouds*, value 1100 *rubles*. Tobacco is now cultivated largely in all parts of the Crimea, and is likely to become an export of considerable importance. In Taganrof plantations are on the increase, and the culture promises well.

San Salvador.—The exports of tobacco in 1884 were 16,113 dollars' worth of leaf, 5898 dollars' worth of manufactured, and 826 dollars' worth of other sorts.

Servia.—It is estimated that there are 4000 acres under tobacco culture in Servia.

Spain.—The port of Cadiz is a great centre of the

PRODUCTION AND COMMERCE. 193

tobacco industry. The imports here in 1878 were:—
123 *kilo.* from Germany, 304,538 *kilo.* from the United
States, and 6,776,900 *kilo.* from Spanish colonies; the
exports were 15,600 *kilo.* to Germany, and 213,846 *kilo.*
to France. Corunna exported 58,280 *kilo.*, value 87,420
pesetas, in 1884. Cadiz exported 514,817 *kilo.*, value
2,574,085 *pesetas*, in the same year.

Sumatra.—This great island is assuming a first-rate
importance in the tobacco industry.

The year 1883 was an exceptionally favourable one,
as the harvest in Sumatra was very good, while prices
for Java tobacco were higher than of late years, in consequence of the short harvest of 1882.

Large quantities of Sumatra tobacco found buyers in
the United States, in consequence of the protectionist
measure introduced in that country in favour of the
home tobacco producers. The duty was raised from 35 c.
to 75 c. per lb. on and after the 1st July, 1883, and great
efforts were made to import as much as possible at the
lower duty before that date.

The principal owners of the plantations are Dutchmen,
and the labour employed is Chinese coolies, brought to
the island principally from the Malaya peninsula. The
crop, according to one of these successful planters, is
scarcely ever reared two years in succession on the same
lands. The jungle is first cleared, and then the seed
planted. After the first crop of tobacco is gathered, it
is the next season used for rice, or something else, and
tobacco is not planted again until the sixth or seventh
year after the jungle is cleared. By adopting this method,
a better result is obtained.

The drying-house is thus described by a recent visitor to the island:—

"The interior is very much like a rick-yard, with tobacco stalks instead of hay-ricks, among which a perfect army of half-clad Chinese coolies, 400 strong, are hard at work sorting, ranging and stowing. So overpoweringly strong is the scent of the half-dried tobacco leaves that a smoker would have nothing to do but to take in an empty pipe with him and enjoy a good hard smoke gratis, merely by inhaling the air through it. But the Chinamen, whether habituated to it by long use, or fortified against it by the superior power of opium, breathe this perfumed atmosphere as easily as if it were the purest air of the sea. 'That is how we measure the heat, you see,' says our host, calling our attention to the hollow bamboos thrust through the heart of each stack, with a stick inside it, which, when pulled out, is almost too hot to touch. 'It must never be above or below a certain point, you know. Instead of stripping off the leaves at once, we hang up the whole plant to dry, and do not strip it till it is quite dried. The Sumatra tobacco, however, will not do for cigars. It is only used for what we call the 'deckblatt' (cover leaf), which covers the outside of the cigar.'"

Consul Kennedy reports that "the main cause of the prosperity in Deli is the tobacco, the first crop of which was shipped in 1869.

"The crop for 1884 will turn out about 122,000 bales, valued at 2,080,000*l*.

"The accompanying table shows the export during the last 11 years:—

Year.	Bales.	Value.
		£
1873	9,238	208,333
1874	12,811	250,000
1875	15,147	291,666
1876	28,947	520,833
1877	36,167	541,666
1878	48,155	750,000
1879	57,544	875,000
1880	64,965	937,500
1881	82,356	1,187,500
1882	102,032	1,750,000
1883	92,000 [Estimated.]	1,583,333

NOTE.—One bale equals 176 English lb.

"Prices for Deli tobacco have ruled on the whole fairly high, the special quality of the leaf lying in the fact of its being light and elastic in texture, with thin fibres, so that it is admirably adapted to serve as cover-leaf, and as such is a good substitute for Havana tobacco. As a smoking-tobacco it lacks flavour. There is a pretty general concurrence of opinion that the seed of the Deli tobacco was indigenous, and obtained from Batak tribes in the interior; and although many experiments have been made with seeds from Java, Manilla, and other places, the planters have invariably come back to the original seed, finding that the new kinds develop a coarseness of leaf attributed to the extraordinary richness of the virgin soil, a soil partly alluvial and partly volcanic, but covered throughout with dense forests.

"The tobacco estates consist of grants of land taken out by individuals or companies, and are as a rule of such an extent that every year a new district can be cleared and used for the coming crop, and this state of things will continue for many years to come; indeed, hitherto only a small portion of the ground cultivated (not one-fifth) has borne two crops, although it is expected that, unless fresh ground is taken up by the planters, a time will arrive when use must be made of old fallow lands, and then guano will be required.

"The planters consist of three or four large companies, principally Dutch—such as the Deli Company, the Amsterdam Deli, and the Batavia Deli—as well as of individual planters of many nationalities, Germany and Switzerland being strongly represented, while there are also a good sprinkling of Englishmen, the principal English firm being the Langkat Plantations Company, with its headquarters in London.

"The grants of land are taken direct from the chiefs before mentioned, and are only valid after confirmation at Bengkalis. The term is for 75 years, and for such a grant a sum of money, by way of premium, amounting to from 1 dol. to 2 dol. per bouw (equal to an acre and two-thirds), is paid in cash, while an annual rent of 40 c. a bouw, payable at the expiration of the fifth year, is also reserved. Such at least are the terms of the last recognised agreements. The whole of the conveniently-situated land in the three districts before-mentioned has now been taken up, and it is only in the outlying regions that fresh ground can be obtained; but as in such outlying regions settled government is not so well established, the Dutch authorities are now very chary in confirming grants in places where the tobacco-growing community would be less under control.

"It is estimated that at least 2,000,000*l*. sterling is now invested in the tobacco industry in the Deli districts.

"The tobacco when ready for shipment is all sent to Clambia on the Langkat river, to the Deli river, or the Sirdang river (as the case may be), and is despatched thence viâ Penang or Singapore to Amsterdam, which is the tobacco mart for the continent of Europe. The United States have also bought the Deli tobacco in the Amsterdam market in late years. Very little of the tobacco goes to England. The leaf remains so moist that the English import duty would press it heavily in comparison with other tobaccos, and this circumstance operates as a check on the import of tobacco from Sumatra into England as compared with tobacco from Java. The principal purchasers are German manufacturers and Dutch middlemen. The latter retail the tobacco over the continent, and supply the several Régies, amongst others the Austrian, Italian, and French. The Americans confine their purchases to dark-leaved, heavy tobacco, requiring 100 leaves or less to the lb.

"It is worth remarking that the whole of the carrying trade in connection with the Deli tobaccos is in the hands of Messrs. Holt's line, the rate of freight from Deli to Amsterdam being about 3*l*. 2*s*. 6*d*. per ton. The shipping season may be said to last from January to June.

"The tobacco crop of 1884 is estimated to yield about 20,000 bales in excess of that of 1883, but the crop in 1883 was a short one owing to unfavourable weather. The 1884 crop is the best one ever obtained, both as regards quantity and quality. Roughly speaking, the Deli tobacco in the Amsterdam market fetches 1s. 4d. per lb. English, and the profits realized may be judged from the dividends given by the most flourishing companies; the shares of the Deli Company being now quoted at 500 per cent. premium. Of course there are exceptions where unsuitable soils have been met with, and losses have been sustained of no inconsiderable amount. These losses have occurred principally on Sirdang lands, where the tobacco grown is reputed not equal to that produced in the other two districts. This comparative defect is disclosed in the burning, the Sirdang tobacco yielding a brown instead of a white ash, and being probably therefore lacking in potash.

"The forests when cleared for the tobacco plantations afford splendid timber, and this is utilized for constructing drying-sheds and coolies' quarters, but a good deal of the wood which might be exported for building or fuel is wasted for want of conveyance and burnt on the ground. As a compensation there can be no doubt that this burnt timber, or rather the ashes of it, supply an excellent manure.

"The labour employed may be distributed under three classes. There are, firstly, Malays and Batak tribesmen, who fell heavy timber, do general clearance, and build sheds; then come the Klings from the Madras districts, who occupy themselves with drainage and road-making; and lastly, we have the Chinese for planting, sorting, and preparation of the weed. The planting is conducted on a co-operative system. Coolies have their fields allotted to them, and plant at their own risk under supervision. Their payment depends on the yield. Reckoning from the estimated out-turn of last year's crop, and that one coolie will raise seven piculs of tobacco in the season, we arrive at the figure 23,000 as representing the total number of Chinese engaged at Deli in tobacco cultivation, to which number 7000 extra hands must be added, employed in pursuits incidental to the industry. 3000 additional Chinese coolies are reported to have been engaged for the coming year. The strength of the Kling community may be taken at about 3000. The Chinamen go into their clearings and begin work during January and February: those not actually in service on the tobacco estates earning money as shopkeepers, pedlars, or gardeners, many of the latter being old hands who, under advances, have taken to planting patches of tobacco on their own account, for which they find a ready sale in Penang. The Klings are also to be met with as drivers of carts and carriages.

"An industrious coolie would, on an average, net in the course of a year 100 to 150 Dutch florins, and on this sum he pays to the Dutch Government 2 per cent. by way of income tax. The coolie, however, arrives in the country with a debt of from 100 fl. to 150 fl., and thus as a rule is not clear and able to leave with a balance in hand till the end of the second year. The coolie is engaged for a year, but he generally re-engages, and takes his departure in the beginning of the third year.

"The Dutch Government regulations with regard to the maintenance of a medical man by every estate and to the erection of hospitals for sick coolies are stringent; and, on the whole, the coolie-lines, considering their temporary nature, are adequate, so that the lot of the coolie in Deli may be regarded as a favourable one, even when compared with places where he is under British control.

"The importing of British Indians, as is well known, is not tolerated, though many have found their way into the country under the stimulus of high wages, the latter running from 7 dol. to 10 dol. a month, according to capacity."

The following report by Consul Eckstein on the export of Sumatran tobacco to the United States, and Dutch dealings in the same in 1882 will be of interest.

Consul Eckstein says "it is not quite three years since a few dealers in tobacco and manufacturers of cigars in the United States had first their attention attracted to Sumatra tobacco, with a view of introducing and using it for cigar-wrappers.

"From this port shipments of the article began to be made during the latter half of the year 1880, and, considering that this trade has only so recently taken its rise, and that by this time it has already assumed rather important proportions, I felt called upon to prepare the present report, giving some information concerning the same.

"In order to show, as nearly correct as possible, the course this trade has taken from its commencement to the present time, I made up the following statement, which exhibits the quantity and value of such tobacco shipped from Amsterdam to the United States during each quarter since such shipments first began to be made, viz.:—

Quarters ending—	Quantities.	Value.
	Bales.	$
September 30, 1880	311	37,694
December 31, 1880	454	52,113
Total	765	89,807
March 31, 1881	None.	None.
June 30, 1881	558	56,958
September 30, 1881	1,162	128,474
December 31, 1881	1,059	114,758
Total	2,779	300,190
March 31, 1882	496	52,203
June 30, 1882	1,464	140,184
September 30, 1882	2,245	254,372
December 31, 1882	2,785	333,254
Total	6,990	780,013

" From this statement it will be observed that the export of the article to the United States is constantly and very largely increasing; and when it is further taken into account that certain quantities of it were invoiced and shipped from Rotterdam and Bremen as well, it may safely be stated that about 9000 bales of Sumatra tobacco entered our markets in 1882.

" What has created, increased, and what sustains this trade appears to be:

" 1st. That certain qualities of Sumatra tobacco in certain dark colours have been found to be peculiarly and advantageously adaptable for cigar-wrappers, and are gaining more and more in favour with manufacturers of cigars in the United States; and

" 2nd. The ever-increasing crops of the article, thus also increasing the supply of the particular sorts especially suitable for the American market.

" The recent animation in this trade has undoubtedly furthermore been stimulated by the removal of the 10 per cent. discriminating duty, formerly payable thereon, being a product of the East Indies, exported from the west of the Cape of Good Hope.

" This will be clearly evident when I state that many shipments, aggregating large quantities of this tobacco, purchased or ordered for months last past, were purposely delayed until late in December, so as not to arrive until after the law abolishing the discriminating duty had gone into effect.

" This unlooked-for introduction and now so considerable export of this staple into the United States has begun to be viewed with great disfavour by cultivators or growers of ' seed-leaf ' tobacco in the United States.

" They apprehend, as I am informed, that the imports of Sumatra tobacco into our country will increase still further in the near future, and seem to consider this would prove greatly detrimental to their interests.

" I am hardly in position or prepared to express an opinion as to how well grounded or justified their fears really are, and, moreover, am inclined to believe that the interested parties are the better judges of this matter, but so far as I can possibly make myself serviceable by giving information which may assist them in reaching correct conclusions on the subject I deem it my duty to do, and do cheerfully.

" Such information may possibly also be of some value to

Congress in its present consideration of our tariff when the article of 'leaf-tobacco' is reached.

"Thus I would report that up to the present the production of the article has increased from year to year without any intermission from the beginning of its cultivation in Sumatra in 1865, when it amounted to only 189 bales.

"In this connection I would respectfully refer and call attention to my report on 'The tobacco trade of the Netherlands in 1881,' dated March 7, 1882, and printed in the volume of monthly consular commercial reports No. 18, of April last, as it contains a statement showing the crops of Sumatra tobacco each year from 1865 to 1880, inclusive, and the average prices realized from its sale.

"The crop of 1881 is represented to have footed up 82,356 bales, valued (approximately) at 5,791,880 dol., being an increase over the crop of the previous year (1880) of 17,433 bales as to quantity, and of 1,260,000 dol. as to the approximate value thereof.

"From the foregoing it will be seen that about one-ninth of the whole crop of 1881 has been exported to the United States.

"The entire crop, excepting about 1700 bales remaining in the hands of the original importers or consignees here, on December 31, 1882, was disposed of at an advance of about 1 cent, United States currency, in the average price as compared with that realized in 1881 for the crop of 1880; or, in other words, the total crop of 1880 brought on the average about $45\frac{3}{4}$ cents, whereas the crop of 1881 averaged about $46\frac{3}{4}$ cents, United States currency, per half-kilogram.

"This refers to the prices originally obtained at the

various sales throughout the year by the importers or consignees, first hands.

"As regards the prices for the particular sorts which during the year found their way to the United States, and which are usually purchased from quite a number of firms in the wholesale tobacco trade through the mediation of brokers, they differed all the way from about 45 cents to 95 cents, United States currency, for the half-kilogram.

"Thinking it might prove interesting, if not important, to parties in the United States in any way concerned in this matter, to be informed as to the extent and quality of the crop of 1882, I made inquiries relating to it, and ascertained as follows, viz.:—'That whilst it is impossible to state, at this early day, with accuracy the yield of the crop, it is generally considered and expected to have been again in excess over the previous one, and that it amounts to about 90,000 bales.'

"Its quality is represented by the planters to be very good, as far as they are able to judge; but this can, of course, only be determined later on, after the tobacco has gone through the process of fermentation.

"The first parcels of this new crop will arrive here about the month of March next, and will be offered for sale about a month or six months thereafter.

"In concluding this report, I would remark that the year 1882 has been a most favourable one for tobacco planters in Sumatra and for those interested in tobacco plantations there, and so have those connected with the trade here realized handsomely by the year's operations.

"I am, therefore, induced to state that so long as the

present general demand for the article continues there will be neither lack of capital nor labour, so long as either can contribute to an increase in its production, and it would seem to be more a question as to the extent of acreage in Sumatra adapted for its cultivation, as only once in four or five years a crop can be raised on the same soil without danger of producing a very inferior quality of tobacco."

Turkey.—The Turkish empire has long been known as producing some of the finest tobaccos in the world. In the sanjac of Drama, which forms the vice-consular district of Cavalla, tobacco is the staple article of production and industry, and some 75,000 acres were devoted to its culture in 1873. The whole crop of 1871 was reckoned at 11,200,000 lb., the exports having been 7,600,000 lb., value 37,825*l.* The tobacco of this district, though derived entirely from one species, is divided into two classes, known as *Drama* and *Yenidji*. The former leaf is larger, stouter, and more potent, and generally of deep reddish-brown colour; the latter is smaller, slighter, less narcotic, with a peculiarly delicate aroma, and the best is of a rich yellow colour, whence its name "golden-leaf." The *Drama* kind is principally grown in the western portion of the district, and is the class supplied to European markets. The differences in the two kinds seem to be due solely to the soil.

The plantations in the Drama district proper occupy both plain and hill-side. The produce of the former is much the more considerable, and superior. The best leaves, distinguished by a stronger and more substantial texture, and a dark-red hue, go to Constantinople; the inferior and lighter-coloured find a sale in Russia. The mountain product is much inferior in quality and is sent chiefly to Europe. When the leaves are petiolate, or furnished with stems, they are made up in *manoks* ("hands") of 10–15, and termed *bashi-baghli* ("head-tied"); when the leaves are sessile, or devoid of stems, they are simply pressed together in small numbers, and called *bassma*. The whole produce of this locality varies from 2,100,000 to 2,450,000 lb. yearly. The growth obtained in the Vale of Pravista is known as *Demirli*. It is inferior, unsubstantial, and dark-coloured, and usually made up as *bashi-baghli*. The annual production is about 2 million lb.; the exports to England were 1,600,000 lb. in 1871. Cavalla affords yearly about 300,000 lb. of inferior quality, chiefly as *bashi-baghli*, and mostly consumed locally. The shipping port for all these places is Cavalla.

The district of Sarishaban produces on the average about 2,000,000 lb. annually, but the crop of 1871 reached 2,800,000 lb. About $\frac{7}{8}$ is as *bashi-baghli*. That grown on the plain and hills is termed *ghynbek*, and forms the bulk; that from the slopes, about 500,000 lb. a year, is the best, and is known as *ghubek*. All is packed up in small *boghchas* (parcels), of 30–50 lb., which are distinguished as *béyaz*, from the white cotton wrappers used for the best sort, and *kenavir*, from the canvas coverings of the inferior kinds. The best goes to Constantinople, secondary to Smyrna and other home markets, and the worst to Europe. The district of Yenidji, near the Gulf of Lagos, affords some 3,500,000 lb. per annum, chiefly as *bassma*, and bearing a very general resemblance to the produce of Sarishaban. The best goes to Constantinople and Russia. Ghiumirgina (Ghumurdjina, or Komuldsina) grows about 300,000 lb. yearly of dark-coloured *bassma*, of the *Drama* class, which is used locally; and Sultan-Yeri gives 400,000 lb. of still darker *bashi-baghli*. The produce of these districts is shipped at Lagos (Karagatch) or Cavalla.

The most delicate and valued of all the tobaccos raised in this portion of European Turkey is the celebrated "golden leaf" from the caza of Yenidji, on the Vardar (Nestus) river. After it, in declining order, come the products of Drama, Persoccian, Sarishaban, Cavalla, and Pravista. Of the whole Drama and Yenidji produce, it is estimated that Austro-Hungary takes 40 per cent. Italy buys annually about 150,000–200,000 *kilo*. France, Germany, and Switzerland receive very little. Russia is a large customer. Before the war, considerable quantities were sent to the countries on the Lower Danube. England imports every year some 10,000 bales, or 400,000 *okes* (of 2·83 lb.) of Pravista tobacco. The *refusa*, or waste leaves, &c., is sent everywhere for making into cigarettes, most largely perhaps to Egypt. A kind of tobacco known as *ayiasoulouk* is grown in considerable quantities in the opium districts, almost exclusively for export to Europe, the natives having a strong prejudice against it.

The necessity for manuring is well understood by the Turks. They dress the seed-beds with goat- and sheep-dung, and manure the fields during winter with horse- and cattle-dung. In the spring, sheep and goats are folded on the land. The soil of tobacco lands will be found quite impregnated with ammonia and nitrate of potash, both absorbed by the plant; the former is thought to influence the aroma, and the latter may be seen in crystals on the surface of the dried leaf. In order to keep the leaves small and delicate, the planting is performed very close, the usual distances being 5 inches apart, and 9 inches between the rows.

The district of Latakia, in the northern part of Syria, has long been celebrated for its tobacco, which is the chief product of the mountainous part. There are several kinds:—(1) *Abu Riha* or *Dgebeli*, found in its best state among the mountains of the Nesseries (Ansaries), which possesses a peculiar and much-admired aroma, derived from its being exposed, from November to April, to the smoke of fires of *ozer* (*Quercus Ilex*, or *Q. Cerris*); (2) *Dgidar*, including a number of kinds, of medium strength, and in great favour locally on account of its low price; (3) *Scheik-el-Bent*, almost equal to *Abu-Riha*, and often substituted for it.

The plain of Koura is remarkable for its tobaccos, which are rather strong, but much admired. The villages of Lebail and Serai produce better tobacco than Koura. The district of Gebail (Gebel) in Kesrasan (Castravan) affords the best and dearest tobacco in Syria; it is very brittle, and its ash is quite white. The country south of Lebanon yields very ordinary qualities, known as *Salili*, *Tanoné*, and *Takibé*, or generically as *Berraoni*; these are mixed with stronger kinds for use. The best of the *Abu-Riha* is yielded by the plant called *Karn-el-Gazel*; the second quality is termed *Bonati*.

The exports of tobacco from Alexandretta in 1879

were:—To Egypt, 91 tons, value 6380*l.*; Turkey, 24 tons, 1920*l.*; England, 51 tons, 2550*l.*; France, 1 ton, 80*l.* The exports from Aleppo in 1878 were 30 tons, value 1200*l.*, to Great Britain. The yield of the crop in Thessaly was 1,116,000 *okes* (of 2·83 lb.) in 1877, 210,000 in 1878, and 890,000 in 1879. The crop of Prevesa in 1878 was 4000 *okes*, value 215*l.* The exports from Dedeagatch were about 260 bales, value 1000*l.*, in 1878; and 600 bales, value 2400*l.*, in 1879. Considerable quantities are grown around Sinope. Tobacco is one of the principal products of the district of Samsoun, and is of good quality. The average yield is 7,000,000 lb. yearly. It is grown near the sea-shore, and not eastward of Yomurah, at Matchka and Trebizonde, and especially at Akché-Abad. But the aggregate crop in these localities is hardly ⅓ of the quantity produced at Samsoun, and the quality is far inferior. The Samsoun product is usually purchased largely on account of the French Government. The exports from Samsoun in 1878 were:—To Turkey, 2,680,000 *kilo.*, value 160,800*l.*; France, 583,500 *kilo.*, 28,008*l.*; Russia, 575,000 *kilo.*, 57,500*l.*; Germany, 400,000 *kilo.*, 7200*l.*; Austria, 327,220 *kilo.*, 31,266*l.*; Great Britain, 87,567 *kilo.*, 1576*l.*; total, 4,653,287 *kilo.*, 286,350*l.* The exports of Turkey-produced tobacco from Trebizonde in 1879 were:—To Turkey, 14,864 cwt., value 44,592*l.*; Russia, 866 cwt., 2598*l.*; Great Britain, 490 cwt., 1470*l.*; Austria and Germany, 204 cwt., 612*l.*; total, 16,424 cwt., 49,272*l.*

In 1884, Damascus imported 1313 sacks of tumbeki, value 1674*l.*, from Bagdad. In the same year Erzeroum imported 9000 *okes*, value 1090*l.*, from Persia.

P

The leaf grown by the Herki Kurds and other cultivators in and around the district of Shemdina is highly prized in Persia. In 1884, the first year of their operations, the employés of the tobacco Régie only succeeded in registering a yield of 25,000 *okes*, but this amount represents less than a fifth of the estimated produce of the vilayet. It is believed, however, that 8000–10,000*l*. Turkish worth of Shemdina tobacco annually crosses the frontier into Persia.

Trebizonde exports in 1884 were 20,167 cwt., value 56,849*l*. Inferior qualities are sent to Europe, good ones remain in Turkey, and the best go to Egypt.

The shipments from Samsoun in 1884 were as follows:—

	cwt.	Price. £ s. d.	£
To Turkey	29,210	4 0 0	116,840
Austria	8,540	5 0 0	42,700
France	5,756	1 4 2	11,512
Egypt	4,176	4 0 0	16,704
Germany	3,579	1 8 6	5,096
Russia	1,730	6 0 0	10,380
Great Britain	832	1 4 2	1,002
Holland	712	1 12 0	1,140
Greece	416	3 0 0	1,248
	54,951		206,622

United States.—The United States of America occupy the foremost rank among tobacco-growing countries. The areas and productions have been as follows:—1875, 559,049 acres, 379,347,000 lb.; 1876, 540,457 acres, 381,002,000 lb.; 1877, 720,344 acres, 489,000,000 lb.; 1878, 542,850 acres, 392,546,700 lb. The crop of 1875 (in millions of lb.) was thus contributed:—Kentucky, 130; Virginia, 57; Missouri, 40; Tennessee, 35; Maryland, 22; Pennsylvania, 16; N. Carolina, 14¾; Ohio,

13½; Indiana, 12¾; Connecticut, 10; Massachusetts, 8½; Illinois, 8. The average yields (in lb. per acre) of the various districts in 1875 were:—Connecticut, 1600; Pennsylvania, 1600; New Hampshire, 1600; Massachusetts, 1350; Missouri, 850; Arkansas, 822; New York, 800; Florida, 750; Ohio, 700; W. Virginia, 680; Maryland, 675; Tennessee, 675; Kansas, 670; Texas, 650; Kentucky, 630; Virginia, 630; Illinois, 550; Georgia, 550; N. Carolina, 500; Indiana, 500; Wisconsin, 500; Alabama, 465; Mississippi, 317. The exports from New York in 1878 were:—37,484 hogsheads, 2561 bales, and 2,218,200 lb. manufactured, to Great Britain; 15,570 hh., 207 bales, and 14,800 lb. manufactured, to France; 35,700 hh., 78,331 bales, and 147,400 lb. manufactured, to N. Europe; 23,150 hh., 6058 bales, and 120,000 lb. manufactured, to other Europe; 4628 hh., 14,360 bales, and 4,780,200 lb. manufactured, to S. America, E. and W. Indies, &c. Baltimore exported 66,039 hh. in 1878. The shipments from New Orleans in 1877–8 were:—1226 hh. to Great Britain, 743 to France, 4552 to N. Europe, 3222 to S. Europe, Mexico, &c., and 4500 coastwise. Philadelphia, in 1879, exported 9,564,171 lb. of leaf tobacco, 52,000 cigars, and 515 lb. of snuff. The total American export of unmanufactured leaf in 1879 was 322,280,000 lb.

The census bulletin on this branch of industry, recently issued, is of a very interesting nature. The tobacco product in the United States is divided into classes, types and grades, the basis of a class being its adaptation to any specific purpose; of a type, to certain qualities or properties in the leaf, such as colour, strength, elasticity, body or flavour. It also applies to the method of curing, such as sun, air or flue curing. Grades represent the different qualities of a type, and vary much in the several types. The classification of American tobacco is threefold, viz. domestic cigar tobacco and "smokers," chewing-tobacco, export tobacco. The domestic tobacco trade comprises the various kinds of seed-leaf of Connecticut, New England, Pennsylvania, Wisconsin, Illinois, New York, Florida and Ohio, as well as the sorts known as White Burley "lugs," fine-fibred wrappers, Indiana kite foot, and American-grown Havana. In the chewing class are included the fine-cut and the plug fillers, principally of the White Burley type from Kentucky, while under the head of export tobacco are the Virginian bird's-eye cutting leaf, and the spinning fillers or shag. It is curious to notice how each market for export tobacco differs in its requirements. The "closed" markets, or those in which the tobacco trade is a monopoly of the Government, are France, Italy, Austria and Spain. The French "Régie" is supplied by wrappers, binders and fillers from Kentucky, Maryland and Ohio; the Italian Régie from Kentucky and Virginia; the Austrian Régie by "strips" from the same States, and the Spanish Régie by common "lugs." The open markets are Germany, to which are sent the tobaccos known as German saucer and spinners; Ohio and Maryland, spangled cigar-wrappers and "smokers" fat lugs; Switzerland, which is supplied with Virginian or Western wrappers and fillers; Holland, with Dutch saucer (a mottled Virginia, Kentucky or Tennessee leaf); Belgium, with Belgian cutter (a light, yellowish-brown leaf, well fired); Norway and Sweden, with heavy types, mainly used for spinning and "saucing." Kentucky, which stands first of all the States for production, the annual produce being 171,120,784 lb., gains her chief profits from the white burley and yellow wrapper; Illinois, from the production of the seed-leaf; Missouri, from sweet fillers and white burley; Virginia, from yellow wrappers, bright "smokers," sun, air and flue-cured fillers. Decidedly the most prosperous tobacco States are those that grow types suitable for domestic consumption, while those that grow it mainly for exportation stand low in the scale, the margin of profit under this head being reduced very low. According to the researches of Dr. Gideon Moore, the largest amount of nicotine is contained in the Virginian heavily manured lots (5·81 per cent.), while the Virginian heavy English shipping has 4·72, the New York domestic Havana but 2·53, the Connecticut seed-leaf 1·14, while the smallest amount of all is found in the little Dutch tobacco of the Miami valley, 0·63. Profits in the culture of tobacco have been in direct proportion—first to its suitableness to domestic consumption; and, secondly, to the amount of fertilization practised by the growers in its cultivation. This is true in every case, except the yellow tobacco districts of North Carolina and Virginia, where poverty in the soil is a condition of success in the production of quality.

Professor J. T. Rothrock is of the opinion that the early natives of California smoked the leaves of *Nicotiana clevelandii*—a species only quite recently described by Professor Asa Gray. It is a small plant with small flowers, and it was found by Professor Rothrock only in association with the shell heaps which occur so abundantly on the coasts of Southern and Central California. He states that perhaps of all the remains of extinct races so richly furnished by that region, none were so common as the pipes, usually made of stone resembling serpentine. The tobacco of *N. clevelandii* Professor Rothrock found by experience to be excessively strong.

A recent report of the Commissioner of Agriculture contains a few pages of sound advice to American planters on the management of this crop, which is worthy of reproduction here.

"The principal points to be attended to if the best results are to be attained may be stated in a few paragraphs—paragraphs which, while referring mainly to shipping, manufacturing, and smoking tobacco as constituting nine-tenths of the tobacco grown in the United States, embody principles and prescribe modes of management nearly identical with those to be considered in the treatment of other tobaccos.

" I. Select good land for the crop; plough and subsoil it *in autumn* to get the multiplied benefits of winter's freezes. This cannot be too strongly urged.

" II. Have early and vigorous plants and *plenty of them*. It were better to have 100,000 too many than 10,000 too few. They are the corner-stone of the building. To make sure of them give personal attention to the selection and preparation of the plant-bed and to the care of the young plants in the means necessary to hasten their growth, and to protect them from the dreaded fly.

" III. Collect manure in season and out of season, and from every available source—from the fence corners, the ditch-banks, the urinal, the ash-pile. Distribute it with a liberal hand; nothing short of princely liberality will answer. Plough it under (both the home-made and the commercial) in *February*, that it may become thoroughly incorporated in the soil and be ready to answer to the first and every call of the growing plant. Often (we believe generally) the greater part of manure applied to tobacco—and this is true of the 'bought' fertilizer as well as of that made on the farm—is lost to that crop from being applied too late. Don't wait to apply your dearly-purchased guano in the hill or the drill from fear that, if applied sooner, it will vanish into thin air before the plant needs it. This is an exploded fallacy. Experience, our best teacher, has demonstrated beyond cavil that stable and commercial manure are most efficacious when used in conjunction. In no other way can they be so intimately intermixed as by ploughing them under—the one broadcasted on the other—at an early period of the preparation of the tobacco lot. This second ploughing should not be so deep as the first; an average of three to four inches is about the right depth.

"IV. Early in May (in the main tobacco belt to which this article chiefly refers, that is to say, between the thirty-fifth and fortieth parallels of north latitude), re-plough the land to about the depth of the February ploughing, and drag and cross-drag, and, if need be, drag it again, until the soil is brought to the finest possible tilth. Thus you augment many fold the probabilities of a 'stand' on the first planting, and lessen materially the subsequent labour of cultivation. Plant on 'lists' (narrow beds made by throwing four furrows together with the mould-board plough) rather than in hills, if for no other reason than that having now, if never before, to pay wages in some shape to labour, whenever and wherever possible horse-power should be substituted for man-power—the plough for the hoe.

"V. Plant as early as possible after a continuance of pleasant spring weather is assured. Seek to have a *forward* crop, as the benefits claimed for a late one from the fall dews do not compensate for the many advantages resulting from early maturity. Make it an inflexible rule to plant no tobacco after the 10th of July—we mean, of course, in the tobacco belt we have named. Where one good crop is made from later planting ninety-nine prove utter failures. Far better *rub out and start afresh the next year*. Take pains in transplanting, that little or no replanting may be necessary. The cut-worm being a prime cause of most of the trouble in securing a stand, hunt it assiduously and particularly in the early morning when it can most readily be found.

"VI. Keep the grass and weeds down, and the soil loose and mellow by frequent stirring, avoiding as much as possible cutting and tearing the roots of the plant in all stages of its growth, and more especially after *topping*. When at all practicable—and, with the great improvement in cultivators, sweeps, and other farm implements, it is oftener practicable than generally supposed—substitute for hand-work in cultivation that of the horse. The difference in cost will tell in the balance-sheet at the close of the operation.

"VII. Attend closely to 'worming,' for on it hinges in no little degree the quality and quantity of tobacco you will have for sale. A worm-eaten crop brings no money.

So important is this operation that it may properly claim more than a passing notice. Not only is it the most tedious, the most unremitting, and the most expensive operation connected with the production of tobacco, but the necessity for it determines more than all other causes the limit of the crop which in general it has been found possible for a single hand to manage. Therefore bring to your aid every possible adjunct in diminishing the number of worms. Use poison for killing the moth in the manner so frequently described in treatises on tobacco, to wit, by injecting a solution of cobalt or other deadly drug into the flower of the Jamestown or 'jimson' weed (*Datura stramonium*), if necessary planting seeds of the weed for the purpose. Employ at night the flames of lamps, of torches, or of huge bonfires, in which the moth may find a quick and certain death.

"In worming, spare those worms found covered with a white film or net-like substance, this being the cocoon producing the ichneumon-fly, an enemy to the worm likely to prove a valuable ally to the planter in his war of extermination.

"Turn your flock of turkeys into the tobacco-field, that they, too, may prey upon the pest, and themselves grow fat in so doing.

"If these remedies should fail, sprinkle diluted spirits of turpentine over the plant through the rose of a watering-pot, a herculean task truly in a large crop, but mere child's play to the hand-picking process, for the one sprinkling suffices to keep off the worms for all time, whereas the hand-picking is a continual round of expensive labour from the appearance of the first worm until the last plant has been carried to the barn. We have no idea that such sprinkling will at all affect the odour or flavour of the tobacco when cured.

"If, as stated by a writer in a California paper, the well-known 'yellow-jacket' be useful in destroying tobacco-worms, by all means win it as an ally. As proving its usefulness, the writer asserts that one of his neighbours, a Mr. Culp, during fifteen years growing tobacco, has never expended a dollar for labour to destroy the worm, trusting all to this little workman, who, he says, carefully searches the plants for the worms, and never allows one to escape its vigilance.

"We cannot speak from our own experience as to many of these suggested means for overcoming the horn-worm, but we have no hesitation in saying to the farmer, try any, try all of them rather than have your crop eaten to shreds, and the labour of more than half the year brought to naught in a few days, it may be, by a single 'glut' of worms.

"VIII. 'Prime high and top low.' While open to objection in particular cases, even with the character of tobacco chiefly under consideration, and altogether inadmissible, it may be, in the management of other varieties of tobacco, this is a safe rule, we think, to follow in general practice.

"We favour 'priming' by all means; for when no priming is done the lower leaves (made worthless by constant whipping on the ground) serve only as a harbour for worms, which are the more difficult to find because of the increased burden of stooping. Moreover, if the bottom leaves be saved on the cut stalk, as most likely they will be, there is always the temptation to put them on the market; and against a *sacrilege* like this we are firmly set, let others say and think what they may.

" Yet another advantage to be gained by the removal of these bottom leaves, which is what the planter terms 'priming,' is the increased circulation of air and distribution of light thereby afforded, both essential factors, the merest tyro knows, to the full development of plant life.

" 'Topping' (the pinching off with the finger-nail the bud at the top of the plant) is an operation requiring considerable skill and judgment. Let it be performed only by hands having these prerequisites.

" That as many plants as possible may ripen at the same time (a desideratum not to be undervalued in aiming, as all should, at a *uniform* crop) wait until a large number of plants begin to button before commencing to top. Going about through the crop, topping a plant here and there because it may chance to have buttoned before its fellows, is a damaging process not to be tolerated.

" No inflexible rule can be given for the number of leaves that should be left on a plant. All depends upon the variety of tobacco, the strength of the soil, the promise of the particular plant, the probable seasons and time left for ripening, &c.

" One of the most successful growers of heavy dark tobacco we have ever known, once stated to us his conviction, after years of observation and practice, that one year with another, taking the seasons as they come, eight leaves would give a better result than any other number.

Our own experience has tended to confirm this judgment.

"IX. See to it that the suckers are promptly removed. It is work quickly done, and with worming may constitute a single operation.

"X. We come now to consider the last operation in the field, 'cutting' the crop. In this, as in topping, a man of judgment, experience, and fidelity is needed. An inexperienced hand, one without judgment, and particularly one who is indifferent to the interests of his employer, will slash away, right and left, not knowing or not caring whether the tobacco he cuts be ripe or green, doing more damage in a few hours than his whole year's wages would compensate for, even could they be garnished.

"Therefore, be on hand to see for yourself, and do not delegate the duty to any less interested party, that a crop managed well, it may be, so far, from the initial plant-bed, should not be spoiled in the closing work by an incompetent or unfaithful cutter.

"Be there, too, to see, in this supreme hour, that injury from sunburn is warded off by the timely removal, to the shade, of the plants that have been cut, or by a proper covering, where they lie, against the scorching rays of the sun. The neglect of this precaution has played havoc with many a crop when brought under the auctioneer's hammer.

"XI. We should have no space to describe the different methods of 'curing' tobacco, as, for instance, 'sun-curing,' 'air-curing,' 'flue-curing,' 'open-fire-curing,' &c., even though the whole subject had not been gone over again and again in previous reports of this Department.

We can only say of this operation, as of all others connected with the production of tobacco, that much depends on its proper doing, and that, as much as possible, it should have the personal superintendence of the owner.

"But the crop may have been brought along successfully even to the completion of this operation and 'lack one thing yet,' if it be not now properly manipulated.

"Therefore, go yourself, brother planter, into your barns, see with your own eyes, and not through the medium of others; handle with your own hands, and *know of a surety* that the tobacco hanging on the tier-poles is in proper order for 'striking' and 'bulking,' and act accordingly.

"When, later on, it is being 'stripped,' 'sorted,' and tied into bundles, or 'hands,' as they are often called, be there again, *propria persona*, to see that it is properly classed, both as to colour and to length, the 'lugs' going with lugs, the 'short' with short, the 'long' with long, &c. Instruct those sorting that when in doubt as to where a particular leaf should be put, to put it at least one grade lower than they had thought of doing. Thus any error will be on the safe side.

"Prize in hogsheads to weigh what is usually called for in the market in which you sell, and, above all, 'let the tobacco in each hogshead be as near alike as possible, uniform throughout, so that the 'sample,' from whatever point it may be taken, can be relied on as representing the whole hogshead,' and that there be left no shadow of suspicion that 'nesting' has been attempted, or any dishonest practice even so much as winked at.

"We sum up the whole matter by repeating :

"1. That overproduction, the production at all, of *low* grade tobacco is the chief cause of the present extremely low price of the entire commodity.

"2. That the planters of the United States have the remedy in their own hands; that remedy being the reduction of area, this reduction to result, from the employment of the means here suggested, in increased crops; and, paradoxical as it may seem, these increased crops to bring greatly enhanced values.

"The whole world wants good tobacco, and will pay well for it. Scarcely a people on earth seeks poor tobacco or will buy it at any price.

"In a word, then, one acre must be made to yield what it has hitherto taken two or three acres to produce; and this double or treble quantity must be made (as, indeed, under good management it could not fail to be) immeasurably superior in quality to that now grown on the greater number of acres. Either this or the abandonment of the crop altogether—one or the other."

The exports from Baltimore were 46,239 hogsheads in 1882, 43,620 in 1883, 43,192 in 1884. The State of New York, in 1883, had 5440 acres under tobacco, producing 9,068,789 lb., value 1,178,943 dollars; and Connecticut, 8145 acres, 9,576,824 lb., 1,292,871 dollars. The production of Minnesota was 65,089 lb. in 1879, 48,437 lb. in 1880, 79,631 lb. in 1881, 62,859 lb. in 1882, 14,744 lb. in 1883.

Venezuela.—The exports from Ciudad Bolivar were, in 1884, 1318 *kilo.*, value 1037 *bolivares*, to the British West Indies; 9618 *kilo.*, 6691 *bolivares*, to the United States; 275,329 *kilo.*, 192,188 *bolivares*, to Germany. The exports of tobacco from this port in decades have been:—

7,650,656 lb. in 1850-59; 2,134,711 in 1860-69; 3,170,812 in 1870-79.

West Indies.—The Spanish possessions in the West Indies are well known for their tobacco. The best is produced on the *vuelta abajo*, or low-lying districts of Cuba, near Havana, which are yearly flooded during the autumn, just before the tobacco is transplanted. To this fact, and the peculiar suitability of the seasons, the excellence of this particular product is attributed. The exports from Havana in 1878 were :—93,603 bales tobacco, 75,212,268 cigars, 203,581 bundles cigarettes, to the United States; 6169 bales tobacco, 66,795,330 cigars, 5,034,774 bundles cigarettes, to England; 32,582 bales tobacco, 9,541,498 cigars, 133,008 bundles cigarettes, to Spain; 582 bales tobacco, 3,861,700 cigars, 8206 bundles cigarettes, to N. Europe; 5671 bales tobacco, 18,327,025 cigars, 797,513 bundles cigarettes, to France; 41 bales tobacco, 900,850 cigars 5,709,442 bundles cigarettes, to other countries. The totals for 1878 were 7,078,904 *kilo.* of tobacco, 182,356 thousand cigars, and 12,816,903 packets of cigarettes; in 1879, 6,371,014 *kilo.* of tobacco, 145,885 thousand cigars, and 14,098,693 packets of cigarettes. The tobacco exports in 1879 from St. Jago de Cuba were 9653 bales to Bremen, 4015 to the United States (chiefly for Bremen), and 1809 coastwise, total 15,477, against 10,249 in 1878. In the island of Puerto Rico, the tobacco-plant thrives well, and the quality, especially in the Rio de la Plata district, is very good. In 1878, the island exported 8 *quintals* (of 101½ lb.) to the United States, 32,109 to Spain, 4198 to Germany, and 18,123 to other countries.

The British West Indies have only recently appreciated the importance of tobacco cultivation. Many portions of Jamaica seem as well fitted for it as the *vuelta abajo* of Cuba, and already Jamaica tobacco in the Hamburg market ranks next to the best Havana, and is considered superior to such Cuban growths as St. Jago, Manzanillo, Yara, &c. Tobacco cultivation may now be said to have a place in the industries of Jamaica, a fact mainly due to Cuban refugees. The most extensive plantations in the island are Potosi in St. Thomas Parish, and Morgan's Valley in Clarendon. Much of the produce goes to the German market, the remainder being made into cigars for local consumption, and said to be quite equal to some of the best Cuban brands. Some experiments made with Bhilsa tobacco have given great satisfaction, on account of the robust habit and immense yield of the plant. It is especially adapted for very wet districts, and its cultivation will be widely extended, if justified by its market value. Tobacco is, and for very many years has been, grown by the peasantry in small patches; from this, they manufacture a smoke-dried leaf, which, twisted together in rope form, sells readily in the home market. The acreage occupied by the crop was 297 in 1874–5, 442 in 1875–6, 331 in 1876–7, and 380 in 1877–8. The slopes of valleys in many parts of Dominica, too, are eminently suited to this crop, particularly the district between Roseau and Grand Bay. The experiment of tobacco culture in New Providence on a large scale has not proved satisfactory, owing to the difficulties encountered in curing and preparing the leaf; the cigars made are fit only for local consumption.

The exports from San Domingo in 1884 were 10,513,940 lb., value 669,500 dollars.

According to a recent Consular Report, it would seem that "Cuban tobacco has lost its prestige through forcing and artificial manures, and has to sustain sharp competition from abroad where it formerly commanded the market; and probably some years must elapse before the soil can recover from the excessive and indiscriminate use of artificial fertilizers.

"A few years ago the leaf harvested in the Vuelta Abajo was not sufficient to meet the large demand, and in order to increase the yield, growers made use of guanos of all sorts, and with such bad results that they find it now difficult to place on reasonable terms more than half, and sometimes less, of their crops, at very low prices; in few localities only the soil has not been spoilt by spurious manures, and the leaf grown there commands very high prices and is warmly competed for by local manufacturers and buyers for the United States.

"Notwithstanding the last crop has been of a better quality than heretofore, growers were compelled to abandon the tobacco cultivation for a certain time, and devote the ground to other purposes.

"It appears that this change of cultivation is absorbing the fertilizers, and restoring to the soil its former good qualities, and, if one can judge from the splendid appearance of the leaf and the ready sale it now meets with, it would seem that the Vuelta Abajo fields are regaining their former renown.

"This has been a hard but healthy lesson the Vegueros are not likely to forget. The soil cannot and should not be taxed beyond a reasonable and natural yield; any attempt to the contrary would only be a repetition of the fable of the golden eggs, as the tobacco growers in the Vuelta Abajo have had occasion to learn to their cost.

"Towards the end of the year buyers, influenced by the pending negotiations of the Spanish-American Treaty, entered the market and operated extensively in the expectation of a great reduction of duties in the United States, paying prices above the established one, and which, a few weeks later, they were utterly unable to obtain.

"Cuban growers complain much of heavy purchases made in the United States for account of the Spanish Government for Peninsular consumption; they say that however low the class of the Cuban leaf may be, it must necessarily be superior to that of the Virginia and Kentucky tobacco, and that they might easily cultivate here the quality required, and place it in the markets at as low a price as any other country.

"Growers are unanimous in denouncing the action of some local merchants and cigar manufacturers in forwarding at the opening of the last season samples of leaf tobacco and cigars in condition that by no means gave a true idea of the quality of the crop, and which necessarily gave a result contrary to the interests of all parties engaged in the trade; and they earnestly protest against a repetition of this injudicious haste.

"The total tobacco production is estimated at between 400,000 and 500,000 *quintals* (one *quintal* about 100 lb.), chiefly from the following districts:—

	Tercios.	
Vuelta Abajo and semi Vuelta Abajo	150,000	to 200,000
Parlida	30,000	50,000
Remedios	60,000	85,000
Cuba and Java	25,000	35,000
Gibara	20,000	30,000
Total	285,000	400,000

(One tercio about 124 lb.)

"As is well known, that grown in the Vuelta Abajo or district west of Havana is the best kind, and has given Cuba its well-earned reputation. About 67,000 acres are cultivated under the denomination.

"I have no reliable statistics to show how much of the raw produce is manufactured in the island, probably not more than one-fourth. Very large quantities of the leaf are exported in bales and rolled abroad.

"It is evident, however, that, given the total production and corresponding result in the manufactured form, but a small portion of the cigars sold in Europe and elsewhere as Havana cigars have the slightest claim to a connection with Cuba.

"The chief and only important manufactories of these cigars are in Havana, and much care and money is expended in producing a handsome-looking article. As much as 40 dollars gold are paid to skilled labourers per 1000 for making up first-class goods. About 17,000 operatives are employed in this manufacture in Havana alone. One of the largest establishments here is that supplying the Henry Clay brands, which is stated to turn out from 80,000 to 120,000 cigars daily; and there are many others of considerable importance with a well-earned and old-established reputation for fine goods.

"The quality of tobacco, like other agricultural produce, depends on seasons, soil, and many natural causes, which may baffle the most careful cultivator.

"There are good and bad years; abundant and scanty crops in succession.

"Except in the case of the few rich owners of plantations in the best districts, brands and names are no guarantees for a permanently good article. Even these favoured few are exposed to bad seasons, if in a minor degree than less fortunate holders.

"There has been no really fine-flavoured aromatic leaf harvested since 1881. Much of that since garnered has been simply bad.

"Great hopes are entertained of the coming 1885 crop, and present indications are in favour of this assumption.

"The manner in which the wholesale trade is carried on in Havana is incomprehensible to an ordinary outsider, to whom it would appear that the manufacturers prefer a prospective loss abroad to a present and certain gain here. They will only execute orders, large or small, for cash over the counter, giving no, or in some cases the smallest, discount. No manufactured goods are kept in stock, but are made to order after sample, and, unless examined in warehouse before delivery, and that means little, must be paid in full on delivery, and the consequence but too frequently is that, on arrival at their destination, they do not correspond with the sample, and the deluded buyer finds that he has made a bad bargain, and (if an Englishman) discovers that he could have bought the same article cheaper in the English market with the additional advantage of examining and testing the goods before purchase.

" I leave the solution of this enigma to the initiated : it probably is that the makers consign very largely, and London importers are too experienced and too wary to pay the full invoice price until well acquainted with the wares, or they get large discounts refused to the cash purchaser in Havana.

" Complaints are heard of the depressed state of the Cuban tobacco trade and of the large unsold stocks on hand. I do not think the traders deserve sympathy, nor have they done anything to ·earn the confidence of foreign customers. My experience leads me to advise intending purchasers to put (I do not advise regular traders) themselves in the hands of reliable London dealers and avoid all direct purchases.

" Intelligent smokers with sensitive palates will find no cheap tobacco here fit to smoke ; 50s. per 100 and upwards is what must be paid at present for really fine-flavoured aromatic cigars ; beyond 80s. or 85s. prices become fancy ones, and are paid for the smart cases and envelopes. Even at the rates I quote it is not easy to find what is wanted. There is abundance of dark powerful tobacco of fine quality at much lower rates, but not light tobacco with flavour or aroma or without strength, such as the educated (I allude to taste) Englishman seeks. I believe that only about 10 per cent. of the tobacco harvested in ordinary years is of the light colour I refer to, hence the difficulty in supplying the demand, and the artifices resorted to to supply the deficiency.

"Cuba's annual tobacco crop may be estimated as between 300,000 and 400,000 *tercios* of 125 lb. each. About 30,000 persons are employed in its cultivation, and its value when harvested may be fixed (according to year's quality) at between 8,000,000 and 12,000,000 dol. of 4s.

" I cannot estimate the number of persons engaged in working plantation (Vegueros) and other cigars for home consumption, nor the quantity thus consumed ; but the higher class of operatives employed in cigar-making for export number about 20,000, and turn out at present probably 200,000,000 cigars annually.

" The export trade has fallen off considerably of late years. In the five years, 1870 to 1874, about 350,000,000 cigars were annually shipped to foreign ports, whereas in the period between 1879 and 1884 the annual average export was only 200,000,000.

" Probably larger quantities have been exported in each period owing to under valuations to escape export duty ; but relative bulk proportions between the two export periods will hardly be affected by this."

The exports from Havana in 1884 were 11,767,200 lb. to the United States, 613,000 to Spain, 252,600 to France, 37,500 to Mexico and South America, 70,000 to Belgium, and 500 to the Mediterranean.

CHAPTER V.

PREPARATION AND USE.

This chapter embraces the manufacture of cut, cake and roll tobacco, cigars, cigarettes, and snuff. It is impossible to indicate the precise form in which each kind of tobacco-leaf is manufactured for use; indeed, no well-defined line marks the qualifications of each sort, and the great art of the manufacturer is to combine the various growths in a manner to produce an article suited to the tastes of his customers, at a price suited to their pockets. But, in a general way, it may be said that Havana and Manilla are probably exclusively consumed in the form of cigars; Virginia is a favourite for cavendish, negrohead, and black twist, and is largely converted into returns, shag, and snuff; Kentucky, Missouri, and Ohio are used for cavendish, brown twist, bird's-eye, returns, and shag; Dutch and German make the commonest cigars, k'naster, moist snuffs, and smoking-mixtures; Java and Japan are selected for light cigars, mixtures, and light moist shag; Latakia, Turkey, Paraguay, Brazil, China, and the remainder, are used up in cigarettes, mixtures, imitations, and substitutes.

Damping.—The tobacco-leaves are received by the manufacturer in all kinds of packages, from a hogshead to a seron (raw hide), and of all weights from 1 to 12 cwt. The first process they undergo is "damping,' which is necessary to overcome their brittleness, and admit of their manipulation without breaking. For this purpose, the bunches ("hands") are separated, and the leaves are scattered loosely upon a portion of the floor of the factory, recessed to retain the moisture. A quantity of water, which has been accurately proportioned to the absorbing qualities of the leaf used, and to the weight present, is applied through a fine-rosed watering-pot, and the mass is left usually for about 24 hours, that damped on one morning being ready for working on the following morning. In England, water alone is admissible (by legislative enactment) for damping, except in special cases to be noted subsequently; but abroad, many "sauces" are in vogue, their chief ingredients being salt, sal ammoniac, and sugar.

Stripping and Sorting.—Quantities of leaf-tobacco are shipped in a condition deprived of their stem and midrib, and are then known as "stripts." Those which are not received in this state, after having been damped, are passed through the hands of workmen, who fold each leaf edge to edge, and rip out the midrib by a deft twirl of the fingers, classifying the two halves of each leaf, and ranging the sorts in separate piles as smooth as possible. The value of the leaf greatly depends upon the dexterity with which the stripping is done, as the slightest tear deteriorates it. Stripts require sorting only. The largest and strongest leaves are selected for cutting and spinning; the best-shaped are reserved for the wrappers of cigars; broken and defective pieces form fillers for cigars; and the ribs are ground to make snuff. For the manufacture of "bird's-eye" smoking-tobacco, the leaves are used without being previously stripped.

Cutting.—Cutting is the process by which the damped leaves, whether stripped or not, are most extensively prepared for smoking in pipes and cigarettes. The tobacco-cutter which is in general use in this country is shown in Figs. 14 (side elevation), 15 (sectional elevation), 16 (front elevation), and 17 (plan). The main frames a are united by stretcher-bolts b; d is a wooden-surface feeding-roller, on which the tobacco is pressed and cut; c are the upper compressing- and feeding-rollers, mounted in e, carriage-plates extended backwards, forming the sides of the feeding-trough, and hinged to the axle m; f are levers; g, links by which the weight w presses down the upper rollers; h, a crank, and i, a connecting-link for working; j, the cross-head to which the knife k is fixed; l, side-levers or radius-bars for guiding the knife, hinged on the eccentric ends of the axle; m, an axle held in bearings at the back of the machine; on its middle part, which is concentric with its own bearings, are hinged the top roll carriage-plates e, whilst on its projecting ends, which are slightly eccentric, the knife-levers l are hinged; n is a worm-wheel segment; o, a worm; p, a hand-wheel for turning the eccentric spindle m through a part of a revolution in its bearings, for adjusting the contact of the knife with the nose-plate q; r, a worm; s, a worm-wheel; t, a worm-pinion for giving simultaneous movement to all the rollers; u, a spindle, "universal jointed" at both ends, for driving the upper rollers in positions varying with the thickness of the feed; v, a saw-toothed ratchet-wheel, moved intermittently by a catch x, link y, and stud-pin z, v being changeable, and the eccentricity of z variable, for the purpose of regu-

234   TOBACCO.

lating the fineness of the cutting. Both ends of the knife move at the same speed, and its surface is made to clear the work by describing a slight curve. The knife

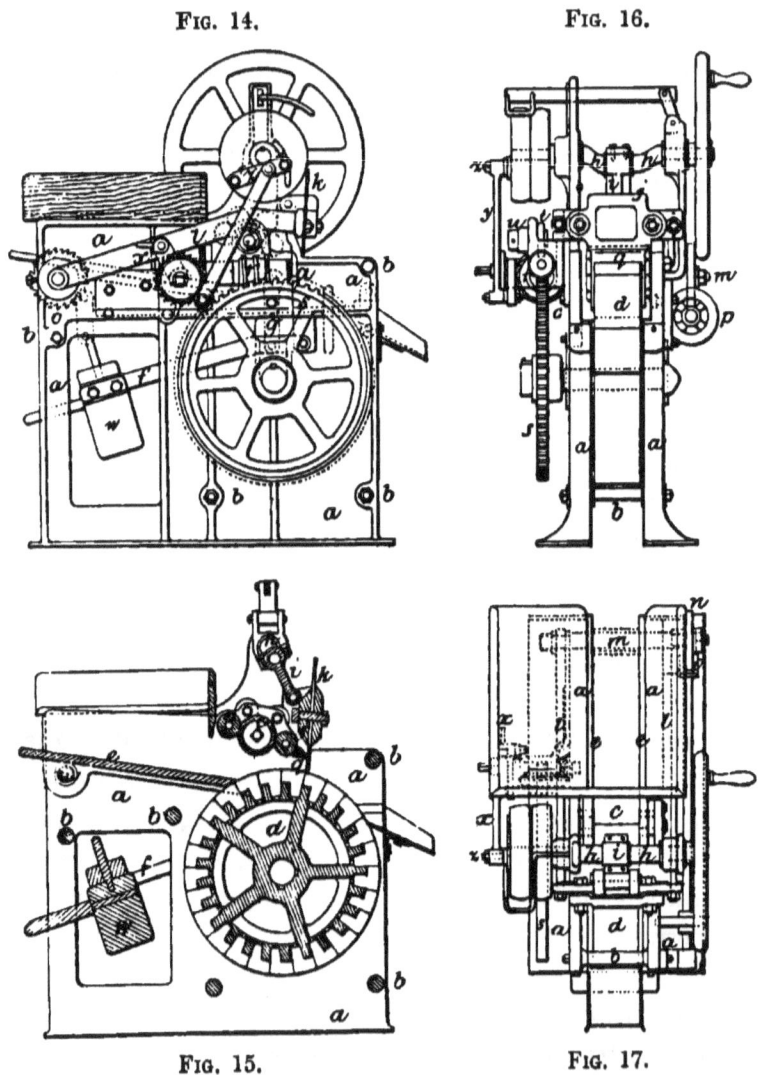

Fig. 14.

Fig. 16.

Fig. 15.

Fig. 17.

is adjusted accurately to the nose-plate, while the machine is in motion, by varying the direction of eccentricity of the axis of the knife-levers to that of the roller-levers. The fineness of the cutting is regulated by varying the eccentricity of a movable stud-pin in a plate on the crank-shaft which gives motion, through a train of speed-reducing gear, to the several rollers. The knives are easily removed and replaced, and require sharpening after every 4-6 hours' working. Two men attend the machine, one to keep the feed-rollers supplied, the other to watch that the knife is doing its work, and to remove the tobacco as fast as it is cut.

Drying.—The cut tobacco, as removed from the machine, is placed loosely in a layer several inches deep in a large trough, provided with a canvas false bottom; steam is introduced between the true and false bottoms, and finds its way up through the tobacco, which is thus rendered more easily workable. It is next transferred to a similar trough having no false bottom, but a steam-jacketed floor instead; here the tobacco is dry-heated, and at the same time lightened up by hand. Finally, it is taken to a third trough, where cold air is forced through the canvas false bottom, by means of a blower or fan. This last operation dries the tobacco ready for use in the course of some hours; but it has the disadvantage of dispersing part of the aroma, and is therefore generally resorted to only when time presses. In other cases, the drying is conducted on canvas trays. However performed, the drying operation needs the greatest attention, to prevent the moisture being extracted to such a degree as to destroy the profit which its presence confers upon the manufacturer. With drying, the preparation of cut tobacco for smoking in pipes is completed.

Cake or Plug.—The manufacture of "cake" or "plug" is little carried on in this country, as the Excise laws exclude the use of sweetening matters, except when carried on in bond. The process is sufficiently simple. Virginian leaf, with or without the addition of flavourings, is sweated for a day or two, to deepen the colour, worked into a soft mass, and next placed in moulds, and subjected to sufficient pressure to ensure the cohesion of the mass. Each cake is then separately wrapped in perfect leaf, and passes through a series of moulds, each smaller than the last, and under increasing pressure in steam-jacketed cupboard-presses, of which there are many forms. The combined effect of the heat and pressure is to thoroughly impregnate the whole mass with the natural juices of the leaf and the flavouring (if any has been used), and to produce a rich dark colour.

A machine for turning out plug-tobacco in ribbons, made by the McGowan Pump Co., New York, is shown in Fig. 18. The tobacco is first weighed out in the proper quantities, and spread in a box placed in spaces in a heavy iron table a. When the latter is filled, it is passed to and fro under the heavy iron wheels b, which are loose on the shaft, and which can be adjusted to exert any desired pressure. Twice passing through suffices. The ribbon is made in lengths of 10 feet, and either $5\frac{3}{4}$ inches or $2\frac{7}{8}$ inches wide, as desired.

Roll or Twist.—Roll- or twist-tobacco is made by spinning the leaf into a rope, and then subjecting it to hot pressure. Until recently, the spinning was performed by

PREPARATION AND USE. 237

hand, much after the manner of ordinary rope-making by hand. But this slow process is now superseded by a

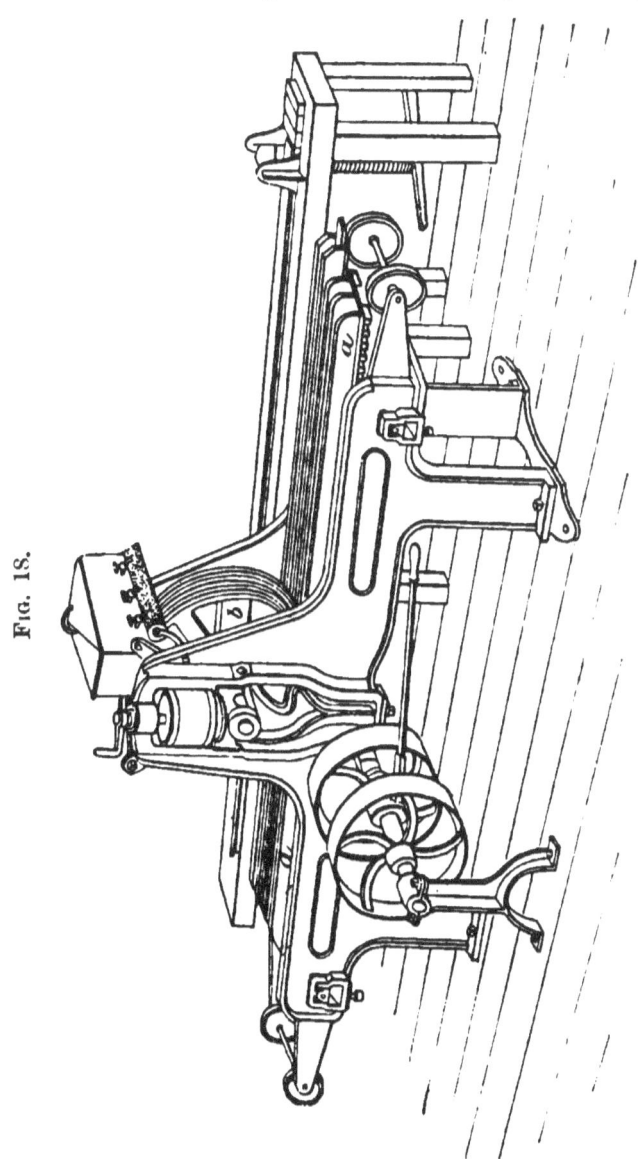

Fig. 18.

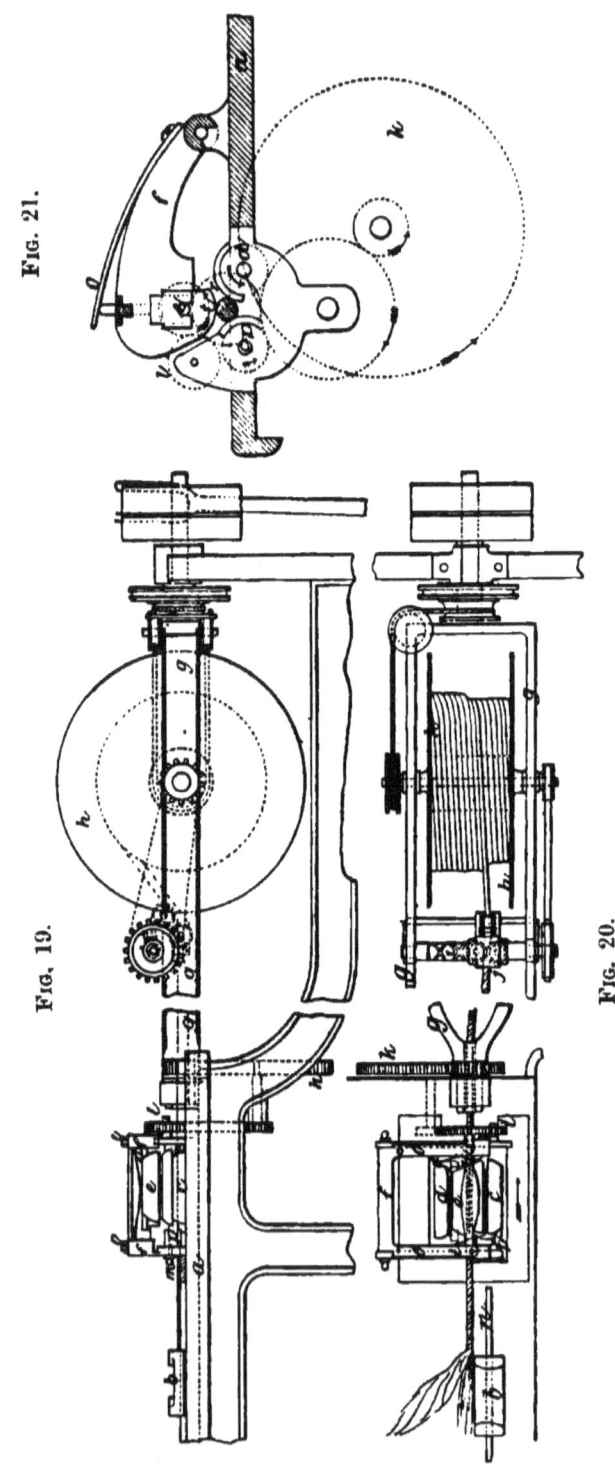

Fig. 19.   Fig. 20.   Fig. 21.

machine made by Robinson and Andrew, of Stockport; it is spoken of in very favourable terms by English manufacturers, and received a diploma of merit at the Philadelphia Exhibition. The machine consists of a combination of 3 rollers, whose surfaces are made of segments, to which lateral to-and-fro motions are given by cams attached to the stands on which the axles of the rollers rotate. The tobacco occupies the central space between the 3 rollers, and it is carried through the machine by the lateral to-and-fro motions given to the segments. The fillers and wrappers are laid on a table joined to the machine. The filler is placed in the cover, and they pass together between the rollers, whose action twists and compresses the tobacco into a roll; this is carried forward and wound on a bobbin, revolving in an open frame, and provided with a guide for equalizing the distribution of the tobacco.

The machine is shown in Figs. 19 (elevation), 20 (plan), and 21 (end view). The tobacco is laid on the table a, provided with a rib n, on which the sliding rest b is free to move to and fro; $c\ d$ are the two lower segmental rollers, the axles of which revolve in stationary bearings; e is the top roller, the axle of which revolves in sliding bearings, fitting in the swing-frame f, and each acted upon by a spring o, pressing on a pin communicating with the bearing, and putting an elastic pressure on the tobacco.

Each segment-roller consists of an axle with four segments, best shown in Figs. 22 and 23. The outer shell of the segments is made of hard wood, fitting an inner shell of malleable cast-iron, the projections on

240 TOBACCO.

which suit grooves on the cast-iron axle. The segments of the rollers *c d* are moved laterally to and fro by the wedge-shaped cams *p q r s*, fixed to the bearings of the

Fig. 22.

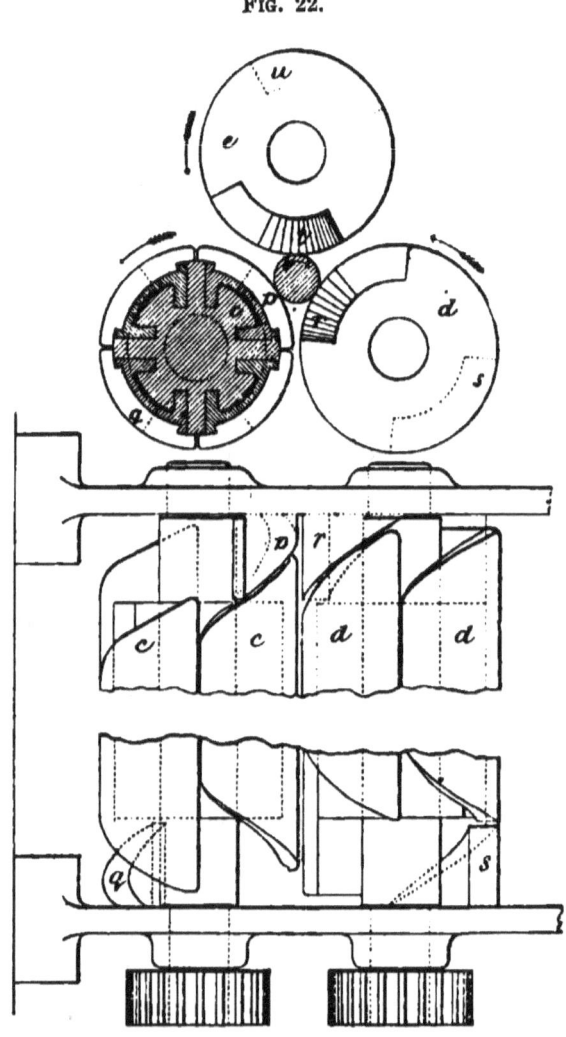

Fig. 23.

roller-axles; and the segments of the roller *e* are moved in the same manner by cams *t u*, fixed to the swing-frame *f*. The tobacco occupies the central space between the 3 rollers, and the cams *p r t* move the segments in the direction of the arrow where they touch the tobacco, while the cams *q s u* move them back. After the tobacco has passed beyond the segment-rollers, it goes through the hollow trunnion of the open frame *g*, in which the bobbin *h* revolves; the other trunnion of the frame *g* is provided with fast and loose pulleys, by which the whole machine is driven. To this trunnion, are also fixed an ordinary friction-break pulley, and a grooved pulley, around which latter passes a band for driving the pulley on the axle of the bobbin *h*. To the other end of the axle of the bobbin, is fixed a pinion, which, by means of a toothed chain, gives motion to another pinion fixed to the double screw *i*; this double screw gives a traversing to-and-fro motion to the guide *j*, for distributing the tobacco evenly on the bobbin, by means of a swivel T-headed stud, connected with the guide, and taking into the thread of the double screw. The guide is provided with two horizontal grooved rollers, between which the tobacco passes, and with two other rollers to guide the tobacco on to the bobbin.

Rotary motion is communicated to the segment-rollers *c d e* as follows:—To the hollow trunnion of the open frame *g*, is affixed a pinion, which drives the wheel *k*, on the same shaft as the change-pinion that drives the wheel gearing into the pinions on the axles of the rollers *c* and *d*, and one of which pinions gears into the intermediate pinion *l*, which drives the pinions on the axle of the roller e. The driving-strap is held upon the fast pulley by a drop-catch acting on a weighted lever, one arm of which is connected by a link to the lower end of a strap fork-lever. When it is requisite to stop the machine, the attendant kicks the point of a catch off the end of the lever, which is then raised by the weight, and so moves the driving-strap from the fast to the loose pulley, the stoppage being virtually instantaneous. The mode of working is as follows:—The spinner and assistants stand at opposite sides of the table; the fillers and wrappers being placed on the table, one assistant spreads out the wrapper and pushes the end towards the filler, which the spinner supplies and holds against the sliding-rest b; the rotary motion of the segment-rollers $c\,d\,e$ twists the tobacco, and causes the wrapper to be wound over the filler, and the rest b, being movable, enables the spinner to regulate its position according to the quantity and quality of the filler and wrapper. The lateral motion of the segment-rollers passes the roll towards the bobbin, on which it is wound, as described. The combined rotary and traversing motions of the rollers consolidate the tobacco, and put the desired face upon the twist. The roller e is supported in a swing-frame, which is lifted off the tobacco when starting the machine. When the machine is at work, the swing-frame is held down by the stud m (Fig. 19). The figures represent a machine suitable for manufacturing Limerick roll; for pigtail and other small descriptions, it is necessary to reduce the diameter of one or more of the segment-rollers.

A more recent improvement in this machine, by

PREPARATION AND USE. 243

J. E. A. Andrew, is shown in Figs. 24 (side view), 25 (transverse section), and 26 (plan). The table *a*,

FIG. 24.

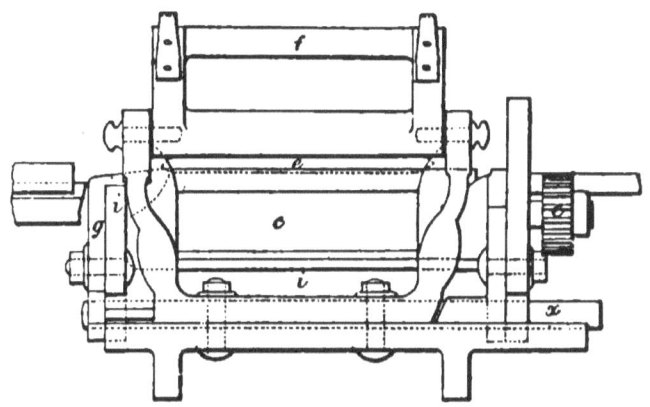

FIG. 25.

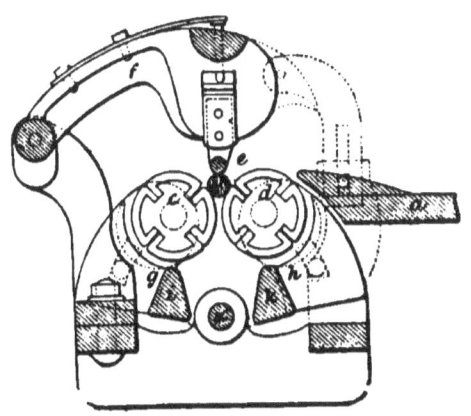

rib *n*, and sliding-rest *b*, and two lower segment-rollers *c d*, are constructed as usual; but the axles of the segment-rollers revolve in bearings *g h*, bolted to the flanges

R 2

of swivel-frames ik, hinged upon the fulcrum-shaft x; the object of thus supporting the bottom rollers cd is to be able to vary the distance between them according to the thickness of the twist of tobacco that is being rolled. When the distance between the rollers is fixed, the bearings are secured by bolts passing through segmental slots. The solid top roller e revolves in centres in sliding bearings fitting in the swing-frame f.

Fig. 26.

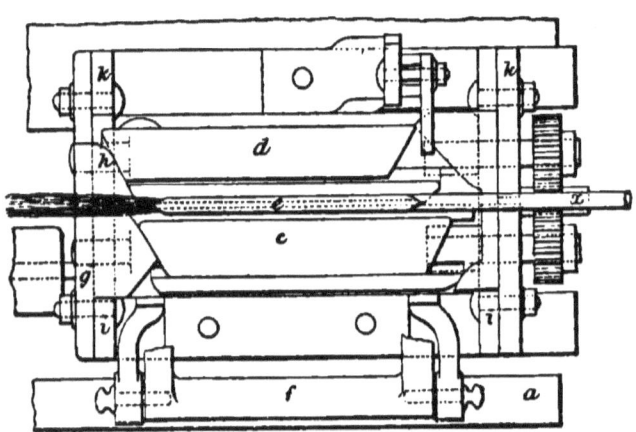

As the bobbin is filled, it is removed, and replaced by an empty one. The rope is then unwound, and formed into rolls, by the aid of a spindle with flanges at the sides, worked by a treadle, under a cushioned weight which squeezes the coils closely together as they are wound. The completed rolls are subjected to great pressure in steam-jacketed presses, in the same way, and with the same object, as the cakes or plugs.

Cigars.—Cigars are composed of two parts, a core

formed of pieces of leaf placed longitudinally, known as "fillers," and a covering formed of perfect leaf, called the "wrapper." Probably all the best cigars are made by hand, the only tools required being a short-bladed sharp knife, a receptacle containing an emulsion of gum, and a square wooden disc or "cutting-board." A portion of perfect leaf is first shaped to form the wrapper of the cigar; then a bunch of fillers is moulded in the hand, and rolled up tightly in the wrapper, the taper end being secured by gumming. Expert workmen make the cigars remarkably uniform in weight and shape. When made, they are sorted according to colour, deftly trimmed at the thick end, and placed in their boxes in cupboards heated by gas-stoves to finally dry or season before being stored for sale.

In America, machinery is introduced wherever possible. Moulds for shaping the cigars are made of hard wood, sometimes partially lined with tin, and of every possible size and form. A machine is made by Dubrul and Co., of Cincinnati, for working 3 sets of moulds at once, 2 being kept filled up under pressure while the 3rd is being filled, or the bunches are being rolled up. A handy little machine for rolling the fillers for cigars is that known as Henneman's, made by Dubrul and Co. The demand for scrap-made cigars, or those manufactured with short fillers, has caused the introduction of machines for cutting and sifting scrap. One made by Dubrul and Co. is shown in Fig. 27. It consists essentially of a cylinder formed of hook-shaped, double-edged steel blades, revolving against 3 series of fixed but adjustable steel blades, thus permitting the size to be regulated at will.

Cigarettes.—Cigarettes consist of paper tubes filled with cut tobacco, with or without an external wrapper of leaf tobacco. Preference is usually given to those made by hand, but machines have been introduced with some

success for making the commoner kinds. A French machine for making cigarettes is shown in Fig. 28. Its work consists in making the paper tubes, and filling them with tobacco. The paper, previously prepared, in a band about 3 inches wide, is unrolled from the coil *a* by means of the carriage *b*, and cut off in pieces about 1 inch long for presentation to the mandrel *c*, temporarily introduced into one of the tubes of the mould-carrier *d*. The mandrel has a clamp which grasps the paper and rolls it, and, at the moment when the latter escapes from the carriage, its free end is brought upon a rubber pad covered with gum, hidden in the illustration. The paper

PREPARATION AND USE. 247

tube is left in the mould, the mandrel being extracted by means of the cam *e*; the mould-carrier is then turned ½ revolution by the cam *f*, a new tube comes into line,

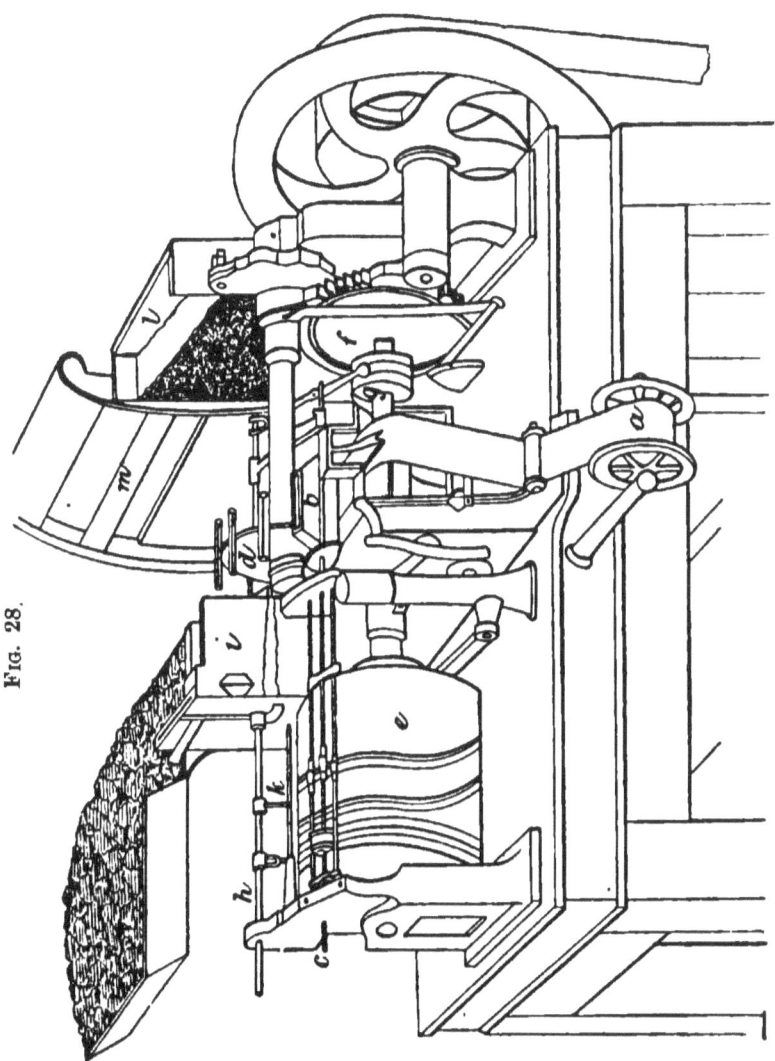

Fig. 28.

and the operation is repeated. When 6 paper tubes are completed, the first one is pushed by a small piston, actuated by the cam g, upon the end of the filling-tube; and immediately the rod h, actuated by the cam e, drives into this tube a portion of tobacco already prepared in the compressor i. In preparing the tobacco, a workman, occupying the seat m, is necessary to dispose the material in regular layers on a carrier, by which it is transported into the compressor. When the cigarette-envelope is filled, the mould-carrier again makes part of a revolution, and the finished cigarette is pushed out of the mould by the rod k, also actuated by the cam e; a device finally lodges the cigarettes in the box l. One workman is said to be able to turn out 9600 cigarettes in 10 hours by the aid of the machine.

Snuff.—Snuff is entitled to the last place in the series of tobacco manufactures, as it is largely made up of the scraps, cuttings, and rejections of the preceding processes. The materials are chopped very fine, placed in heaps in warm damp cellars, "doctored" with various flavourings, left to ferment for several weeks, and then ground to powder in edge-runner mills, some kinds even undergoing a slight roasting. When ground, the mass is passed through "mulls," wood-lined, bottomless bowls, let into a bench, where the snuff is softened and rendered less powdery means of pointed pins, resembling domestic rolling-pins, which slowly travel around the sides of the bowls. Snuff represents a highly profitable article manufactured from materials that are otherwise useless, and depending for its favour chiefly upon the perfumes and flavourings used.

Hence these last are kept profoundly secret by the manufacturer.

From refuse tobacco which is unfit for any other purpose, is made a decoction for washing sheep and destroying vermin; often the waste is ground very fine, and used by gardeners, presumably to keep noxious insects away.

Miscellaneous Appliances.—The customary ingenuity of the Americans has invented a profusion of admirable labour-saving machines for almost all the operations of the tobacco manufacturer. A few of these only can be noticed in the present article.

Fig. 29 shows a portable resweating-apparatus, intended for darkening the colour of tobacco to suit the dealer's market. It measures 4 feet long, 3 feet wide, and 5 feet high, being just large enough for one case (400 lb.) of tobacco, including the case; it consists of a water-tank a, a pipe b for conducting the water into the metallic pan c, at the bottom of the apparatus, which is heated by gas-jets d. The tobacco is introduced by the door e, which is fitted with a thermometer. The roof is sloped so as to determine the flow of the water of condensation. The steaming occupies 3–5 days, and needs occasional watching. The apparatus is made by C. S. Philips and Co., 188 Pearl Street, New York.

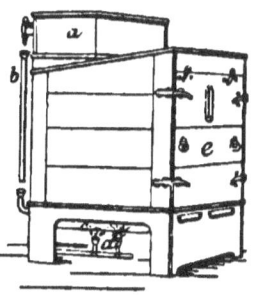

FIG. 29.

Fig. 30 illustrates a complicated machine, introduced

by C. C. Clawson and Co., of Raleigh, N. Carolina, for putting up large quantities of tobacco in parcels of 2 oz. upwards. It consists of a central table provided with automatic scales for weighing out the portion; four equidistant guides which determine the form of the package;

Fig. 30.

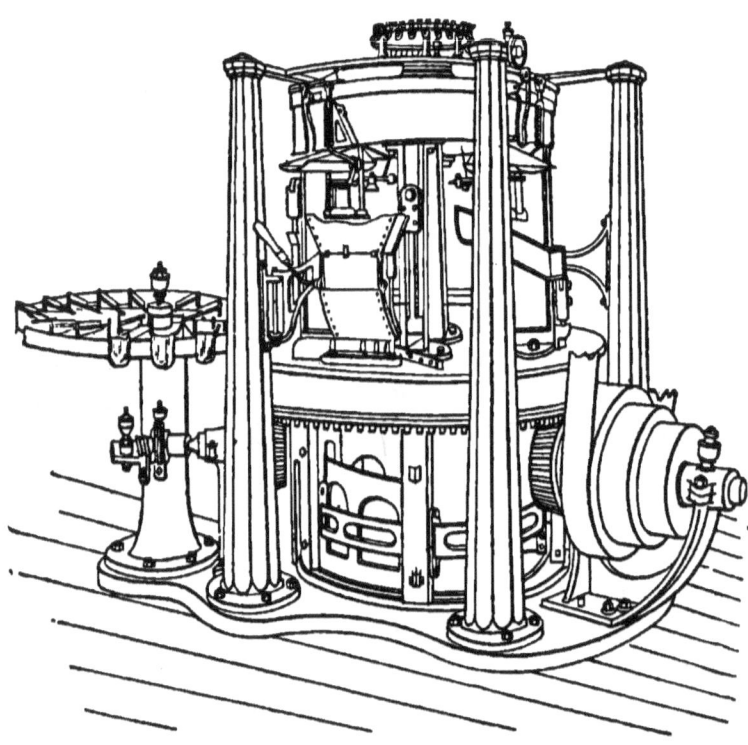

a plunger for packing, and a follower for raising the package; a side-table carrying tongs for holding the empty bags; and another to receive the packages, and hold them during tying. The hopper being supplied with tobacco, and the machine put in motion, each form takes a bag from the tong-table, and the article having been weighed, is carried to the form by a shute, when it drops into the bag, is packed by the plunger, and transferred to the tying-table. With 2 girls or boys, it is said to weigh, pack, and tie 30 bags a minute.

The New York Tobacco Machine Co. make two forms of machines for granulating tobacco, chiefly for making "Killickinick" and cigarettes, their working capacity ranging from 200 to 2000 lb. a day. The cutting-rollers are covered with cross-millings at right angles to each other, those running lengthwise being deep; the fixed cutters are adjustable, so that the cutting may be either coarse or fine. When working, the action is like that of a pair of shears, except that the cross-millings reduce the strips to a granular state. Both stems and leaves may be worked up. The great advantage claimed for these machines is that, though the tobacco should be dry, the percentage of dust escaping is reduced to a nominal figure.

A cutting-machine made by the same Co. is shown in Fig. 31. It is adapted to cut leaf, stem, scrap, plug, or any form of tobacco, to any required degree of fineness, turning out 300-400 lb. a day. The action is almost precisely that of a chaff-cutter. The Co.'s sifting-machine consists of an adjustable cylindrical wire sieve, with a rattan-broom screw-roller revolving inside. The stems are stripped and worked out at one end, while the remainder is broken up, and passed through the sieve, falling upon a perforated tray, through which pass the finest particles for snuff-making. A machine largely used in America is the stem-roller, for crushing and flattening the stems so that they may be used like leaves for making cigars. Great benefit is anticipated in the United States from the adaptation of Ryerson's "attrition mill" to snuff-grinding, owing to the fact that the pulverization is accomplished without the particles being heated in the least degree. Of cigarette-making machines, there are many kinds; the best are those which deal with the tobacco in a comparatively dry state, thus preventing shrinkage after packing.

Indebtedness is acknowledged to Hy. Archer and Co.,

FIG. 31.

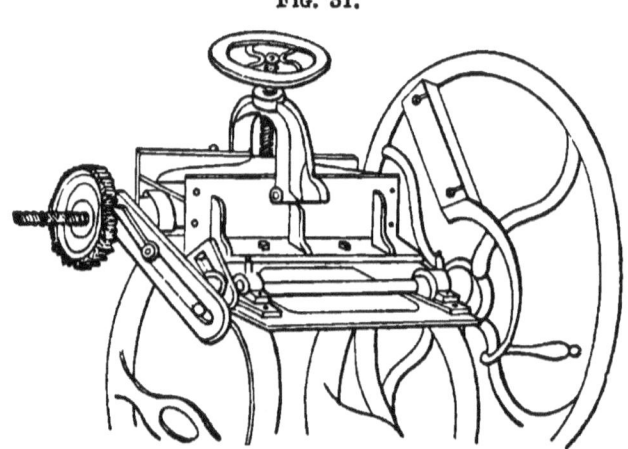

Borough, S.E., and T. Brankston and Co., Carter Lane, Doctors' Commons, for opportunities of inspecting their thoroughly representative works, and for much information readily given concerning the manufacture in this country; to W. Jollyman, of W. D. and H. O. Wills' London house, for having revised these sheets before going to press; and to Hy. A. Forrest, 61 Broadway, agent of the New York Tobacco Machine Co., for valuable material relating to American machines and processes.

CHAPTER VI.

NATURE AND PROPERTIES.

THE active principle of tobacco is a volatile, highly poisonous alkaloid, called Nicotine ($C_{10}H_{14}N_2$). Although green tobacco-plants contain generally more nicotine than the leaves after they have been prepared for the market, yet the odour is only perceptible after the fermentation of the leaves has set in. It has been ascertained that young leaves 2 inches long contained 2·8 per cent., and leaves 10½ inches broad and 16 inches long, as much as 5·6 per cent. of their weight of nicotine. The amount increases as the plants become ripe, and decreases on their becoming overripe.

Though the narcotic effects of tobacco experienced by the smoker must partly be attributed to nicotine, it cannot be said that they are solely due to it. It is well known that the products of combustion of quite harmless substances are often stupefying. Good Syrian tobacco contains no nicotine, yet smokers consider cigars made from this tobacco to be strong. It is evident that the strength of a cigar, as judged by the smoker, depends greatly on the circumstance whether the tobacco burns well or not. If it burns well, a greater amount of nicotine is consumed and decomposed, and less of the narcotic products of combustion are created, than when it burns badly. Cigars of the latter description, containing little nicotine, are more narcotic in their effects when smoked than well-burning cigars containing much nicotine.

The amount of nicotine in tobacco varies very much, according to the sort of plant, the climate, the nature of the soil in which the plant grew, the treatment received during its growth, and the course adopted to prepare the leaf for the market. Dr. Nessler found that good Syrian tobacco contained no nicotine, Havana tobaccos between 0·6 and 2·0 per cent., and German tobaccos between 0·7 and 3·3 per cent. Schlösing found in French tobacco nearly 8·0 per cent. of nicotine. Fine tobaccos contain generally little or no nicotine. Broughton found that the amount of nicotine in Indian tobaccos varies very much. The conditions favourable to the development of nicotine in the plants are:—Soil in a bad physical state, strong nitrogenous manure, a dry atmosphere, and probably a low temperature during the growth.

According to Nessler, green and newly-cut tobacco-plants contain no ammonia; it is developed during the drying and fermentation of the leaves, especially when they assume a brown colour. Tobacco-leaves, which have undergone a strong fermentation, contain more ammonia than those slightly fermented. Fine tobaccos contain generally less ammonia than coarser ones. In various smoking-tobaccos, Nessler found:—Havana, 0·2 per cent. of ammonia; Cuba, 0·3; Syrian, 0·6; German, 0·9 per cent. Schlösing found Havana tobacco to contain 0·8 per cent.

Nitric acid, consisting of nitrogen and oxygen, is formed in animal and plant substances when decomposed under the influence of atmospheric air and a sufficiently high temperature; whereas ammonia, consisting of nitrogen and hydrogen, is formed when those substances decompose in the absence, or nearly so, of atmospheric air. Organic substances decomposing under the latter condition emit an objectionable pungent odour, which must partly be attributed to the formation of ammonia. Tobacco, soon after harvesting, commences, according to the conditions under which it is placed, one of these decompositions. The extent of the decomposition the tobacco has gone through may be partly judged from the colour the leaves have attained. If leaves be dried so rapidly as to remain green, the decomposition is probably confined to the formation of carbonic acid. A yellow colour indicates the formation of nitric acid; and a dark-brown or black colour, that of ammonia. The conditions under which nitric acid and ammonia are formed being known, it is possible to control their development. When the tobacco is hung far apart, so that the air has free access, the formation of nitric acid will take place; but if the air be excluded more or less, by hanging the tobacco very close, or pressing it in heaps or pits, the formation of ammonia is engendered.

Nitric acid generally promotes the combustion of plant substances, by supplying a portion of the needed oxygen, and has undoubtedly a similar effect in tobacco; its occurrence in the tobacco is therefore a desideratum with the cultivator and manufacturer, and to supply any deficiency, the manufacturer often resorts to impregnating his tobacco with a solution of saltpetre. From this, however, it must not be concluded that every tobacco containing a large amount of nitric acid will necessarily burn well. Schlösing and Nessler have shown that the well-burning of a tobacco does not always correspond with a great amount of nitric acid, thus indicating that other substances or other conditions also affect the combustibility. The effect of the nitric acid will most probably vary with the base with which it is in combination.

The nitrogen in the forms of nicotine, ammonia, and nitric acid, constitutes only a small portion of the total amount present in tobacco; by far the greater portion ($\frac{2}{3}-\frac{7}{8}$) exists in the form of albuminoids. Nessler found that the nitrogen under this form varies from 2 to 4 per cent., which is equal to 13–26 per cent. of albuminoids. Substances rich in albuminoids generally burn badly, and emit a pungent noxious odour. On the condition of these albuminoids, and on the presence of other substances, as nitric acid, alkalies, &c., in the tobacco, mostly depend the burning qualities of the leaf, and the flavour of a cigar. The Eastern habit in smoking, from Malaysia, Japan and China, through India, Persia and Turkey, even to Hungary, is to inhale the smoke into the lungs, and natives of these countries maintain that a tobacco should be of full flavour without burning the throat or catching the breath. Western nations do not admit the smoke further than the mouth, and therefore require a strong, rank flavour.

Whilst drying and fermenting, the tobacco undergoes great changes. Some substances are decomposed, others are newly formed. The highly complicated compounds, the albuminoids, undergo first decomposition, and in doing so give rise to more simple combinations. Nitric acid, ammonia, and other substances less known are chiefly, if not entirely, derived from the products of the decomposition of albuminoids. The substances that cause the objectionable pungent smell in tobacco are formed from the broken-up constituents of these high combinations. The conditions under which these bad-smelling combinations originate are not properly known; but it is probable that they are developed with, and under the same conditions that cause the formation of, ammonia, as the disagreeable pungent flavour is found generally in tobacco that has undergone fermentation to a great extent. It is believed that the conditions that favour the development of nicotine are also conducive to the formation of albuminous substances in the leaf, viz. fresh nitrogenous manure, bad physical state of the soil, &c.

According to Nessler, the quality of tobacco depends to a great degree on the amount of cellulose it contains. He found that a good tobacco invariably contained more than a bad one, Havana yielding as much as 46 per cent. The fact that tobacco burns better after being stored for a time may be partly due to an increase of cellulose in it.

Every tobacco contains more or less fat, gum, ethereal oil, &c. It is not properly known in what way fatty matters affect the quality of tobacco. Many other organic matters exist in tobacco in combination with substances from which it is most difficult to separate them; they have not as yet been quantitatively ascertained, and are therefore little known. Most of them are only developed during the drying and fermenting

s

of the leaf; their presence, however, considerably affects the quality of the tobacco.

The amount of ash constituents in the tobacco is considerable, varying between 16 and 28 per cent. There cannot be said to exist a definite relation between the total amount of ash in the tobacco and its quality, as tobaccos yielding much ash are sometimes of good, and at other times of bad, quality; a good tobacco may yield much or little ash. The relative proportion in which the ash constituents exist is, however, of the greatest importance. It has been ascertained that the presence of some special mineral elements modify to a great extent the quality of the tobacco. Of all ash constituents, potash (K_2O), more correctly speaking potassium carbonate (K_2CO_3), affects the quality of tobacco in the highest degree. Schlösing has pointed out that the good burning qualities of a tobacco depend on the presence in it of potash in combination with a vegetable acid; that a soil deficient in potash is unfit to produce tobacco of good quality. Numerous analyses have tended not only to corroborate the assertion made by Schlösing, but to demonstrate also, that it is not the total amount of potash, but the potash found as a carbonate, which existed in the plant in combination with a vegetable acid, that is the constituent chiefly affecting the combustibility of a tobacco. The complete analyses of Nessler have shown that, although a tobacco may contain a great amount of potash, it does not necessarily follow that the tobacco burns well. He found that some German tobaccos contained more potash than Havana, although the latter burned much better than the former; and that a great amount of potash did not always indicate a great amount of carbonate of potash. Although tobaccos yielding a great amount of carbonate of potash in their ash generally burn well, there may be conditions which neutralize the good effect of this combination, as a large proportion of albuminoids. It may therefore be said that the combustibility of a tobacco is improved in proportion as its ash yields more carbonate of potash, other conditions being equal.

Among the minor salts, the chlorides deserve most attention. It has been found that they generally retard the burning of tobacco, and that as they increase, carbonate of potash decreases. Lime is invariably found more or less in the ash, but it has not been ascertained to what extent its presence affects the quality of the tobacco; good tobacco may contain much or little, so that its presence is probably not of great importance. The same may be said of soda, magnesia, and phosphoric acid. According to Nessler, their proportions may vary thus:—Potash, 1·95–5 per cent.; lime, 6·5–9·2; soda, 0–1·63; magnesia, 0·12–0·99; phosphoric acid, 0·57–1·39.

In connection with the chemistry of tobacco, and the rational manuring of the crop, the name of Prof. S. W. Johnson, Chemist to the Connecticut State Board of Agriculture, must be placed in the foremost rank. Indebtedness is acknowledged to Prof. Johnson for a copy of his valuable report, quoted in the Bibliography at the end of this work.

In November, 1884, a paper was read by Dr. John Clark, on the composition of tobacco, before the Society of Chemical Industry, which is sufficiently interesting to be quoted at length.

Dr. Clark remarks that the "tobacco plant is very extensively cultivated in various parts of the world, and after it has reached its maturity it is cut and dried on poles. When the plant is in proper condition, the leaves are stripped from the stalk, sorted and cured, by which means they are converted into the tobacco of commerce. The good leaves are called 'wrappers,' and the infirm or defective ones, which are separated from the others, are called 'mediums and fillers.' The term 'strips' is applied to tobacco leaves, from which 20 to 25 per cent. of the stem or midrib has been removed to suit the requirements of manufacturers in this country more especially. Tobacco is largely imported into the United Kingdom, partly in the manufactured state, but principally in the unmanufactured or leaf form.

"Through the kindness of a well-known firm of tobacco manufacturers, I have been furnished with authentic samples of the principal varieties of leaf tobacco, imported into this country, and the accompanying table gives the proportions of mineral matter or ash, alkaline salts, and sand, which these contain. For the sake of comparison the results are all stated in the dry tobacco, and in order to ensure greater accuracy, the analysis was, in each case, made with several leaves, which were separated into laminæ and stem, and the whole of each incinerated. The difference in the composition of the laminæ and the stem is very marked, especially as regards alkaline salts, and is of importance more especially to the snuff manufacturer.

NATURE AND PROPERTIES. 261

COMPOSITION OF VARIOUS KINDS OF LEAF TOBACCO.

	Whole Leaf. Dried at 212° F., per cent.			Laminae. Dried at 212° F., per cent.			Stem. Dried at 212° F., per cent.		
	Ash.	Alk. Salt.	Sand.	Ash.	Alk. Salt.	Sand.	Ash.	Alk. Salt.	Sand.
U. S. Kentucky	19·11	6·84	2·57	18·93	5·43	3·06	21·69	13·51	·68
do.	18·50	6·68	1·82	15·50	2·77	2·39	26·07	16·68	·38
do.	25·99	9·69	3·51	24·88	6·70	4·17	29·36	20·01	1·10
do. Strips	15·73	4·31	2·61	15·57	4·07	2·71	16·95	6·35	1·37
U. S. Missouri	20·96	5·07	4·63	20·46	2·62	5·27	22·61	12·72	1·90
do.	22·01	6·32	3·51	21·36	4·96	3·88	23·62	12·37	1·53
do.	18·88	4·81	2·61	17·18	2·88	3·21	22·17	10·68	·92
do.	18·36	4·60	3·44	17·05	2·50	4·07	22·39	11·10	1·49
U. S. N. Carolina	14·50	5·99	·63	12·98	3·92	·74	18·64	11·72	·23
Paraguay	30·80	8·15	12·32	31·07	6·37	14·41	30·37	14·78	4·91
Brazil—Carmen	20·54	7·81	·42	20·42	7·24	·46	20·86	9·37	·31
Holland	21·83	11·37	·13	20·16	8·99	·55	25·15	17·20	·12
Turkey—Cavallo	13·79	5·05	3·06	12·47	2·94	3·45	18·14	11·76	1·87
do. Latakia	19·50	7·19	·55	21·86	8·28	·72	15·44	7·73	·24
do. Samsoun	18·39	6·98	·49	17·59	5·32	·44	21·72	13·42	·60
Japan	15·67	6·86	·50	14·60	5·59	·54	19·84	11·55	·35
China	18·58	2·40	6·30	17·94	1·66	6·94	20·57	5·27	3·61
Havana	20·99	8·19	1·02	20·91	7·51	1·04	21·02	10·33	·92
Manilla	21·80	6·54	·14	21·25	5·49	·13	22·50	9·09	·14
German	22·27	3·76	1·79	22·12	2·78	1·87	23·13	4·63	1·39
Sumatra	18·61	7·20	·13	18·71	6·59	·09	18·14	9·11	·28

	Average of Whole Leaf, per cent.	Average of Laminæ, per cent.	Average of Stem, per cent.
Ash or Inorganic	20·32	19·21	21·92
Alk. Salts	6·47	4·98	11·41
Sand	2·48	2·86	1·15

"The unmanufactured tobacco which is imported into this country, is converted into roll or spun tobacco, cut tobacco and cigars, and the refuse is used for making snuff. Roll tobacco is the staple manufacture in Scotland and Ireland, and cut tobacco the staple article in England.

"In the manufacture of roll tobacco, the leaves are moistened with water, spun into various sizes of twist, made up into rolls, and pressed. The liquid or juice which exudes under pressure is used as a sheep dip. Cut tobacco is made by moistening the leaves, cutting them into the desired size, and drying on plates. Sometimes it is made into cakes in the first instance, and afterwards cut.

"When we compare the composition of roll and cut tobaccos with that of the leaf from which they are made, we find that the difference lies almost entirely in the amount of moisture, and as manufacturers are not allowed to add anything but water and a little oil to tobacco, you will not err very much in assuming that as a rule the cheapest qualities of roll and cut tobaccos contain most water. Thus in 15 samples of the cheapest roll tobacco I found an average of 41·66 per cent. of water.

"The lowest qualities of cut tobacco, such as are

largely manufactured and consumed in England, contain as much water as the cheapest roll tobacco, whereas the finer qualities of cut tobacco contain as a rule from 14 to 22 per cent. Cigars, even the cheapest, are comparatively dry, and contain, as a rule, only from 10 to 12 per cent. of water.

"The difference in cheap cigars is due chiefly to the weight of the material, but also to the quality of the tobacco and the labour, machinery being used in the manufacture of the lower qualities, whereas the higher qualities are nearly all hand made.

"The large quantity of water contained in the cheapest tobacco, and which frequently amounts to about 50 per cent., is not, in my opinion, introduced to please the palate of the working man, but simply on account of the keen competition between rival manufacturers, and the low price at which tobacco is sold; and in the interest both of the working classes and of tobacco manufacturers themselves, I think it is very desirable that some limit should be placed to the amount of water which may be sold as tobacco.

"Snuff.—I stated that the refuse tobacco was employed in the manufacture of snuff. This refuse consists of stems, tobacco smalls, and sweepings. These are moistened with water, subjected to a process of fermentation, which lasts from about six weeks to two months, then ground, mixed with alkaline salts to preserve the snuff, and flavoured when desired. Nothing is allowed to be added to snuff except the carbonates, chlorides, and sulphates of potash and soda, and carbonate of ammonia. It is also provided by Act of Parliament that any snuff found to contain, after being dried at 212° F., more than 26 per cent. of such salts, including those naturally in the tobacco, will be liable to forfeiture and a penalty of 50*l.* From my table of analyses you will observe that not only does the proportion of alkaline salts vary in different tobaccos, but the stem contains a much larger proportion than the leaf. On this account it is necessary that the snuff manufacturer should know the quantity of alkaline salts in his snuff material, in order to obtain an article of uniform composition. Some manufacturers go by rule of thumb, and in attempting to work close to the legal limit, they run a serious risk of unintentionally incurring the penalty. As a matter of fact, three samples of snuff, in 1883, were condemned by the Somerset House authorities because they contained an excessive proportion of alkaline salts, and the manufacturers were prosecuted. The more intelligent of the snuff manufacturers, however, analyse their snuff material, and are thus able to keep within the legal limit.

"The principal alkaline salts which are added to snuff are chloride of sodium or common salt, carbonate of potash, and carbonate of ammonia, all of which are allowed by Act of Parliament, and therefore no exception can be taken to their addition, so long as the total quantity does not exceed 26 per cent. in the dry snuff. In addition to alkaline salts, snuffs usually contain from 25 to 45 per cent. of water, with the exception of a kind of snuff called 'High Toast or Irish Blackguard,' which is very dry and contains from 5 to 8 per cent. Sometimes they also contain a considerable quantity of sand. In the several hundred samples of snuff which I have had occasion to examine for different manufacturers the average quantity of sand was about 5 per cent. in the dry snuff, and sometimes fell as low as a half per cent., but in many samples the quantity exceeded 10 per cent., and in one case I found as much as 30·94 per cent. of sand in the dry snuff. The greater part of this sand is probably derived from the sweepings of tobacco, on which duty has been paid, and I have no doubt the snuff manufacturer considers himself justified in selling it as snuff. But it appears to me to be very desirable in the interest of snuffers, that some limit should be placed on the quantity of sand which may be sold as snuff: more especially as the particles of sand are frequently very sharp, and have a tendency to produce inflammation of the mucous membrane of the nose, and it is to this, probably, that we owe the popular notion that snuff is sometimes mixed with ground glass to give it additional piquancy.

" When from any cause snuff is spoiled, the manufacturer may export it, and obtain a drawback of 3s. 7d. per lb. on the real tobacco which it contains.

" The Government standard for tobacco is as follows:

	Per cent.
Organic matter	70·52
Inorganic	15·48
Water	14·00
	100·00

" This is equal to 18 per cent. of ash or inorganic matter in the dry tobacco. This standard is in my opinion too high, as the average percentage of inorganic or ash in the dry leaf tobaccos which I have examined is

20·32, and the stem from which snuff is largely made contains still more. The result is that the tobacco manufacturer not only loses the value of the tobacco over and above the duty, but also a part of the duty which he has paid. This matter concerns the tobacco manufacturer alone, but I would point out that the authorities in Somerset House in fixing such a high standard for tobacco are benefiting the public at the expense of the manufacturer, whereas in the case of milk the low standard which they employ is a loss to the public and gain to the dishonest dealer."

CHAPTER VII.

ADULTERATIONS AND SUBSTITUTES.

It is said that in Thuringia, over 1000 tons yearly of dried beetroot-leaves are passed off as tobacco. These leaves, and those of chicory and cabbage, are similarly employed in Magdeburg and the Palatinate. Many of the *Vevey* cigars of S. Germany are entirely composed of cabbage- and beetroot-leaves which have been steeped in tobacco-water for a long time. Other leaves, such as rhubarb, dock, burdock, and coltsfoot are also used. These are all principally for cigars. For smoking-tobacco, chamomile flowers, exhausted in water, then dyed and sweetened with logwood and liquorice, and dried, have been mixed with tobacco in such proportions as 70–80 per cent. In America, a specially-prepared brown paper, saturated with the juice expressed from tobacco-stems and other refuse, is most extensively used, not only for the "wrappers" of cigars, but also for "filling." Various ground woods, starches, meals, and pigments are introduced into snuff.

A New York paper mentions that a great quantity of brown straw paper lately reached Havana, which was to be employed in the manufacture of Havana cigars. Straw paper impregnated with the juice of tobacco stalks is wound up with the leaf in such a way that it is often impossible to detect the adulteration. Dr. Jacobson, writing in the *Industrie Blätter*, remarks that there is no difficulty in escaping detection, if the paper be specially prepared for the purpose out of suitable raw materials. It has long been known that cigar paper soaked in a solution of soluble glass gives forth no smell of paper on being burnt.

Patent No. 210,538, issued from the United States Patent Office, December 3, 1878, states the ingredients of a "substitute" to be—spikenard, red clover, hyssop, hops, slippery-elm bark, tarred rope, pennyroyal, mullein leaves, kinnikinic, wild cherry bark, and ginseng. This is an ingenious combination intended to approach in effect, appearance, and aroma, tobacco; and in so far it might be said to be a success: as mullein leaves are reputed to be feebly narcotic, hops are known to possess anodyne properties, clover and hyssop are pectoral in effect, and slippery-elm febrifuge. Ginseng is aromatic and pungent, and has a great reputation among the Chinese as a stimulant and restorative. The tarred rope, we presume, is intended to add to the pyrognostic value of the mixture. The great point in selecting material for the fabrication of a mixture of this description is to get leaves containing a fair percentage of nitrate of potass, as does tobacco; on this depends its pyrognostic value, and that, next to aroma, is everything.

"Tobacco, like those who smoke it, is credited with many sins of which it is guiltless. The 'loss of health' so often laid at its door is probably due in many instances not to tobacco itself, but to some villainous compound bearing its name. A story told by the principal of the laboratory of the Inland Revenue Department in his report for the past year shows how easily this may happen. The supervisor at Birmingham, observing that an article was being sold at a very cheap rate in packets, under the name of 'smoking mixture,' sent a sample to the Inland Revenue laboratory for examination, and it being found to contain a large proportion of vegetable matter resembling the broken-up heads of camomile flowers, further inquiry led to the discovery of the manufactory. The process of manufacture consisted in exhausting the bitter principle of camomile flower-heads with water, and then dyeing and sweetening them with a solution of logwood and liquorice, which brought them, when dried, somewhat to the colour of tobacco. The heads, when broken up, were then mixed with from 20 to 30 per cent. of cut tobacco, according to the price at which the mixture was to be sold. The mixture was supplied to retailers in packets labelled 'The New Smoking Mixture, Analysed and Approved,' and as agencies had already been established in several towns, an extensive trade would no doubt soon have arisen had the manufactory not been suppressed at an early stage of its existence."

The United States Consul at Smyrna puts the following statement in his report of January 15, 1883.

Since the establishment of the tobacco monopoly in Turkey, snuff may be said to be one of the several articles that undergo the most unscrupulous adulteration. Owing to the high amount of duties imposed on tobacco by the Turkish Government, and the large profits licensed manufacturers expect to make on the same, the poorer classes cannot afford to use the products of doubtful purity coming from the factories, and so are altogether at the mercy of the clandestine manufacturer and retailer, who, in order to make the most he can of his vile industry, adulterates his snuff to such an extent that it can be safely said that his products contain on an average from 60 to 70 per cent. of inferior Persian tobacco (tumbeki), fragments of country tobacco leaf, and tobacco of cigarettes picked up in the streets by beggars, the 30 to 40 per cent. consisting of walnut sawdust, terra umbra, fine sifted sand, and scum of lead (lead oxide), covered with inferior black writing-ink.

The snuff is manufactured in Smyrna, as follows:

The conscientious manufacturer uses Persian hookah tobacco (tumbeki) and the fragments of country tobacco leaf coloured with black ink. These tobaccos, ground as fine as possible and mixed with grape molasses, are put in a covered barrel to ferment. Two or three days later the snuff is taken out and spread in the sun to dry partly, and then rubbed with the hands and passed through iron wire sieves to be granulated.

The product is afterwards scented with powdered orris root, tonka beans, and geranium oil; the superior qualities are scented with essences of roses and jessamine and put up in packages.

The adulterated article is manufactured in the same manner with the addition of the above-named substances.

The only persons using genuine snuff in this city are the Catholic priests, who import it directly from France, Italy, Spain and Holland, and enjoy the privilege of paying no custom-house duties.

CHAPTER VIII.

IMPORTS, DUTIES, VALUES, AND CONSUMPTION.

A COMPARISON of the taxation of the chief nations of the world for the consumption of tobacco has been published in the *Imperial Statistics of Germany*. Of the countries where the sale is a Government monopoly, France last year stood first, the gross duty, with profits, amounting to 7s. 1½d. per head of the population annually, the net revenue from the article being 5s. 8¼d. per head. In Austria the gross was 5s. 5¾d., the net, 3s. 5d.; in Hungary, the gross 3s. 3½d., the net 1s. 7d.; in Italy, the gross 3s. 11d., and the net 2s. 8¼d. In Great Britain, the duty and licenses brought in 4s. 10¾d. per head of the population for the year, and in the United States 4s. 4½d. In Germany, on the other hand, where the duty was very light, the average was no more than 7¾d. per head of the population.

The duties on unmanufactured tobacco are 3s. 6d. a lb. when it contains 10 per cent. or more of moisture; 3s. 10d. a lb. when it contains less than 10 per cent. of moisture. Snuff containing no more than 13 per cent. of moisture, 4s. 10d. a lb.; 13 per cent. and upwards, 4s. 1d. a lb. Cigars pay 5s. 6d. a lb. Cavendish of foreign manufacture pays 4s. 10d. a lb.; that manufactured in bond, 4s. 4d. Other sorts, including cigarettes, pay 4s. 4d. a lb.

The approximate relative values in the London market are as follows:—Maryland, fine yellow, fine, and good coloured, 7-9½d. a lb.; colory, 5-7d.; light-brown and leafy, 5-7½d.; ordinary and brown, 4-4½d. Virginia: Fine Irish and Scotch spinners, 7-10d.; good and middling, ordinary light and dry, 6-10d.; fine black sweet scent, and middling do., 6½-7½d.; part blacks, 5-6d.; ordinary and heated, 3-5d.; mixed parcels, ordinary and good, middling and fine, 5½-6½d.; stripped leaf, 4d.-1s. Kentucky: fine long light leaf, 7-11d.; good to middling do., 5½-7½d.; fine and middling blacks, 6-8d.; ordinary and mixed, 2-5d.; stripped leaf, fine, light leafy, middling and ordinary, 4½-11d. Negrohead, 11d.-1s. 6d. Cavendish, 4½d.-1s. Amersfort and German, 2¾d.-1s. 6d. St. Domingo, 5-7½d. Havana, Cuba, and Yara, 1s. 2d.-6s. Turkish and Greek, 2½-9d. E. India, Japan, and China, 2-9d. Java, 5d.-2s. Colombia (New Granada), 5d.-2s. 6d. Manilla, 8d.-4s. Manilla cheroots, 4s.-7s. 6d. Havana cigars, 5-40s.

Imports, Duties, and Values.—Our imports of tobacco in 1879 were as follows:—

(a) Unmanufactured: From United States, 25,743,880 lb., value 682,253l.; Holland, 6,215,930 lb., 266,109l.; China, 1,444,192 lb., 36,265l.; Turkey, 1,214,319 lb., 32,627l.; Japan, 805,928 lb., 24,003l.; France, 651,350 lb., 14,585l.; Belgium, 515,009 lb., 15,501l.; Argentine Republic, 470,309 lb., 10,870l.; Germany, 426,139 lb., 25,602l.; Straits Settlements, 267,258 lb., 29,718l.; British India, 246,305 lb., 3605l.; New Granada, 241,638 lb., 9621l.; Canada, 121,920 lb., 3473l.; other countries, 497,043 lb., 14,256l.; total, 38,861,220 lb., 1,165,488l.

(b) Snuff: From all countries, 7719 lb., value 92l.

(c) Cigars: From Spanish W. Indies, 495,518 lb.,

IMPORTS, DUTIES, VALUES, AND CONSUMPTION. 273

value 494,974*l.*; Germany, 150,460 lb., 46,318*l.*; Holland, 116,218 lb., 31,348*l.*; Philippines, 80,199 lb., 21,738*l.*; France, 73,348 lb., 24,071*l.*; Straits Settlements, 51,191 lb., 13,822*l.*; China, 48,762 lb., 11,240*l.*; Belgium, 46,536 lb., 14,211*l.*; British India, 33,208 lb., 10,898*l.*; United States, 14,625 lb., 5461*l.*; other countries, 43,978 lb., 19,184*l.*; total, 1,154,043 lb., 693,265*l.*

(*d*) Cavendish or Negrohead: From United States, 2,247,557 lb., value 84,422*l.*; other countries, 45,052 lb., 1964*l.*; total, 2,292,609 lb., 86,386*l.*

(*e*) Cavendish, manufactured in bond: 33,069 lb., 7126*l.*

(*f*) Other sorts, including cigarettes: From United States, 52,206 lb., value 7999*l.*; Holland, 25,273 lb., 1372*l.*; Channel Islands, 15,470 lb., 1279*l.*; Germany, 14,474 lb., 4472*l.*; France, 9497 lb., 2368*l.*; Belgium, 7939 lb., 2086*l.*; other countries, 12,328 lb., 3845*l.*; total, 137,187 lb., 23,421*l.*

Following are statistics of the imports of tobacco for the year 1884, being the latest available.

UNMANUFACTURED TOBACCO.

	Quantity.	Value.
	lb.	£
From Germany	1,464,350	57,435
,, Holland	5,728,744	246,795
,, Belgium	299,863	10,994
,, France	733,207	23,975
,, Spain	1,265,347	24,370
,, Malta	81,026	1,160
,, Turkey	1,114,143	46,545
,, Algeria	85,580	3,081
,, British East Indies	918,066	11,082
,, Philippine Islands	45,989	3,785
Carried forward	11,736,315	429,222

T

TOBACCO.

Unmanufactured Tobacco—continued.

	Quantity.	Value.
	lb.	£
Brought forward	11,736,315	429,222
From China and Hong Kong	1,813,221	63,566
,, Japan	1,876,787	46,081
,, British North America	150,056	5,188
,, United States of America	37,186,980	1,183,102
,, Spanish West India Islands	361,095	17,972
,, United States of Colombia	122,570	3,589
,, Ecuador	76,642	2,085
,, Argentine Republic	131,013	2,970
,, Other Countries	75,728	2,476
Total	53,530,407	1,756,251

Cigars.

	Quantity.	Value.
	lb.	£
From Denmark	2,349	1,243
,, Germany	151,650	46,512
,, Holland	78,471	22,231
,, Belgium	109,388	32,789
,, Channel Islands	2,501	1,645
,, France	49,313	24,061
,, Gibraltar	1,437	982
,, Malta	1,008	390
,, Greece	1,750	600
,, British Possessions in South Africa	1,615	687
,, British East Indies	188,354	45,218
,, Philippine Islands	201,652	56,208
,, China and Hong Kong	25,659	6,242
,, Australasia	3,740	883
,, United States of America	166,740	98,510
,, British West Indies and Guiana	2,313	1,198
,, Spanish West India Islands	467,315	453,610
,, Danish West India Islands	2,448	1,519
,, Mexico	59,727	37,249
,, United States of Colombia	1,004	686
,, Brazil	4,519	2,089
,, Other Countries	4,127	2,008
Total	1,527,080	836,560

CAVENDISH OR NEGROHEAD.

	Quantity.	Value.
	lb.	£
From Channel Islands	78,569	5,156
,, British North America	64,910	3,244
,, United States of America	1,243,720	59,780
,, British West India Islands	16,332	2,764
,, Other Countries	32,315	1,646
TOTAL	1,435,846	72,590

SNUFF.

	Quantity.	Value.
	lb.	£
From Brazil	4,099	830
,, Other Countries	96	24
TOTAL	4,195	854

OTHER MANUFACTURED TOBACCO.

	Quantity.	Value.
	lb.	£
From Germany	9,993	2,920
,, Holland	20,657	1,173
,, Belgium	7,740	1,616
,, France	17,985	2,818
,, Malta	5,968	1,592
,, Turkey	5,444	1,674
,, Egypt	31,662	13,306
,, Algeria	6,410	1,580
,, United States of America	76,472	20,039
,, Spanish West India Islands	6,259	865
,, Other Countries	9,625	1,968
TOTAL	198,215	49,551

CHAPTER IX.

BIBLIOGRAPHY.

J. Neander.
    Tabacologia.   Lugduni-Batavorum : 1622.

B. Stella.
    Il Tabacco.   Rome : 1669.

S. Paulli.
    Treatise on Tobacco, &c.   London : 1746.

P. Winther.
    Tobaks-plantning.   Kjoebenhavn : 1773.

J. Carver.
    Culture of the Tobacco-plant.   London : 1779.

Villeneuve.
    Culture, Fabrication et Vente du Tabac.
                                      Paris : 1791.

W. Tatham.
    Culture and Commerce of Tobacco.
                                     London : 1800.

Jens Fr. Becker.
    Kort anviisning til tabaks-platning.
                                      Viborg : 1809.

J. E. Normann.
    Tobaksplantens dyrkning i Norge.
                                    Christiania : 1811.

M. de Truchet.
    Culture du Tabac en France.   Paris : 1816.

M. R. Flor.
    Om Tobakavl.   Christiania : 1817.

Hermbstädt.
    Gründliche Anweisung zur Cultur der Tabakpflanzen.
                                                      Berlin: 1822.

T. Brodigan.
    Art of Growing and Curing Tobacco in the British Isles.   London: 1830.

J. Jennings.
    Practical Treatise on Tobacco.   London: 1830.

H. J. Meller.
    Nicotiana.   London: 1832.

K. C. Antz.
    Tabachi historia.   Berolini: 1836.

L. A. Demersay.
    Du Tabac du Paraguay.   Paris: 1851.

Babo und Hofacker.
    Der Tabak und sein Anbau.   Karlsruhe: 1852.

V. P. G. Demoor.
    Culture du Tabac.   Luxembourg: 1853.

F. Tiedemann.
    Geschichte des Tabaks.   Frankfurt: 1854.

C. Fermond.
    Monographie du Tabac.   Paris: 1857.

A. Steinmetz.
    Tobacco.   London: 1857.

H. B. Prescott.
    Tobacco and its Adulterations.   London: 1858.

F. W. Fairholt.
    Tobacco; its History.   London: 1859, 1876.

M. C. Cooke.
  The Seven Sisters of Sleep.　　　London: 1860.

H. Raibaud L'Ange.
  Du Tabac en Provence.　　　Paris: 1860.

Nessler.
  Der Tabak.　　　Mannheim: 1860.

J. L. P. Fèvre.
  Le Tabac.　　　Paris: 1863.

C. E. Guys.
  Culture of Latakia Tobacco.
  　　　Technologist, London: 1863.

Maling.
  Tobacco Trade and Cultivation of the District of
    Cavalla.　　　*Technologist*, London: 1863.

R. de Coin.
  History and Cultivation of Cotton and Tobacco.
  　　　London: 1864.

Holzschuher.
  Der Tabakbau.　　　Gotha: 1864.

G. A. Henrieck.
  Du Tabac.　　　Paris: 1866.

A. Imbert-Courbeyre.
  Leçons sur le Tabac.　　　Clermont-Ferrand: 1866.

S. W. Johnson.
  Tobacco; Report of Chemist to the Connecticut State
    Board of Agriculture.　　　1873.

A. de Bec.
  Culture du Tabac en France.　　　Aix: 1875.

F. A. Allart.
    Culture du Tabac.   Abbeville: 1876.

B. T. Creighton.
    Culture of Tobacco in Ohio.
        Pharmaceutical Journal, London: 1876.

D. Décobert.
    Culture du Tabac.   Lille: 1876.

Hofacker und Babo.
    Der Tabakbau.   Berlin: 1876.

A. Nouvel.
    Le Tabac.   Brive: 1876.
    Notes sur la Culture des Tabacs.   Paris: 1876.

R. E. Burton.
    Cultivation of Tobacco.
        Sugar Cane, Manchester: 1877.

G. Cantoni.
    L'Industria del Tabacco.
        Annali di Agricoltura, Rome: 1879.

K. Schiffmayer.
    Tobacco and its Culture; Report of Agricultural Department, Madras Presidency.
        Madras: 1879.

F. Alfonso.
    Tabacchi della Sicilia.   Palermo: 1880.

F. Anderegg.
    Tabakbau in der Schweiz.   Chur: 1880.

O. Comes.
    Tabacco in Italia.
        L'agricolt. meridionale, Portici: 1881.

K. W. van Gorkom.
 De Oost-Indische Cultures. Amsterdam: 1881.

J. H. Zimmermann.
 Tabaksbaubüchlein. Aarau: 1881.

J. Clark.
 Composition of Tobacco.
  Journal Soc. Chem. Industry, Manchester: 1884.

A series of Prize Essays on Tobacco Culture in the Southern States of America, published in pamphlet form by the Orange Judd Co., and containing much valuable information.

INDEX.

ADULTERATIONS of tobacco, 267–70
Afghanistan, tobacco in, 137
African tobacco, 138
After-cultivation, 54–60
Albuminoids in tobacco, 256
American tobacco, 210–22
Amersfort tobacco, 6
Ammonia in tobacco, 255
Analyses of tobacco, 261
—— —— —— plants, 22
Area of nursery, 59
—— to plant, 53
Artificial heat for drying tobacco, 89, 91
Ash of tobacco, 258
Australian tobacco, 141
Austro-Hungarian tobacco, 141

BARRELS for tobacco, 125, 127
Best kind of tobacco to grow, 33
Betun, 117
Bibliography of tobacco, 276
Big Frederic tobacco, 34, 37
—— Orinoco tobacco, 35, 37
Black soil for tobacco growing, 10
Blue prior tobacco, 37
—— stalk tobacco, 35
—— vitriol for killing caterpillars, 58
Books on tobacco, 276
Bornean tobacco, 142
Bourbon tobacco, 143
Boxes for tobacco, 126
Brazilian tobacco, 143–7
British tobacco, 164–6

Brittle stem tobacco, 35
Building drying-sheds, 86, 90, 95
Bulking tobacco, 121–5
Bull tongue tobacco, 35

CAKE tobacco, 236
Calabrian tobacco, 3
Californian tobacco, 3
Canary Island tobacco, 148
Cases for tobacco, 129
Caterpillars, destroying, 55–60
Cellulose in tobacco, 257
Central Asian tobacco, 3
Chemical ingredients of tobacco soils, 9
Chemistry of tobacco, 259–66
Chinese tobacco, 148
Chlorine compounds to be avoided in tobacco manures, 25
Choosing sort of tobacco, 31–7
Cigarettes, 246–8
Cigars, 244
Classifying tobacco, 109–21
Clay as a tobacco soil, 9, 10
Climate for tobacco growing, 7
Cochin China tobacco, 149
Commerce in tobacco in Afghanistan, 137
—— Africa, 138
—— Australia, 141
—— Austro-Hungary, 141
—— Borneo, 142
—— Bourbon, 143
—— Brazil, 143–7
—— Canary Islands, 148
—— China, 148
—— Cochin China, 149
—— Costa Rica, 149

Commerce in tobacco in Ecuador, 149
—— Fiji, 150
—— France, 150–6
—— Germany, 156–64
—— Great Britain, 164–6
—— Greece, 166
—— Holland, 166
—— India, 167–76
—— Italy, 176
—— Japan, 176
—— Java, 176
—— New Zealand, 177
—— Nicaragua, 177
—— Paraguay, 178
—— Persia, 178–91
—— Philippines, 191
—— Roumania, 192
—— Russia, 192
—— San Salvador, 192
—— Servia, 192
—— Spain, 192
—— Sumatra, 193–205
—— Turkey, 205–10
—— United States, 210–22
—— Venezuela, 222
—— West Indies, 223–30
Conditions of drying-house, 78
Connecticut seed-leaf, 34
Consumption of tobacco, 271
Corn as a shelter for tobacco, 65
Costa Rica tobacco, 149
Crops adapted for rotation with tobacco, 31
Cuban drying practices, 101
—— harvesting practices, 83–6
—— manuring practices, 15
—— planting practices, 51–4
—— tobacco, 2, 3, 34, 37
Cultivation of tobacco, 7–66
Curing practices in Cuba, 83–6
—— tobacco, 67–136
Cutting machine, 251
—— tobacco for smoking, 233–5
—— —— plants, 68

Damping tobacco, 231
Destroying insects, 55–60
Distance in planting, 50
Doctoring tobacco, 133–6

Drying-house, 75
—— -sheds, building, 86, 90, 95
—— ——, sizes of, 90
—— tobacco, 86–104
—— —— for smoking, 235
Dung for tobacco soils, 14
Dutch tobacco, 166
Duties on tobacco, 271
Dyeing the leaves, 119

Ecuador tobacco, 149
Elements needed by tobacco, 11–29
European tobacco plant, 4
Examining tobacco while drying, 88

Fermenting tobacco, 121–5
Fertilizers, principles of, 18–22
Field, preparing, 48–50
Fiji tobacco, 150
Filling vacancies, 53
Flavouring tobacco, 133–6
Flowers of tobacco plants, 3–6
Foliage of tobacco plants, 3–6
Fowls, protecting seed-beds from, 46
French tobacco, 150–6
Frost at harvest time, 79
——, protecting seed-beds from, 43, 47

German tobacco, 156–64
Grades of tobacco, 109–21
Graham tobacco, 35
Granulating machine, 251
Greek tobacco, 166
Green-soiling for tobacco, 14
Guano for tobacco soil, 16
Gypsum for tobacco soil, 26

Hands of tobacco, 107
Hanging leaves in sheds, 88, 93, 95
—— split leaves, 81
—— tobacco, 72
Harvesting for small planters, 76
—— tobacco, 67–86

INDEX. 283

Hoeing plants, 54
Hogsheads for tobacco, 126, 128
Hot-bed for seedlings, 44
Hungarian tobacco, 3

IMPORTS of tobacco, 271-5
Improving tobacco, 133-6
Indian tobacco, 167-76
Italian tobacco, 176

JAPANESE tobacco, 176
Javanese tobacco, 176
Judging condition of leaf, 74

KAINIT for tobacco soil, 24
Kentucky leaf, 36

LATAKIA tobacco, 2, 3
Levant tobacco, 3
Lime for tobacco soil, 28
Literature on tobacco, 276
Little Frederic tobacco, 34, 37
—— Orinoco tobacco, 35, 37
Loading cut tobacco leaves, 70
Loam as a tobacco soil, 10

MAGNESIA for tobacco soil, 28
Manilla tobacco, 3
Manuring, principles of, 18-22
—— seedlings, 41
—— tobacco, 11-29
Maryland tobacco, 1
—— —— as a crop, 33
Mat for keeping frost off, 47
Mexican tobacco, 3
Moth of tobacco worm, 56

NATURE of tobacco, 253-66
New Zealand tobacco, 177
Nicaraguan tobacco, 177
Nicotine, 253
Nitrates for tobacco soils, 13
Nitric acid in tobacco, 255
Nurseries, 38-48
——, shelter for, 38

Nurseries, situation for, 38
——, soil for, 38
Nursery, area of, 39

ORGANIC matter in tobacco soils, 8

PACKING tobacco, 125-33
Paraguay tobacco, 178
Pegging tobacco, 71
Pennsylvania seed-leaf, 37
Persian tobacco, 3, 178-91
Philippine tobacco, 191
Picking tobacco, 104-9
Planting out, 50-4
Plug tobacco, 236
Pole-burn, 78
Potash for tobacco growing, 11, 27
Preparation of tobacco, 231-52
Preparing field, 48-50
—— seed-beds, 38, 41, 43, 44
Pressing tobacco in casks, 128, 131, 133
Priming, 62, 65
Principles of manuring, 18-22
Production of tobacco in Afghanistan, 137
—— Africa, 138
—— Australia, 141
—— Austro-Hungary, 141
—— Borneo, 142
—— Bourbon, 143
—— Brazil, 143-7
—— Canary Islands, 148
—— China, 148
—— Cochin China, 149
—— Costa Rica, 149
—— Ecuador, 149
—— Fiji, 150
—— France, 150-6
—— Germany, 156-64
—— Great Britain, 164-6
—— Greece, 166
—— Holland, 166
—— India, 167-76
—— Italy, 176
—— Japan, 176
—— Java, 176

INDEX.

Production of tobacco in New Zealand, 177
—— Nicaragua, 177
—— Paraguay, 178
—— Persia, 178–91
—— Philippines, 191
—— Roumania, 192
—— Russia, 192
—— San Salvador, 192
—— Servia, 192
—— Spain, 192
—— Sumatra, 193–205
—— Turkey, 205–10
—— United States, 210–22
—— Venezuela, 222
—— West Indies, 223-30
Properties of tobacco, 253–66

Qualities of tobacco, 109–21
Quantity of manure for tobacco, 12
Quicklime for tobacco soil, 24
Quincunx planting, 52

Rate of growth of tobacco, 24
Removing superfluous leaves, 62, 65
Resweating apparatus, 249
Ridging land, 49
Ripeness, influence on tobacco, 61
—— of tobacco, judging, 70
Ripening, 61
River bottoms for tobacco growing, 10
Roll tobacco, 236–44
Rotation for tobacco soils, 29–31
Roumanian tobacco, 192
Russian tobacco, 192

Saltpetre as tobacco manure, 13
Salts added to snuff, 264
—— in tobacco, 259
Sandy bottoms for tobacco growing, 9
San Salvador tobacco, 192
Saving seed, 37
Scaffolding for tobacco, 75

Seed, 37
—— -beds, 38–48
—— ——, area of, 39
—— ——, preparing, 38, 41, 43, 44
—— ——, protecting from fowls, 46
—— ——, —— —— frost, 43, 47
—— ——, shade frames for, 48
—— ——, shelter for, 38
—— ——, situation for, 38
—— ——, soil for, 38
—— ——, time for sowing, 41
Seedlings, hot-bed for, 44
——, planting out, 50–4
——, thinning out, 40, 48
——, top-dressing, 41
——, watering, 40
——, weeding, 40, 46
Seed required for an acre, 39
——, sowing, 39, 45
Servian tobacco, 192
Setting out plants, 50–4
Shade frames for seed-beds, 48
Sheds for holding tobacco as gathered, 68
Shelter for nurseries, 38
Sheltering tobacco from wind, 10
—— —— lands with corn, 65
Shiraz tobacco, 3
Signs of ripening, 72
Situation for nurseries, 38
—— —— plantations, 10
Sizes of tobacco barns, 90
Snuff, 248, 263
—— tobacco, 61
Soil for nurseries, 38
—— —— plantations, 8–10
Sorting tobacco, 109–21
—— —— for use, 232
Sort of tobacco to grow, 31–7
Sorts of tobacco grown in America, 33–7
Sowing seed, 39, 45
Spanish tobacco, 37, 192
Spearing tobacco, 72
Species of tobacco, 1–3
Splitting tobacco, 72
Sponging the leaves, 119
Stacking gathered tobacco leaves, 67
Straw mat for keeping frost off, 47

Stripping tobacco, 104–9
—— —— for use, 232
Substitutes for tobacco, 267–70
Suckering plants, 60–6
Sumatran tobacco, 193–205
Sun-curing shed, 83
—— -drying cut tobacco leaves, 68
Sweating tobacco, 121–5

T<small>AUARI</small> wrappers, 143
Temporary hanging for tobacco, 68
Teymbeki, 179–91
Thinning out seedlings, 40, 48
Time for harvesting tobacco, 69
—— —— topping, 60, 61, 63
—— of day for cutting tobacco, 77
—— required for curing, 92
Tobacco horse, 72
—— plant, 1–6
Top-dressing seedlings, 41
Topping plants, 60–6
Tumbeki, 178–91
Turkeys as grub-eaters, 55
Turkish tobacco, 2, 3, 205–10
Twist tobacco, 236–44
Tying tobacco for hanging, 97

U<small>NITED</small> States tobacco, 210–22
Use of tobacco, 231–52

V<small>ALUES</small> of tobaccos, 271
Varieties of tobacco, 1–3
Venezuelan tobacco, 222
Ventilating drying-sheds, 88
Virginian tobacco, 2, 34–7

W<small>ASHING</small> tobacco when sorting, 117
Watering plants when setting out, 51
—— seedlings, 40
Water in tobacco, 262
Weeding seedlings, 40, 46
Weighing and packing machine, 250
West Indian tobacco, 223–30
Windrowing tobacco, 124
Wind shelter for tobacco, 10
Wood-ashes as tobacco manure, 14
Worms, destroying, 55–60

Y<small>ELLOW</small> prior tobacco, 37

LONDON:
PRINTED BY WILLIAM CLOWES AND SONS, LIMITED,
STAMFORD STREET AND CHARING CROSS.

USEFUL BOOKS FOR THE COLONIES.

COFFEE AND CHICORY; the Culture, Chemical Composition, Preparation for Market, and Consumption, with simple tests for detecting adulteration,' and practical hints for the Producer and Consumer, by P. L. SIMMONDS, F.S.S., author of 'The Commercial Products of the Vegetable Kingdom,' 'Dictionary of Products,' etc., etc., *illustrated by numerous wood engravings*, post 8vo, cloth, 2s.

THE YOUNG FARMER'S MANUAL, detailing the manipulations of the farm in a plain and intelligible manner, with practical directions for laying out a farm, and erecting buildings, fences, and farm gates; embracing also 'The Young Farmer's Workshop,' by S. E. TODD, *numerqus woodcuts*, new edition, 3 vols., crown 8vo, cloth, 21s.

TROPICAL AGRICULTURE, or the Culture, Preparation, Commerce, and Consumption of the Principal Products of the Vegetable Kingdom, as furnishing Food, Clothing, Medicine, etc., and in their relation to the Arts and Manufactures; forming a practical treatise and Handbook of Reference for the Colonist, Manufacturer, Merchant, and Consumer, on the Cultivation, Preparation for Shipment, and Commercial Value, etc., of the various Substances obtained from Trees and Plants entering into the Husbandry of Tropical and Sub-Tropical Regions; by P. L. SIMMONDS, second edition, revised and improved, in one thick vol., 8vo, cloth, 21s.

TALKS ON MANURES; a series of familiar and practical talks between the Author and the Deacon, the Doctor and the other neighbours, on the whole subject of Manures and Fertilizers, by J. HARRIS, crown 8vo, cloth, 7s. 6d.

CULTURAL INDUSTRIES FOR QUEENSLAND. Papers on the Cultivation of useful Plants suited to the climate of Queensland, their value as Food, in the Arts, and in Medicine, and methods of obtaining their products, by L. A. BERNAYS, F.L.S., F.R.G.S., 8vo, half calf, 7s. 6d.
The same in cloth, 6s.

SPONS' INFORMATION FOR COLONIAL ENGINEERS, edited by J. T. HURST.

No. 1. **CEYLON**, by ABRAHAM DEANE, C.E., 8vo, boards, 2s. 6d.
CONTENTS:
Introductory Remarks—Natural Productions—Architecture and Engineering—Topography, Trade, and Natural History—Principal Stations—Weights and Measures, etc., etc.

No. 2. **SOUTHERN AFRICA**, including the Cape Colony, Natal, and the Dutch Republics, by HENRY HALL, F.R.G.S., F.R.C.I., 8vo, *with map*, 3s. 6d.

No. 3. **INDIA**, by F. C. DANVERS, Assoc. Inst. C.E., *with map*, 4s. 6d.

E. & F. N. SPON, 125, Strand, London.
New York: 35, Murray Street.

SPONS' ENCYCLOPÆDIA

OF THE

INDUSTRIAL ARTS, MANUFACTURES, & COMMERCIAL PRODUCTS.

EDITED BY C. G. WARNFORD LOCK, F.L.S., &c., &c.

In Super-royal 8vo, containing 2100 *pp., and Illustrated by nearly* 1500 *Engravings.*

Can be had in the following bindings :— £ s. d.
In 2 vols., cloth 3 10 0
In 5 divisions, cloth 3 11 6
In 2 vols., half-morocco, top edge gilt, bound in a
    superior manner.. .. .. 4 10 0
In 33 monthly parts, at 2s. each.

Any Part can be had separate, price 2s., postage 2d.

COMPLETE LIST OF ALL THE SUBJECTS.

	Part		Part		Part
Acids	1, 2, 3	Dyestuffs	14	Narcotics	21, 22
Alcohol	3, 4	Electro-Metallurgy ..	14	Oils & Fatty Substances	
Alkalies	4, 5	Explosives	14, 15		22, 23, 24
Alloys	5, 6	Feathers	15	Paper	24
Arsenic	6	Fibrous Substances	15, 16	Paraffin	24
Asphalte	6	Floor-cloth	16	Pearl and Coral ..	24
Aerated Waters ..	6	Food Preservation ..	16	Perfumes	24
Beer and Wine ..	6, 7	Fruit	16, 17	Photography ..	24, 25
Beverages	7, 8	Fur	17	Pigments and Paint	25
Bleaching Powder ..	8	Gas, Coal	17	Pottery	25, 26
Bleaching	8, 9	Gems	17	Printing and Engraving	26
Borax	9	Glass	17	Resinous and Gummy	
Brushes	9	Graphite	18	Substances	26, 27
Buttons	9	Hair Manufactures ..	18	Rope	27
Camphor	9, 10	Hats	18	Salt	27, 28
Candles	10	Ice, Artificial	18	Silk	28
Carbon	10	Indiarubber Manufac-		Skins	28
Celluloid	10	tures	18, 19	Soap, Railway Grease,	
Clays	10	Ink	19	and Glycerine ..	28, 29
Carbolic Acid	11	Jute Manufactures ..	19	Spices	29
Coal-tar Products ..	11	Knitted Fabrics (Ho-		Starch	29
Cocoa	11	siery)	19	Sugar	29, 30, 31
Coffee	11, 12	Lace	19	Tannin	31, 32
Cork	12	Leather	19, 20	Tea	32
Cotton Manufactures	12, 13	Linen Manufaturers ..	20	Timber	32
Drugs	13	Manures	20	Varnish	32
Dyeing and Calico Print-		Matches	20, 21	Wool and Woollen Manu-	
ing	13, 14	Mordants	21	factures	32, 33

E. & F. N. SPON, 125, Strand, London.
New York: 35, Murray Street.

www.ingramcontent.com/pod-product-compliance
Lightning Source LLC
Chambersburg PA
CBHW032050230426
43672CB00009B/1542